Tears of Jupiter

The Cosmos and the Camino

Shima Shanti

Peace Waters

Tears of Jupiter

ISBN 978-0-9915481-3-2

Publishing Consultant, Project Manager and Book Interior Layout and Cover Design by Karen Saunders, www.KarenSaundersAssoc.com

Edited by Barbara McNichol Editorial, www. BarbaraMcNichol.com

Editing Consultant: Suzanne Merritt, www.SuzanneMerrittArt.com

Cover – Original artwork and photos by Shima Shanti

Published by
Peace Waters
San Diego, CA 92128
www.shimashanti.com

Preface

D ear Reader and Friend,
Then and now...

It has been ten years since I walked the *Camino de Santiago* in May 2012.

Within weeks of returning home, my blisters healed and the physical pain lessened. Months afterward, the emotional pain began to fade, leaving a beautiful sadness and traces of poignancy. My life settled into a comfortable routine with my beloved husband, Jim Kelly, in our San Diego and Montana homes.

For two years, I wrote and rewrote and retraced every step of my journey. As I kept memories alive, deeper revelations were unveiled. I was no longer physically walking the *Camino*; instead, I walked it in my dreams. I knew there were still more gifts to be given, rewards to be received, and Truth to be realized.

My *Camino* continued until my writing was done in 2014.

When my edited manuscript was ready to publish, I went to work. So good was my story, I thought, that it merited being put into the world by a traditional publisher: *Me, a married, fiftyish woman alone in a foreign country with nothing but a backpack walking nearly 500 kilometers in unyielding rain to find Truth.*

"Readers will connect and resonate with that," I mused. "Our paths may be different, but aren't we all on our own quest to find what is Truth for us? Soul-seeking? Searching? This powerful story was mainstream. Raw and real and exposed."

And so, I queried for a literary agent. And I queried and queried and queried. But to no avail.

Finally, in late fall 2015, to clear my head of this diligence and disappointment, I took a break. And on a whim, I signed up for an encaustic workshop. Encaustic—the ancient art form of painting with beeswax and fire. "Interesting," I thought. "A distraction away from the left-brained task I had assigned to myself for far too long."

Encaustic painting proved to be the creative outlet my soul was seeking.

I was surprised by my feelings this art form evoked. I immediately fell in love with the lusciousness of beeswax, the sensuous fragrance of the grasses and wildflowers radiating from melting pots of wax straight from the hive. I sensed a Merlin-like magic to the alchemic elixir of wax melting beneath the flame of a torch. Its luminosity and translucency born of earth elements were, at the same time, grounding and ethereal.

With the same inspired passion that propelled me on the *Camino*, I immersed myself in this art. Jim renovated an old work shed into a state-of-the-art studio where I painted and prayed in a meditative ritual that connected me to Spirit and Self. Days turned into weeks, into months, into years.

Now, it is 2022. Having gained international recognition in contemporary fine art exhibits, my work is sought by art collectors, interior designers, and art consultants nationwide.

I didn't know then that what started as a simple diversion was my Divine purpose: Shima, the Encaustic Artist. Thus, the wisdom and enlightenment I glimpsed, grasped, and actualized on the *Camino* became real. My encaustic artwork speaks to its viewers. My writing speaks to its readers. I am the Silent Partner. This is who I AM.

When you become it and are it—when you are just being—all separation disappears, and without separation, there is no individuality or identity. It just is.

If there is one gift to share from my journey that ended all my searching and seeking, it is this:

Wherever God is I am, and wherever I am God is. I stand on holy ground wherever I may be.

And what of *Tears of Jupiter*, the story of my *Camino?* My manuscript sat patiently on the shelf for six years. Until now—where it has found its way into your hands.

Wishing You Peace All Ways,
Journey OM

Shima

June 2022

Also by Shima Shanti

Journey OM, A Soul Journeyer's Adventure

The Soul Journeyer's Companion, A Cosmic Re-memoir
(Companion to *Journey OM)*

Ascension Kis, Opening the Doorways to Light

Hats I Am
(A children's book of who you are with a message for all)

Chapter 1

The glare of the airport pulsed with morning energy. It was a Wednesday. A workday. The plane, having touched down at the *Madrid Aero Puerto* only minutes before, had jolted me out of a hard sleep. My eyes stung and tears fell. I cinched my pack over my shoulder, adjusting and readjusting. This, it suddenly occurred to me, was an activity that would likely consume me for weeks.

I fell in line with the flow of rustling arms and legs, of rolling suitcases and duffle bags, of mouths spewing indecipherable conversation. I had no choice but to go with the flow. This had become my airport travel mantra: Go With The Flow.

The cool but stale building where I would await my final flight to *O'Porto, Portugal,* was the last leg of my pre-journey—the last leg before I set foot on the *Camino.* A rush of electricity, a throbbing of my heart, moved through me. This was happening! All my preparations, all my planning and studying and packing had paid off. This would be the last round of pushing through gates, checkpoints, and escalators—

the last leg of sitting in rigid seats, watching the clock to meet my next flight.

I turned a corner and bumped shoulders with a narrow man wearing a suit. I could smell tobacco on him. His long, manicured fingers gripped a thin leather case.

"Pardon," I blurted.

He paused briefly, his eyes taking me in, telling me (I felt certain) he knew I was foreign. "American," he said, before disappearing into the flesh and bone of humanity that zipped up and down the concourse like a stream of busy ants. I blinked hard, trying to focus.

I resolved I would speak only when spoken to and only when necessary. Sure, I would nod greetings to indicate a hello, a good morning, or a thank you. And I could say my name and announce: "My shirt is pink" in Spanish. My face flushed at the depth of my unpreparedness for this part, the *real* part. Yet I knew I would sail along with the breeze once on the ground, blue skies above me, as I walked the *Camino*. And even though every Spaniard I'd encountered so far was fluent in English, I noticed that Spaniards found amusement in withholding that knowledge. I supposed they took sport at the sight of a squirming foreigner—an American—who pained over the simplest of questions such as "Where is the restroom?" Finally, one of them gave in and politely answered this question for me. He was rotund with a happy shine to his eyes. He dressed in a neatly pressed navy-colored uniform with buttons that seemed to scream for dear life as they held back his belly. He smiled so widely when I approached him, the gold of his molars glinted beneath the airport lights. "Yes, ma'am, you will find the water closet down the walkway and to your left," he said in English before ambling back behind a counter nearby.

As I strode away, I considered that my incomprehension of the language—and the quiet buffer it created—offered me a sense of invisibility *if I so chose*. And I kind of liked it.

The Microcosm

The airport lights flickered intermittently. The hallways were modern, sleek, with white tiled walls and floors. Surprising. I supposed I'd expected the place to be heavy with archways and columns. But of course this was the *aero puerto* and a newish building by any standards. Plastic, color-coded placards in yellow, red, and blue signaled each exit and entrance, clearly marked for those who didn't understand the language.

I cinched my teal-blue sweater around my waist, crumpled and stale from travel, and pressed my shoulder through the bathroom door. Peering into the small rectangular mirror while washing my hands, I noticed new creases around my eyes and puffiness from the flight. I brushed my teeth, the minty paste cool and sweet on my tongue. And then I watched, mesmerized, as the suds of paste mixed with the running water, encircling the porcelain sink, aminiature hurricane.

**All of life comes down to this: the spiral,
the vortex—the cosmos!—
the microcosm within the macrocosm.**

I glanced back toward the mirror. I was smiling.

I strode back into the stream of travelers outside of the bathroom, my booted feet aching and sweaty. My pack suddenly felt too heavy; although a scant twenty pounds, it felt like I was lugging a box of rocks. This sort of travel—in the stale confines of buildings and planes—was the true test. Once on land, on dirt, and breathing the unfiltered outdoor air, I knew I would gain my stride.

Sinking my teeth into an apple I'd tucked in my pack back home in California staved off my need for breakfast—or whatever meal my body clock was aching for. But I still had one more flight and a stopover in a hotel before hitting the trail. So I followed the herd going to Customs, mentally shoring up my energy.

I Asked for This?

Standing in the queue for Customs, I became acutely aware of the many zippers, clips, buttons, and straps dangling from my pack and my body—and so my incessant quest for comfort kept me zipping, buttoning, and fiddling. I fumbled around the inside pouch secured around my neck feeling for my tickets and my passport with the frequency of a manic. Check and recheck. Tuck and zip. Stay present. Be mindful.

Focus! The words bounced back and forth in my head, reprimanding me.

Then a thought drifted in—a good thought—whispering that this lengthy layover would be a perfect time to call Jim. Yes, Jim. My eyes scanned the scene: I was gaining forward movement in the line and didn't want to lose my place. But I didn't want to dial out while surrounded by so many prying ears, so many blinking stares. I needed privacy and quiet to talk. Maintaining my bearings in this foreign airport, I realized, did require all of my focus. The blank faces floated above me, below me. Shining foreign eyes stared back at me as if to ask, "What are you looking at?"

I gulped down my rising fear, or was it a longing? I wanted to connect with my husband Jim. I hadn't moved an inch, yet I could feel my heart beating against my cheeks. Had I made a mistake?

Gradually, I talked myself down from this ledge of longing, this aching for Jim, for home—silently in my mind, of course. I wasn't about to cause a scene so early in my adventure. But I knew there was no turning back—not now, not at this final airport stop. I had landed, boots on the ground. And nothing to do but rely on my own instincts, my own wits. There would be no Jim standing by with an answer or a funny joke; no Jim offering a strong arm to carry my twenty pounds of rocks; no Jim with one of his all-encompassing hugs and his quiet words of reassurance; no Jim and his unyielding love.

And I had asked for this! I had methodically planned it. This was my doing (or my undoing).

There would be no one to ease my burden, no one to soothe my soul. No one. Only me.

I couldn't add Jim's worries to my pain. Too much. I had my own torrent of rain and pain to soak in. Jim's worries had to be his own. His anxieties of what was happening to me—what dangers were facing me—were built on knowing me, yes. But they also came from his own experiences traveling alone in Europe as a young man. His imaginings of me were his own. Now, he had time to bring his fear to life after being dormant for thirty years. If I were to think about Jim's anguish, I would have to own it. After all, my going on this trip had uprooted his

uncertainties and reopened the wounds of his insecurities.

No, I concluded. I had my own backpack of worries to carry, and Jim had his own. I couldn't carry his load, too.

Together, we were mired in our own fears— and each other's.

Fatherly Taxi Driver

The skies dumped rain all day, drumming hard on the taxi's roof, adding to my frayed nerves and keeping me on high alert. Zipping from the airport in *Madrid* to my first stop for the night, a hotel in the suburb *Maia* outside *Porto*, the driver maneuvered the slick streets with precision. He'd been kindly from the start, letting me keep my pack by my side rather than in the taxi's trunk, as if priceless breakables were hidden inside. He'd been mindful of my personal space, too, opening my door and gently cupping his hand around my arm to help me into the seat.

"You remind me of my father," I said, as I scooted across the plastic-covered bench. But as soon as the words left me, I could tell he didn't quite understand. "My father—you remind me of him. You understand? *Entendes?* My papa. *Mi pai,*" I added, trying to break through the language barrier. He nodded with a hint of recognition and then smiled before shutting my car door. I folded my jacket in my lap, taking in the damp tobacco scent of the car's interior.

My thoughts flitted around, trying to ascertain how I could explain my father to this man—or anything else about myself. I suddenly felt compelled to tell him about my father. I also wanted to explain to him (or anyone who would listen) how this trip's genesis began more than four years ago and now I was here (and it was as real as the bags beneath my eyes and the stains on my sweater). But it wasn't at all how

I had imagined it. Not at all. I wanted to tell him, tell someone. I craved connection.

"I'm a pilgrim, a *peregrino*," I said finally, peering into his dark eyes through the rearview mirror. "The *Camino*—*entendes*? You know—the *Camino*?" I laughed a little. He nodded his understanding and chuckled, just to kindly go along with me like he was laughing at a joke he didn't get. But we'd communicated. I'd struck pay dirt! And I could tell he was kind. A memory of my dad barreled into my thoughts.

> *I had just turned fifteen and my rebellious, unbridled anger had become too much. My dad and mom had five other children to think about, after all. For the sake of the family, it was best for everyone that I be given away to a foster family.*
>
> *It was only me and my dad on that 400-mile drive. The closer we got to the foster family's home, the more terrified I became. I begged, "Please don't give me away!" I bartered, "I'll do anything you ask!" I broke down.*
>
> *In a mixed mist of our tears, Dad turned the car around. This shattering of our hearts pieced together was the closest to love I would ever allow from my dad. By never mentioning this day—ever again—it never happened, and life went on. Until now.*

He never mentioned the pain or the sorrow. Typical for my dad. "Let me live in Disneyland," he would say. He was generous and unyielding with his love. But for whatever reason, I could have heard "I love you" a thousand and one times and still needed more. I was a sieve and all of his love poured clean through me.

**In this moment I realized—
I was the one who hadn't let him into *my* heart.**

I blinked hard pushing back tears, then I sat up, my back rigid against the seat. I had not bargained for this part nor anticipated this range of emotion. No, I'd carried around vision after vision of my *Camino* trip filled with purpose and strength, with blue skies and strong bones, with enlightened thoughts and the ever-present sense of a possible transcendence.

I'd been the girl with sugar plums floating in her head. A fool.

**But the reality of the rain, my aching feet,
my longing for all the lost time with my dad—
and my utter and complete aloneness—
was what the trip was shaping up to be.
And I hadn't even set foot on the *Camino*!**

Mindful of my breath, mindful of my racing heart, I peered into the streets. Outside, another green taxi car spun around the corner, a wake of water fanning from beneath its spinning wheels. I wondered if this taxi driver was as caring as mine.

I turned to look at my driver, his fingers tapping the worn leather of the steering wheel. He was moving to the beat of *fado*, the Portuguese folk music softly wafting from the radio. Beneath his sagging lids, his eyes shifted from the streets to the rearview mirror (and his view of me) every few minutes. It was as if he were duty-bound to watch the road *and* keep an eye on his precious cargo—me. I must have looked fragile or crazy or both.

I pushed at my hair, combing through it with my fingers. I pulled lip balm from my pack and moistened my lips. Before long, his gaze, darting from the road to me, comforted and surprised me at the same time. It wasn't like me to take solace from a complete stranger.

But no one is a stranger on life's journey, right? Not really.

I laughed at my foolishness, at all the platitudes rolling through my thoughts. The power of now; love is the answer; all you need is love. "Deep breaths, deep breaths," repeated in my mind like a mantra.

"You need air?" the driver asked in his choppy English.

"I just need to—to breathe. But thank you, I mean, *obrigado*. I need to breathe—is all." Yes, I thought, air is all I need, all I need is air—and air is love—everything is love.

"You okay?' he asked, checking on me again.

"I'm a little tired, that's all," I said, looking into the mirror, wondering if I had been talking aloud. "But, yes, I am well. *Muito bem*," I added, trying to convince myself as much as him.

A Welcome Comfort

Just the thought of another soul watching over me in this foreign land was a welcome comfort that I accepted with no apology. I took another breath and imagined my dad sitting by my side, proud of me for my independence, for testing my limits. Outside the window, blurred images of moving people flashed in and out of view, their umbrellas—yellow, green, and red—vivid against the gray.

After a while, the swishing wiper blades and the pounding rain helped calm my thoughts. I dozed off. When my kindly driver pulled over, I jolted forward. I paid him and stepped to the sidewalk above the curb. That's when the elements immediately engulfed me. It was as if the clouds had dropped low, churning barely above the rooflines spitting into the streets. The driver rushed around the car and popped open an umbrella above me.

"Lots of crying today," he said, looking up. He placed his hand on my back, the way my dad used to. "*Cuiadadoso*. Be careful," he said, and then he opened the hotel door, sending me on my way.

The weather report had promised clear skies for the week ahead. But for today, I could tell this storm was stalling out, hanging above me and this land I had entered—the countryside of Portugal.

And like me, this storm was due to roam across the landscape, pouring itself out.

Checking In

The clerk behind the desk smiled, spoke to me in perfect English, and then busily clicked away on his computer keyboard. He pulled up my reservation in an instant, then yanked a newly programmed key card from the computer terminal. This efficiency—with all the blinking and pinging his computer was emitting—was not what I had imagined to find in Portugal. But then I reminded myself I was still in *Porto*, the second largest city next to *Lisbon* with a sizable population.

I turned back toward the polished doors of the lobby and saw my taxi driver pulling away. Suddenly, I could barely swallow. A new wave of fear coursed through me, a fear manifesting in the flesh—roaring, clamoring to jump out of me. Thank goodness the fatherly taxi driver had vanished. *Emotionally, I couldn't manage any more kindness.*

To get grounded, I scanned the lobby. Businessmen huddled in groups, smoking and talking, their hair shining beneath the lights. I tried pushing away thoughts of my husband Jim from my mind. *I can't think of him now, not in public anyway, for fear I would*

12

sob and never stop. I had transformed into some kind of damsel in distress and I hated it.

But I was here now. At the beginning of my lone journey. Oh, how I had prattled on about the *Camino* for so long. And now my hidden doubts bobbed so close to the surface, I could hardly hold them back. The clerk stared at me in between looking at his paperwork. Another nervous laugh escaped me like a hiccup.

"How are you?" I managed to ask him.

He offered a wincing sort of smile. "I am very well," he said, his perfect enunciation forming around each word. I guessed he could tell something wasn't quite right with his lone American guest, this middle-aged, maniacal woman dressed like a hiker, but was likely more comfortable in a garish American shopping mall.

As he ripped the invoice from the printer, I turned and glimpsed at the bar behind me just beyond the lobby. The shine of polished brass flickered along its edges, the glow of cigarettes floating on the air. A woman dressed in black slacks sitting on the end laughed heartily before she sucked her cigarette. Then she tossed back her hair, a thick mass of curls, and she leaned in toward the bartender and a man seated to her right. As she sipped her wine, she looked like she'd be a mess of good fun—like me when I was a young twenty-something—with all that attention, all that laughing, all that hair. I smoothed down the wrinkles in my jeans with my palms, knowing it was only my loneliness enticing me to the bar.

I took my invoice, folded it, and slipped it into my pack with finality.

"Would you like a wakeup call?" the clerk asked.

"Oh, no. No, thank you. *Obrigado*," I said, taking my credit-card-size room key.

My "Ordinary" Trip

Still, I lingered at the counter, thinking to ask the clerk if he'd ever met a lone pilgrim, a lone female. But I held off. Of course he had. My research told me that many pilgrims walked alone—men and women both. This was ordinary: A middle-aged woman walking alone across a foreign country with a backpack and no reservations. Ordinary. Shirley MacLaine had done it. *Yeah, and she's ordinary!* I thought, laughing again. *The Saintly Queen Isabela of Portugal—hadn't she walked it in 1325? (probably barefoot, too)*. I laughed a little more.

Yes, this meticulous preparation—all the weighing, folding, and packing—added to my carefully orchestrated plans of waltzing across the countryside in the elements *alone* while my perfectly ordinary husband stayed home in California. *Yes, this is definitely an ordinary trip.*

"*Señhora?*" the clerk was now leaning in, a pained look on his face. "Can I help you with anything else?"

"No, no. Thank you, again—*obrigado*," I said before I turned, hitched my pack over my shoulder, and headed for the elevator.

"No," I hollered back. "I just need to find my sanity, gain my bearings. I'll be on the *Camino* tomorrow," I added, not caring that he hadn't the slightest idea what I was saying.

Chapter 2

I'd missed a day in air overseas and thus lost all sense of time. After being aloft, my body ached to connect with Mother Earth—foot to ground. A quick survey of my "could be anywhere" room told me I didn't have to leave America for this. The thought prodded me to get outdoors. The rain was hard and cold, a winter rain—not a spring shower, not drizzle—rain. Only by the clock did I know it was still daytime.

Prior to departure, the guidebook's author stressed the importance of obtaining a *Credencial,* or "Pilgrim Passport." And even though I didn't consider myself a pilgrim in the traditional sense I took his advice and early on contacted the Society of Saint James for mine; if for no other reason as a souvenir to mark my journey. The *Credencial* is the modern-day version of the letter of safe-conduct carried by medieval pilgrims which allowed them safe passage through the neighboring kingdoms. Today's version certified the legitimate status of a pilgrim, proof she journeyed by foot. Arriving at the final destination of *Catedral de Santiago,* the *Casa do Dean,* would issue the coveted Certificate of Completion called the *Compostela* if the pilgrim had met the Dean's condition: a passport stamped by churches, cafes or hotels for each day on the route. It all seemed so very Catholic to me, just another novena to prove one worthy or unworthy of God's merit. Even though I continued to affirm I was not walking the *Camino* as a traditional pilgrim, I followed the rules all the same. My *Credencial* was pocketed safely next to my US Passport. Its unmarked pages and finely creased edges were not yet inked and tattered, not yet the witness to my journey ahead. That would come later. For now I was anxious to receive my *selo,* or stamp from *Catedral Se* in *Porto*. It would be my first.

I went in search of the public *Metro* to get to the cathedral.

The *Metro* was so foreign to me; it would have been more believable if the station was a space hub and the train a space ship, with its hi-tech and high speed. But I was okay once I understood that each red, green, and orange line represented a color-coded route. The one I wanted was orange.

With a whizz and a swoosh, I was on the train then off, dropped at the end of the orange line. As long as I stayed along the tracks, I knew I wasn't lost. But now with the roads and their roundabouts (no lefts or rights), I was mixed up.

The Baroque buildings with their angels, nymphs, and gargoyles all looked like cathedrals to me; any one of them could have been the *Catedral Se*. On a sunny day, I imagined their medieval architecture as magnificent, but today the granite façade looked ominous against the dark slate sky.

No one I saw spoke English, but I continued to ask anyone who would listen. Finally, just minutes before it closed, I stumbled into the *Turismo Centro* outside the cathedral and received my precious stamp. Now an official pilgrim, I climbed a steep embankment to enter the mammoth cathedral.

Once I stepped inside, it felt cold and damp,
darker even than the sunless outdoors.
I hastily reminded myself visiting cathedrals
was not why I journeyed.
I immediately walked out.

Getting Lost

Being in *Porto* took practice. Practice. Practice makes perfect. I'd had a piano teacher in grade school who used to tell me that. I practiced, but I never was perfect, or even good.

This is only practice, I told myself. I was navigating a foreign city—not even on the *Camino* yet—marching up and down winding streets in the rain, reading foreign maps without Jim, my beloved scout. All of this would at least test my mettle. In fact, it *was* testing my mettle, for I could see I might be a little bit lost and the rain was coming down in sheets and it would be dark soon and I was just plain tired.

Spiraling back from the cathedral on the *Metro*, then getting off at *Maia* where I began, I walked and walked and found I had landed where I'd begun—back at the station. I had been walking in circles! But I felt certain the hotel was only minutes—a few blocks perhaps—from the station. I saw no familiar landmarks to signal the direction—north, south, east, or west. Gray clouds shrouded the sun.

Still, I bounced along, appearing (I hoped) like I knew where I was headed, acting as if I was enjoying it even. I walked a few blocks in each direction, praying I'd recognize something, anything, that would point the way to my hotel. A grocery store came into view, so I thought I would pick up bottled water. *I can always use water. Yes, stocking up on provisions seems like a good idea. Plus, stopping gives me a purpose—an activity that distracts me from my growing concern about finding the way back to my hotel.*

As I moved toward the store, I noticed a small shop with blue gloves displayed in the window. My hands were cold—raw and cold. *I need those gloves.* I pushed my way inside, locked eyes with the shopkeeper, and then pointed to them like a mute. He raised three fingers (like a mute, too) and then tapped his fingers on the counter. I knew he meant three euros; money has its own language. I handed over that amount, put on the gloves, and then rushed back into the streets, my hair whipping in the wind and rain, the skies growing darker.

Once inside the grocer's, I pecked around waiting for the check-out line to dwindle, hoping the cashier spoke English and could help me find my hotel. When I asked her how I might find my way, a wide, gummy smile spread across her face. She nodded while handing me my bag and change. "*Si, si,*" she said, smiling even wider. Clearly, she hadn't a clue what I had asked.

Getting Unlost

Back on the street, I retraced my way to the *Metro* station. The attendant, a twenties-something woman, had perfectly arched brows and a stack of bracelets up her arms that jangled with each movement of her rotund yet utterly feminine body. *How comfortable the Portuguese women seemed to be in their skins.* I stood taller, allowing my curves to relax beneath my clothes, searching for words to translate into her language. I recognized her as the person who helped me purchase my ticket and board the correct train earlier in the day. *Would I understand a little something? Would she understand me?*

I smiled, she jangled; both of us nodded to the other. I assumed she'd be impressed that I'd made my way back. Or maybe it was only I who was impressed with myself for finding the station. She was simply doing her job, jangling along, taking tickets.

"*Donde está Hotel Central Parque?*" I asked, louder this time.

"*No se,*" she said, turning to shove tickets into a drawer.

Just then, a man—thin and wiry, leaning against the wall and smoking an unfiltered cigarette—called out "*trescientos metros.*" He must have understood my broken Portuguese and offered directions toward the hotel. It was now dark. I was shivering, and as he spoke in his choppy English, I felt the urge to hug him—to drop to my knees and offer my thanks.

"Thank you, thank you," I said, feeling the tightness in my throat soften. And with each swift stride toward my destination, my limbs loosened. When I reached the hotel entrance, I gladly slipped through the familiar glass doors into the warmth of the *Hotel Central Parque*.

In that moment, I fought off the growing sense I was in over my head.

At Dinner

In the hotel *café* bar, the waiter had set my table with a simple dinner—salad, baguette, tomatoes, and cheese—prearranged and waiting for me. I scooted into my seat and scanned the bar, searching for the young woman with the long wild curly hair. Nowhere in sight.

In fact, the entire bar and restaurant were empty of patrons except me. The bartender nodded toward me and continued polishing glasses. I settled in, pulled out my maps, and began planning my first walking day's journey. Because of the heavy rain, I decided it was best to take an alternate route via the *Metro* to *Vila do Conde Ponte* and then walk 9.8 kilometers to the village of *Arcos* and *Quinta Sao Miguel. I am not a purest—and a little zip on the Metro here and there wouldn't be horrible.*

Then once I've settled at the *Quinta,* I would venture to *Megalitico do Fulom,* my first designated sacred site. The guidebook described it as a burial chamber dating back to 3000 BC.

For me, it was the first spiritual gateway where I would consecrate my journey and truly begin the purpose of my pilgrimage.

I sipped my water feeling content with my well-laid plans between bites of bread. This moment couldn't have been more perfect.

A sense of calm smoothed out the tension that had gridlocked me for the past few hours. Any second-guessing, any regret for having made this trek, was fading.

Chapter 3

I'm okay being lost. This is what I told myself when, yet again, I found I'd turned down a side street thinking it would take me to the *Metro* station. In fact, it landed me in the dead end of a dirty alleyway. *Only day two, but being lost seemed to be my new norm.*

I turned around, picking my way through puddles, and I tried to go with the flow. After all, no one was waiting for me and this *Camino* walk was my own journey. I had no one to report to, nowhere else to be. So I kept walking.

More than hour after I stepped off the *Metro* on the outskirts of *Vila do Conde,* I searched for the yellow arrows of the *Camino.* There was nothing remotely signaling the *Camino* and no one to ask—until I came upon a white country home, freshly painted and connected to a small barn. A lean and handsome Portuguese man stood in the pasture training his horse. The seeming wealth of his clean paddock, orderly stable, and whitewashed fence appeared out of the ordinary in this countryside of the poor.

"Donde está?"

"Cuando?" He asked and then switched to English,

saving me from my poor attempt to speak his tongue. "How can I help you?"

I clutched at my chest, even bowed a little in gratitude, and felt surprised by the jolt of emotion rushing through me. Instantly, the thought about pretending I was "okay with being lost" jumped into my head.

Next came a pleading inside. Could this handsome man help me find my way?

"I am a *peregrino.*" My words gushed forth. "I am a *peregrino* on the *Camino de Santiago.*" I searched his eyes for some kind of recognition. "Do you know where I might I find the yellow arrows?" I asked, well aware that the *Camino* was not a common path in these parts of Portugal, and that few pilgrims ever choose this route. Plus those who did were not initiates like me; they tended to travel the French and Spanish routes first. It was only on their second, third, or even seventh pilgrimage that they chose this or another of the twelve *Camino* routes.

But as I asked him how he might help me, I realized I was unclear where I wanted to go. My stomach tightened. I knew I had to find and follow the yellow arrows to my ultimate destination, *Santiago*, the city in Spain more than 400 kilometers away. This I knew. But this was all I knew.

Sure, I had my map in hand. It offered squiggly lines and foreign words—that was it. I smoothed my hands over it, feeling foolish. Here I stood on this this quiet farm in front of this beautiful stranger, and I wasn't sure what to ask, or how to explain my journey, or what my intentions were in walking to *Santiago*. As the farmer walked closer, I fumbled for my guidebook while the horse dipped his head to nosh on the grass. Once the man stood next to me (not as tall as I had thought but just as handsome), I pointed to the closest town to where I thought I was.

**He nodded recognition. Good.
We're getting somewhere.**

My face burned hot the more I tried to come up with questions to ask, so I remained quiet and let him peruse my book and map. He squinted and leaned in, his finger sliding over the pages, soon pointing to what he must have assumed I was looking for—the starting point of the *Camino*.

"*Obrigado,*" I said, again gushing with gratitude. I wanted to kiss him! Two days alone in a foreign country and I was as giddy as a child over a few moments of kindness. "*Obrigado,*" I repeated as I folded my map, closed my book, and tucked them inside my backpack.

"*De nada.*" He stepped back and waved his hand, swatting at the cool, muggy air. We nodded our farewells, and I set out in the prescribed direction.

Walking Steady and With Purpose

Ah, what beauty there is in having only one thing to do—no decision except to put one foot in front of the other and walk. The movement of walking, steady and with purpose, gave me a sense that, for once in my life, I was doing the right thing. And when I cleared the corner and away from the farmer's view, I began to cry. It wasn't a cry of fear or frustration, or even sadness.

It was his kindness and graciousness that had touched me.

Tears rolled from my eyes quietly and steadily. And it wasn't until another hour and many kilometers later when I realized he had pointed me to the *Estrada* (the highway!) and not the *Camino*. Nearly three hours had passed, and I was nowhere near my first day's destination.

The sheer folly of my adventure seemed like too much, but this time, I was too tired to cry. I was a fool, a tired fool. What could I do but find a place to stop and rest my foolish limbs before deciding what to do next.

Before long, I made it to the countryside *Metro* station and boarded the train to backtrack to *Santa Clara*. There, I hoped to find another starting point.

Locals milled about the station at *Santa Clara* waiting for their trains. To anyone nearby, I asked, "Do you speak English? *Falas Englis, por favor?*" The young ones did, and in between inhales and exhales (everyone smoked in these parts), they kindly tried helping me—this foreign woman, this American—as best they could. But I sensed the perplexity in their expression. *Who is this foreigner—a woman traveling alone with feathers in her hair and a knapsack heavy on her back?* I'm sure they wondered. My rugged, mountaineering appearances (complete with boots and backpack) stood out among the narrow-hipped males and their counterpart slender females with full lips and lavish hair. Still, I fit in with the people there long enough to get a bit of direction. At least they didn't shun me. And because the *Camino Santiago* wasn't well known in these parts, I ascertained they didn't quite understand what I was asking.

I wandered away from the crowd-filled station and peered off into the distance, squinting into the clouds. *What a majestic place—a town encircled by rugged hills standing tall beyond the rooflines.* That's when I noticed the elegant stone arches appearing to be floating between the hills—an ancient Roman aqueduct like the one pictured in my guidebook.

The structure loomed like a castle in the sky— a beacon of hope.

The Wrong Town!

I stopped short and sat on a rock, rechecking my guidebook. Two dots finally connected so I could discover my error. *I'd been looking for landmarks in the wrong town.* I was in the *Vila do Conde* when I should have been in *Vila do Conde Ponte.* A few letters in the name—one little word—made all the difference.

No time for self-recrimination or regret. My pace quickened as I headed in its direction and stumbled on road signs to the *Turismo!* The Tourist Office. The people there would help me get on track.

I flipped open my book and glossed over the pages to confirm the spelling of T-u-r-i-s-m-o. Yes! I had found my way to *Vila do Conde Ponte.* Knowing I was on track—feeling sure of each step with the adrenaline flowing—bolstered me forward, my strides long and agile. Yes, Jim would have found the trail by now and with ease. Sure, he probably never would have been lost in the first place. Or he would have known we'd been going the wrong direction long before setting out from the farmer's house.

But Jim wasn't here. *I need to trust my own instincts.* I had relied on Jim for too long and my father before him.

On my way to the *Turismo,* I strolled along the perimeter of the central square. Shops and taverns lined the cobbled street. I came upon a single-story building covered in green ivy adorned with tall shuttered windows. With its whitewashed door and straggling red flowers in pots along either side of the entrance, it seemed inviting enough. The woman behind the desk, a bookish-looking person with a pinched nose and glasses perched atop her head, glanced up and flashed her scowl. Then she turned and walked through a side door, leaving me alone.

I set down my pack and waited in the chilly entry-way expecting her to return. Outside, sounds of car motors hummed past every few minutes, a group of people strolled along. I waited. When she finally returned, she caught sight of me, and her stunned eyes told me she was surprised I was still there. "Did you think you scared me off?" I asked, expecting her not to understand my English. She stared at me, boring her eyes into mine for longer than I felt comfortable. Maybe she hadn't really noticed me in the first place.

"I was just kidding," I said.

Then I leaned in toward the desk offering the most gracious smile I could muster. "*Bom dia, por favor falas Englis?*" I asked.

She adjusted her glasses and pulled open a drawer, still completely ignoring me. She rummaged around a bit and then shut the drawer with a heave.

I asked again, "*Falas Englis?*" Maybe she had understood me.

She grabbed my guidebook and pointed to *Vila do Conde Ponte*, where I already knew I was. "*Quinta Sao Miguel?*" I ask. Now she was waving and barking in my direction but refusing eye contact at this point. She then grimaced as if she'd just eaten rotting meat.

"*Arcos! Quinta Sao Miguel* is in *Arcos*," she offered in English. "Not here," she barked again before shooing me out the door.

Too Angry to Cry

I picked my way back to the town square. Her rudeness fueled my drive to push on. *How dare she! This is her job! To help tourists like me! Who does she think she is, some noblewoman? Some Portuguese Queen? Worse, who does she think I am? Some foreigner unworthy of her help? What have I done to be on the receiving end of such rudeness?*

I was too angry to cry. Crying was overrated anyway and not useful at this moment. What I needed was a roof, a meal, and a bath for the night. Jim might have found her funny—or ridiculous, at least. He would have scoffed before launching into a charming exchange that would have led to securing directions. He had this healthy way of inserting humor into situations such as this—humor and charm. "Why let some curmudgeon ruin your day?" he would say.

And what did I offer? I was surly and not friendly enough, perhaps. But she worked at the *Turismo*! *Wasn't it her job to ingratiate herself to me? I was a tourist in her country! Why did I allow others to dump on me like that? What was so wrong with me that she had refused me?*

At this, I did begin to cry—a childish cry, too, a kicking-at-puddles kind of angry-cry. And that's when

I noticed a rather worn-looking Portuguese man who looked up and caught my stare.

"Por favor . . . " I began.

"Si, si, yes, I know *Sao Miguel* in *Arcos.* Not far,"he said, smiling. And in his limited English, he assured me he knew where I was going and promised he could get me there. Francesco, this nice man, whisked me the fifteen kilometers to my destination. In his dusty car sitting in the back, I laughed out loud and with gusto, my pack at my side. *This quick jaunt on wheels took only minutes, yet I had walked four hours on foot to go nowhere.*

Again, I was reminded of the folly of my journey, but I had wanted to walk. To *walk.* I would walk tomorrow. I would begin again.

**But for today, I told myself,
it truly was about the destination.
Tomorrow it would be once again
about the journey.**

Chapter 4

I arrived at *Quinta Sao Miguel* feigning an air of calm as the innkeeper Antonio—a strong man of the land, ruggedly handsome, around age forty (I'd guessed)—escorted me to my room. I glanced at my image in a small mirror while also trying to keep up with him. Screaming inside, I looked tired, worn out. I needed rest, and I'd barely begun my journey. Antonio moved along in long but quick strides, leading me up a flight of stairs opening into an ornate sitting room, all the while proudly sharing the history of his home and the land and *Sao Miguel.*

When he flipped on the light and revealed the fifteenth-century stone and millwork (what I had expected), I gasped audibly at the contrasting glare of its furnishings.

"You okay, *Señhora?*" he asked in perfect English. I nodded an affirmative and stepped inside, surrounded by the methodical design I saw. Such effort had been expended, such thoughtfulness, with the color orange central to its theme.

Yes, this room was a shrine to the color orange. I guessed that the designer, his wife, had hoped to diminish the otherwise dank wood and stone of the medieval building. Orange-painted walls, orange throw rugs, orange curtains, and matching orange bedspread were splashed, it seemed, from floor to ceiling.

"So bright! I won't need lamps!" I teased.

He ignored me, eager to return to his work in the fields before the last of sunlight. Then he pushed open the door to the bathroom—also decorated in orange. Even the bowl of fruits on the bureau were oranges— plastic oranges—thoughtfully placed next to an orange-scented candle. The sight, scent and texture of every item were so purposefully matched nothing could be ignored; yet the careful selection and placement of each adornment was hard not to smile, even if it affronted my taste for décor. I appreciated the effort, if nothing else. My room walled me in a case of citrus bliss.

"Ah, yes. Well, thank you," I said, as he waited for my approval, busying himself with puffing the pillows as if throwing bales on my orange bed.

"Well, this is nice." I dropped my pack onto the floor.

It was early in my journey and already I was forced to abandon any remnants of grandeur I'd held when dreaming up this trip.

But the mind can play tricks as I chuckled—just a little. I realized it was a nervous chuckle, a disappointed and nervous chuckle. Antonio, who had cracked the window to let in much-needed fresh air, stared at me quizzically.

"*No—Nada*. It's nothing," I said, smiling at him. He nodded again and pulled fresh towels from a cabinet, setting them on the bed. I could see there was nothing to do but accept things as they were. And *Quinta Sao Miguel* was definitely ancient and orange.

I was able to marvel at the difference between Antonio and the mean lady at the *Turismo*. I longed to talk to someone about this—about how striking it was to be treated so poorly only to find respite and kindness a few kilometers away. My encounters that day felt heavy with meaning and seemed to carry a message I needed to understand.

Meanwhile, as my thoughts wandered, Antonio pointed out all the amenities and quirks—hot water in the bath but the drain was slow, windows faced west but were hard to open. "But if you could manage to open them," he said as he struggled with the latch, "they offer a lovely view of a tiny garden."

Outside, I could hear doves cooing—a sign that meant peace.

Piece of Peace

Yes, peace was finally with me, for I had reconciled these events in my mind: I had gotten lost and found the farmer; I had happened upon the mean lady at the *Turismo*; I had wandered down this path. In the process, I was accepting the good with the so-called bad events, realizing none of them were bad after all.

Therefore, the mean lady of *Turismo* was only bad

if I chose to carry her in anger with me. Instead, I opted for carrying peace within me. I was too tired to hold the anger, anyway. If I had met her in the bright sun of San Diego, I would have had enough bed rest and energy to fight her negativity. Then I laughed at the thought of seeing the lady of *Turismo* at my doorstep. I would have gladly welcomed her inside for a cup of tea and a warm bed.

And so that afternoon in Portugal at *Quinta Sao Miguel,* peace filled me to the brim. Peace was my friend.

After Antonio left, I dropped onto the bed full of doubting thoughts.

This was no stroll. This walk was lonely.
This walk was foreign and
downright unglamorous.

Not that I'd expected champagne and roses—who wanted champagne and roses. But what had I wanted? Certainly not this—not this!

My reasons for walking the *Camino* were suddenly hard to pin down. And while I had prepared by building my physical strength, mapping the trail, and making reservations, I hadn't given a thought to my emotional strength. I had assumed I was impenetrable, rock solid, steady.

I had let go a little sob but stopped. Truthfully, I was afraid if I really let go—if I went for a shoulder-shaking kind of sob—I might lose control completely. Then Jim would have to fly out and extract me from a

Portuguese mental hospital. *Do they even have mental hospitals here? I hadn't seen any listed in my guidebooks.*

Who is This Person?

I stood up and went toward the mirror gazing at this person—at my reflection. At that moment, I remembered I'd hoped for a sense of peace, of inner power. I had always seen myself as independent, confident, and secure. "Ha!" I laughed into the mirror, taking in the depth and color of the dark circles under my eyes. It was a fake and angry laugh. "Ha!"

But these traits—confidence and independence—had vaporized two days ago when Jim kissed me good-bye. It occurred to me that, so far from home, I was unable to draw his life force into my own. I blushed at the thought that I'd been like a vampire lapping up his energy—a thief! It never occurred to me how much I'd relied on him—for the everyday things, yes, groceries and gas, reminding me where I left my phone. He was the key to my freedom—never having to explain why I am the way I am. Now I wonder.

Alone and in a foreign country, I was a child, an orphan, or worse, an idiot.

I went for my pack and pulled out my essential oils. *Yes, I had come prepared. Who brings essential oils on the Camino? I do.* Was I talking aloud? I honestly didn't know. I quickly dabbed calendula under my eyes and pushed the vial back inside my pack.

And, in an effort to (number one) subdue the orange overwhelm and (number two) stop thinking so much, I pulled out all of my clothes and messily threw them around. I tossed my blue sweater on the orange bed and a black pair of leggings on the orange 1970s-style bubble chair in the corner. Now the room looked messy, but at least Antonio wasn't here to witness my disapproval of the orange decor.

Inside the tiny orange bathroom, I scrubbed my hands and splashed cool water on my face and neck. All the while, my sense of dread rumbled inside my stomach, rising into my throat. *Nothing is working. What was I thinking when I chose to walk alone?*

It was late afternoon—still enough time to venture out to *Megalitico do Fulom,* a place of death and re-birth, and where I had chosen to consecrate my journey. *I'd rather nap for a while, but if I didn't go now, I'd be delayed another day, or I'd miss it altogether; not an option.* To bypass this ceremony would seem sacrilegious. *Why would I have come all this way and not stop there?* I knew the path would be easy to find less than a kilometer away.

A patchwork of farmland crisscrossed the lane made of hand-placed cobblestones—scores of them—the same lane that would carry me across two entire countries. Breathing in the clean air, taking in the bright green of spring growth, and catching sounds of new life buzzing in the trees—all of this galvanized my good spirits. It left no room for doubt whenever I might cast my memories back to those moments lost in *Vila do Conde.*

**Nature was communicating with me,
inviting me to open up to a sense of God
everywhere around me.**

Suddenly, two yellow birds darted daringly close to my face. After wandering into a glade of a pine forest and finding the site of the *Megalitico do Fulom,* a rush of excitement shot through me. *Megalitico do Fulom* was a burial chamber dating back to 3,000 BC. This was my first sacred site, the gateway into the realm of the *Camino* and my initiation as a pilgrim.

A breeze lifted the tree limbs above me, the air feeling light around my face and arms. Here, like any number of sacred places I'd visited, I entreated the Devas and Elementals to welcome me. I'd come to know them as pure Earth energy, the very essence of the plant and animal kingdom. Greeted by a tiny insect, I smiled in its fairy-like presence. I sensed a warm gentleness emanating from the ground, and despite the ominous weather pending, I enjoyed a sense of peace in this place.

Among a few delicate blooms, fiddlehead ferns were pushing up through the earth, belying their appearance of tenderness. I felt the springtime ground lush and marshy, soft underfoot. I stepped farther and noticed a stand of eucalyptus and pine had been clear-cut, boughs and branches scattered on the forest floor.

Beyond the manmade opening, a remaining stand of eucalyptus trees encircled two giant earthen mounds each the size of a truck. One tree, bigger than the others by ten times, stood out boldly. He had shed his bark and stood bald and stark, the sun warming the smooth skin of his limbs. *The grandfather guarding the family remains.*

It was not lost on me that beneath the ten-feet high bunkers were unseen manmade rock caves housing ancient tombs. I had enough space to walk between the two hills down an aisle-like pathway ending at a tree stump. Both a sense of eeriness and reverence formed in my throat. I sat at the base of the mounds and began to pray.

**Now, finally at Megalitico do Fulom,
my doubts and fears dissolved into dust
that made room for only prayer.**

Dearly Beloved,
Reveal Thy Self. Open my heart to allow,
accept, and surrender to All That Is.
Allow me to walk in rhythm held in
Your protection. Guide me to the places
You will have me go as Your vessel of
Light and Wisdom and Illumination.
I choose All Ways Thy Divine Will to walk
in Grace and reverence. Peace All Ways.

Tomb or Womb?

Sitting in the stillness atop the tombs, I waited for a feeling, a sign. A bright green worm inched by, its multitude of tiny legs spinning. The sun crept higher, breaking through an opening in the trees. I thought about the one letter—the "T" of tomb—that had changed from the "W" of *womb*. And I chuckled. *What a difference one letter makes. All the difference! We arrive in a womb, and we leave in a tomb.*

Both are ostensibly closed spaces yet are gateways to a new dimension. Aren't they each the side of the same coin? I once again laughed out loud at such thoughts flitting through my brain. *Nothing like a little time alone. All this quiet gives me time and space to hear myself think—or not think—for that matter.*

Jim would have found my tomb/womb comparison silly, I imagined. And we would have laughed together. But for the first time ever, it was okay that I laughed alone. I was with myself and not in a panic. *Is this the core reason for my trip, to make peace with myself? To be my own friend? Yes.*

I embraced my newfound comfort level at being alone with my thoughts—no need to receive outside approval, assurance, or commentary. I sat on the damp earth in the stillness, the dust of long-gone souls holed up in the tombs below. Yet I sensed their imprint on this place. They were with me. The space felt alive, vibrant. *This sensation would have gone undetected if I hadn't come alone.* I could feel it. Or was it simply the idea of it? Or the reverence and energy of humanity that kept this space sacred, venerating the land. Was this what I felt?

No matter, for if all Earth was treated as sacred and worth honoring, we just might find ourselves in Eden. The possibility thrilled me.

No Holding Back

Such emotions—such thrill—spoke a language, too. It's one that until now I'd felt compelled to restrain or, more correctly, was taught to do so. I could hear my mother admonishing me. *Don't you cry now,* or, *stop giggling* followed by *wipe that frown off your face.* Perhaps the noise of joy and heartache or the clamor of pain and fear was part of the gift.

The tears began to roll. For once in my life—a life controlled by restraint—I did not hold back. It wasn't an anguished cry; it was a soft and happy cry, a cry of release, a cry of acceptance. It said this: *To be alone and free was enough.* I could let my feelings out and express whatever surfaced—without shame, without embarrassment.

A roadway nearby hummed with the intermittent sound of trucks and cars, seemingly marring the silence of this space. But then again I wondered, *why bother comparing the pristine countryside to the advancement of technology or judge the latter in the negative way?* The sense of peace I had not yet known until sitting at the *Megalitico do Fulom* was enough to lessen any perception of the modern world displacing nature. For that, I was grateful. *Enough battling played out on earth. Anyway, why would I choose to fight what is ephemeral, fleeting, and not eternal?*

The clouds lifted revealing blue skies, my connection to earth and the heavens palpable. Those who lay beneath me had left their human bodies, transcending into another time, another space. Or perhaps they truly were with me at that moment although out of my time, out of my perception.

Build an Altar

The wind picked up, shifting me from stillness into action. I jumped up, inspired to build an altar. Poking around for rocks, I set out to outline the perimeter of a circular indentation in front of the tree stump where I'd been sitting. I gathered eucalyptus twigs and formed a cross in the center of the circle. On the cross, I laid more twigs to create an X. In the center, I placed the stone and blessed it with a sprinkle of Peace Waters. I heard a church bell chime in the distance. Only once. *Oneness.*

**I deemed my altar the circle of life,
the beginning and the end.
All the struggles from the day had melted away.**

If nothing else, I was happy for the peace of this moment and for my connection with life.

Chapter 5

"If you are here to help me,
you are wasting your time.
But if your liberation is bound in mine,
then take my hand and we will walk together."
— Dr. Nicandro Castañeda

Back in my room, I reached out and dialed home. Then I sat on the edge of the bed waiting for Jim's voice on the other end. As each ring blared into my ear, I imagined him picking up and telling me everything was okay. He would laugh at my description of the medieval orange room and my being lost. Most important, he would try to convince me it wasn't too late to come home. He would give me the permission that I wouldn't give myself.

The phone rang again. "Pick up, Jim," I pleaded into the air.

Then I realized my cell phone wasn't working. It was charged, sure, but the connection was spotty and, after the fourth ring, it clicked off and was replaced by blaring beeps. I had yet again (in the space of only a few seconds) projected a mental scene in which

Jim would be laughing, chatting, and imploring me to return home. But the reality was that *I* was alone and that I needed to rely on myself. So I pulled on a sweater and went downstairs, hoping I'd run into Antonio—perhaps help him feed the goats or milk the cow or anything, just to have someone talk to me.

Seeing anyone would feel welcoming.

When I entered a small alcove near the front door, I sat down on a small couch tucked along the wall. It looked as if it had been there since the building's construction hundreds of years ago. Beside it was a small aquarium, bulbous and squat, the kind you'd buy a child. A lone goldfish wiggled around inside it. And like most children's amusements when play turns into a chore, it was mossy with neglect.

This fish tank shared space with assorted knick-knacks: a wooden statue of St. Francis with a dove on his shoulder, a few books, and a Barbie doll, the kind with thick eyeliner from the early 1960s. A plastic Sophia Loren look-alike! *Funny thing,* I thought, gazing into her blank eyes. I suspect Antonio had become so familiar with this room, he no longer noticed the dust and clutter or the forgotten fish. (It appeared to me it survived by living on algae.)

The Gift of a Phone

I sank deeper into the belly of the couch, almost but not quite grateful for the companionship of the abandoned fish. I would be lying to myself if I didn't admit I was hoping for Antonio to appear. I tapped at my Droid phone with foolish faith, silently begging God to connect me to Jim. My struggles weren't so silent, though. That's when another pilgrim—an American—refreshed and clean, walked in. And without hesitation, he leaned in and handed over his phone. "I have good service here," he said, gesturing for me to take it.

I set down my useless Droid and accepted his offer of a phone. "Thanks. Thank you," I stammered, thrilled to hear his perfect American English. "So, you're okay with me calling out of country?"

"What other kind of call would you be making? The baker in town? The candlestick maker?" he said, a bright grin spreading across his face.

"True enough." I dialed and turned slightly away. The American turned a little, too, eyeing the goldfish, the books, and the Barbie doll. We shared a quick smile just as Jim picked up the phone.

"Hello?" I was certain my voice sounded desperate, even panicky, but I didn't care. I *was* desperate and panicky. "Jim? Can you hear me?"

"Hello," I could hear Jim say. "Hello my love? Is that you? Yes, I can hear you. I didn't recognize this number."

I didn't know where to begin. But I immediately knew I didn't want to hog the minutes on this nice man's phone. Then a newfound concern to appease Jim washed over me. "Yes, it's me and I'm okay. I'm fine."

All that inner whimpering and crying that had played out in my mind over the course of the past minutes were held inside.

I turned away from the man a bit more, which caused him to move farther into the dining room. *He is only being kind, allowing me a bit of privacy.*

"It's fine. And I don't expect you'll be hearing from me much," I told Jim. "The phone service isn't reliable, so we'll have to make do. There is no need to worry, though. Really. I'm doing well. And there are other pilgrims around—Americans." I looked over to the American. "I borrowed this nice man's phone because mine isn't working. No need to worry. I'm holding up fairly well. Really."

Jim seemed to buy it and then told me he missed me and loved me, which nearly broke me. I sat taller and brushed away the tears springing up in my eyes, trying to hold my composure within the folds of the sofa. I glanced over to the American. He had walked to the far end of the dining room and was peering out the window, a true gentleman out of earshot and unable to hear my goodbyes to Jim.

This began my friendship with a fellow countryman.

Dr. Nicandro Castañeda—*with a tilde*

The American was tall and lean, with large muscular hands and finely chiseled fingers. "I've had my share

46

of bad phone service," he said. "It can be unnerving when you're unable to contact loved ones to let them know you're alive and well."

"I know my husband was glad to hear from me. I'm sure of it. So, thank you. He'll sleep better tonight."

"I'm Nick, by the way–Doctor Nicandro Castañeda– 'with a tilde'." He offered a firm American handshake, said he was from California in fact, and traveling the *Camino* alone. I wondered if he was as thrilled as I was to have met someone from the States.

At dinnertime, it made sense to sit together. I flashed on Jim and knew he would understand. *It isn't as if we are on a date.* I could feel myself blushing. Not at all; I was a pilgrim dining with another pilgrim, who happened to be a man. Harmless.

"Are you okay?" Nick searched my eyes before breaking off a new piece of bread.

"I am fine, perfectly fine. I am missing Jim, my husband. That's all."

"Ah, right. That's one of the greatest challenges, isn't it?" He took a bite.

It felt better now that I'd invoked Jim's name. Nick seemed to key into my nervousness and began to chat about anything that might lighten the mood.

We shared our reasons for embarking on this journey, both of us laughing a little at how easy it was to plan it, yet how radical and life changing it seemed to actually be here.

"I feel as if home is a dream, and I need to hold the memory of it for fear I'll lose touch," I said.

"Yes, I think it has to do with the slowing down, the walking, the quiet contemplation. You'll soon find a nice pace. On a vacation different from this—this is no vacation, after all—we are programmed to let go of our lives, forget all the woes, stop all the busy-ness, all the worries," he said, sparking me to laugh out loud. "But here on this journey, we're called to slow down and search within ourselves."

"Yes! That's exactly it," I jumped in.

Common Threads

Nick had already been traveling the *Camino* for nearly a month, having started in *Lisbon*; taking his time along the way to experience the Feast Days of Holy Week and other cultural festivities. I was beyond impressed.

"The blisters finally got me," he winced, looking at his tennis shoes. "It was brutal for a time there." He motioned to Antonio to bring more wine.

"Well, I'm glad for you that those blisters are healing." I could have dropped to the floor and shouted. *Thanks to the universe for delivering this English-speaking soul to my dinner.* But of course I only smiled and scooped up another helping of vegetables.

Jim would have liked Nick. He was courteous and a great conversationalist. I liked him. He felt safe and familiar.

We both marveled over the fact of being so far from home yet practically neighbors in California.

We lightly touched on our backgrounds, politics, religion, but in a careful and measured way. We shared our favorite books and both gushed over learning we both had loved *The Alchemist* by Paulo Coelho.

I thought about my room, the plastic oranges and the bubble chair, and smiled at the quick turn life can take. *How wonderful to find such a comrade.*

Soon, other couples streamed into the dining room. We easily related to Klaus and Renata, our new German friends at the next table who were also walking the *Camino* for the first time. Both were retired physicians who had ten grandchildren, and among other wildly ambitious endeavors, they'd sailed the Baltic and now were walking the *Camino*. Both looked healthy and beautiful in that way people do after spending what I imagined was a lifetime of hearty physical outdoor activity. I liked them.

Another couple, young and in the throes of love, sat by the window; the two leaned into each other, kissing and cooing, and barely touched their food. The young man, obviously still not close enough to his lover, finally picked up his chair and scooted it next to hers.

Nick interjected, "I have a girlfriend who's also walking the *Camino*. She started in France, and we'll meet up in *Santiago*. We're both supportive, for the most part. We understand we had to take this journey for different reasons. We're not sure where we'll end up after—together, I mean." He swirled the wine around in his glass. "I'm grateful for that," he added.

I understood all too well. Without Jim's support and blessing, I couldn't imagine how I would have been able to make the trip. For the first time, I'm grateful Jim is *not* here because of the reasons Nick cited about his girlfriend. *I can't imagine walking alone, only to learn our relationship was over. Still, I wish Jim were here meeting Nick and sharing so much with him. I will keep a journal and take notes.*

"I miss my husband terribly," I said to Nick.

Not Alone After All

Then this thought suddenly occurred to me: *I wouldn't have to spend the entire Camino walk alone after all.* Of course, I reminded myself I had wanted the time alone. But a few hours sharing stories over dinner was more than nice; it was saving my sanity.

My dinner companion, I soon learned, was Doctor Nicandro Castañeda (with a tilde). He made sure I knew the importance of the tilde and his name's spiritual link to the author and soul journeyer Carlos Castañeda. Sometime during our dinner, I mentally dropped the *k* in Nick. He was simply Dr. Nic.

With so many commonalities, we quickly established a bond, but I refrained from being too overt. I didn't want to appear in the slightest way forward.

50

And while we chatted like old friends, both of us carefully held a sense of propriety, good manners. I liked him even more for this.

"It's as if I've met you before," he said, as Antonio cleared his plate. "Wouldn't that be something if we had? It isn't entirely impossible. I've visited San Diego many times."

His déjà vu feeling of finding an old companion felt true for me, too. I laughed along with him, happy to have found such a compatible dinner mate this early on my journey.

As we waited for dessert, Dr. Nic leaned down, looking toward his feet. "Enough!" he said. "Enough with these ridiculous blisters. I never dreamed they could cause such discomfort. I had no choice but to wait it out and allow them to heal."

"Look at you!" I teased. "Here you are the doctor yet suffering a patient's plight."

"Yes! But it's the nurses who tend to blisters. Where is a nurse when you need one?" He kidded, as he criss-crossed the dining room, his eyes shining. "Ah, my feet are as good as new now," he said. "And there's an upside after all. I'm glad I stopped here. We wouldn't have met otherwise."

He then raised his water glass and we toasted our meeting and our new friendship.

"I was thinking I'd like to welcome you to join me in the morning. We could walk together for a time. If you'd like."

"That would be great! Yes," I said. "Yes, I'd love that." *I didn't dare tell him how often I'd been lost and that I'd yet to discover if there truly are yellow arrows marking the way.* I was brimming—gleeful—that things had turned around. Dr. Nic would be my guide. He'd set me on the path and in the right direction.

Chapter 6

B reakfast at Antonio's was laid out buffet style: *pan*, biscuits, breads, pastries, rolls, and more bread served with two choices of morning-picked *naranjas*, juiced or whole, and Portugal's staple, *café com leite*. These were all lovingly prepared by Antonio's invisible wife. With little time between last night's dinner and this morning's breakfast, our bellies were more than full to meet the *Camino's* demand.

Antonio stamped our passports with his special *Sao Miguel* seal and imprinted kisses on both our cheeks. My final *bom dia* included my orange room, the goldfish, *Quinta Sao Miguel,* and the village *Arcos* as I followed my new companion out the gate. We headed toward *Barcelos,* twenty-three kilometers away.

A light steady rain made for muddy trekking on the country roads, but I was light-footed and nimble as I skirted the puddles to keep my boots relatively dry. Nic's tennis shoes and windbreaker were no match for the rain. That's my assessment.

It's also my opinion that Nic wasn't faring quite as well as me. Still, if he was feeling any discomfort, he didn't show it. I felt grateful for all my waterproof layers, thankful my rain pants passed the weight-to-value test when I was deciding if they were worthy to carry—in, then out, then in.

With Dr. Nic, I walked and talked the time away.

Step by step, we got to know each other and ourselves. The more familiar we got, the deeper became the inner probing of who we are and why we're on the Camino.

In Dr. Nic's reflection, I saw my hidden and internal *whys*.

Why Do Pilgrims Journey?

There are many reasons a pilgrim journeys, but what is *my* reason?

I know I'm not following the early Christian path to atone for my sins or earn heavenly indulgences. (Well, maybe heavenly indulgences.) Mine's a spiritual quest, but then everything I do is spiritual. None of us travel like our medieval brothers on horseback or donkey nor are we among the modern-day pilgrims on bicycles.

"Why are you a pilgrim, Nic? I wondered. *"For religious reasons? For sport and the challenge of walking for weeks in a foreign land? Or, is there some-inescapable-one thing you are running from?"*

"Why do you take this journey, Shima, alone and so far away from home?"

These were the unanswered questions underfoot.

Hearty Welcome

Estavao's *café* in the village of *Pedra Furado* made famous by my guidebook obliged us to stop, though neither one of us was hungry or needed rest in that moment. Entering a luxury eatery adjoining the popular pilgrims' *café*, we were greeted by two grandmotherly sorts—most likely Estavao's mother and aunt—who immediately seated us amid silver, crystal, linen, and chandeliers before we could realize our mistake and object.

Our sodden, disheveled appearance did not deter the women's hearty welcome. In the way only mothers can command, we stripped our wet layers to modest decorum. They hung our clothes to dry on backs of empty chairs, giving the appearance other diners sat in them. Grandma *Vovo* took my boots to place them by the fire, but I could see they'd be too close to the flames for my comfort. Instead, I kept them under the table like a precious pet.

Stripped to our underwear, we ate more than our fill of delicious food. Course after course, without request, the entrees kept coming.

**I had to keep swallowing or start crying;
these nurturing women reminded me so of Jim.**

I may as well say "I don't love you" as to refuse one of his—or their—exquisitely prepared meals, no matter how full.

We kept eating until Grandma *Vovo* and Aunt *Tia* deemed enough. Sated more than we dared acknowledge for a noontime meal, we redressed just as the formal mid-day diners attired in their finery took our places.

With another stamp in our passport, we departed.

The Mystical *Fonte da Vida*

"Dr. Nic," I stuttered, fearful of revealing too much too soon and hasten Nic's good-bye. "I'm in search of the mystical *Fonte da Vida*. Its healing waters are said to be the fountain of life. It's somewhere on *Monte Franqueria*, very close by, only five kilometers farther."

My invitation left out two factors: it's straight uphill 140 meters and I have only my intuition to guide me.

"If we imbibe this mystical elixir," I implored in my theatrical voice, "it will fortify us with its Light and Grace and move us into higher states of consciousness. It promises eternal gifts. I can't wait to find it! Want to come with me?"

I stood ramrod waiting for his physician's logic to fell me. It wouldn't be the first time I'd bared my mystic love, only to be left alone with my fantastical truths. But his boyish sense of adventure and affable charm wasn't suffused.

He enthusiastically agreed to join in my treasure hunt for God's fountain of life. I breathed with joy.

Sacred Stone Geometry

The steep climb up the curving mountain road carved through eucalyptus and ancient oaks opened to a hilltop clearing. There, huge stone slabs were strategically placed atop each other at perfect right angles. On either side marking their perimeter were two smaller stone slabs held perpendicular by two sturdy stones.

Immediately drawn into the sacred stone geometry, I marveled to Nic, "We are witnessing the work of indigenous people from an ancient . . . " and before I could say, "civilization," my visions of antiquity vanished in Nic's burst of unrestrained laughter.

"These are picnic tables and benches!"

Not ready to give in to my embarrassment, I choked, "In the wild, they could easily be ancient henges!" *Being on foot has a way of making things ominous and wild.*

This time Dr. Nic stood firm but kind in his knowledge that these picnic tables and benches were meant for the guests and parishioners of the chapel nearby. In that defenseless moment of pure silliness we'd just become real friends.

Finally, atop the *monte,* we rested. And from our henge, we breathed the Atlantic Ocean—so far, far away yet within sensual reach. We did not linger long; the day was waning. We had yet to find the *Fonte da Vida.* From there, it was still six more kilometers to get to *Barcelos.*

**Our spiral descent was marked by twelve huge
stone crosses towering more than fifteen feet each.**

This time, I wasn't fooled by their sacred geometry, for each symbolized the sorrowful ritual of the Stations of the Cross. Candles long since extinguished marked some but not others.

There was a time when these symbols of Jesus's suffering would have lured me, but not today. Today they did not represent the revelation of Jesus. Yet I continued walking and, with every step, I felt the energies of Christ's Light transforming the old ideas that mourning, suffering, and depletion were the way to God. I recognized Jesus as Christ. I saw Resurrection and Ascension, not crucifixion.

The Enchanted Forest

Not far from the Stations of the Cross, we came to a sign pointing to *Castelo de Faria*, an historical castle in the parish of *Gilmonde*. It would be another half kilometer out of our way, but it wouldn't take us much time to go.

As soon as we turned off the main road, the air stilled. It felt heavy and moist.

**Patches of sunlight shone through in veiled
prisms from the sky hidden behind a canopy
of ancient oak and pine.**

58

The moss, ferns, and lichen had grown meters thick in the rarified air. Pine needles and fallen leaves remained undisturbed where they had fallen season after season. The combined growth and decay gave a spring to our steps as we sunk into nature's mattress. Giddy with the feeling of stumbling into an enchanted forest, thoughts of Hansel and Gretel danced in our heads. With Nic's physician's logic abandoned, nothing could be further from his reality than this scene. A boyish adventure fully engaged his spirit.

To the left of the pathway was a huge boulder, a gatekeeper, guarding the sacred space we were about to enter. I stopped as if entering someone's house— in this case, the home of the Elementals and Devas. I asked for their blessings to continue, knowing that entering this natural cathedral was a spiritual passage. I took it seriously, for it would affect my pilgrimage and beyond.

Hidden beneath the heavy wooded overgrowth lay random piles of overturned squared boulders, remnants of a fourteenth century Roman fortress left in ruins. Smothered under the Roman-built remains thousands of years older than the ancient fortress were the invisible remnants of a prehistoric settlement called a *Citânia* dating back to the Iron Age 1200 BCE. We were hushed by the sheer antiquity surrounding us. Marvel and awe consumed our thoughts and silenced our chatter.

Next to the gatekeeper boulder stood another huge rock. It was smaller than the gatekeeper but still huge. Miraculously, from this rock grew a gnarled, decades-old tree. Its root system was embedded in the rock with its trunk and roots easily five feet above the ground. It appeared healthy and alive in partnership with the boulder. We realized how the mineral kingdom supports its life, nourishing the tree with all it needs to thrive.

We stood at this place of changing realities, seeing with certainty the rocks and crystals and stones pulsing with life force energy. They may not be at the level of consciousness or vibration as humans are—or even the other kingdoms of nature, angelic, elemental, and devic who call Earth home—but they contain a life force all the same.

The tree growing from the rock revealed a consciousness in everything, showing me that every molecule of creation can be a source of unlimited potential.

**I was stunned to silence in awe of what I saw.
I walked around in reverence seeking
something I wasn't sure of.**

Nic followed. *Perhaps he was more sure than me.*

Prodded to Move On

My quest for *Fonte da Vida* impatiently prodded me so I unduly moved on. We walked out of the forest back to the road and stepped out of our sacred trance. I had been led to this most sacred spot, but in my quest for the fountain of life, I did not give it its due.

We were on the road only a short while when the enchanted forest called to me again. I felt happy to have Nic with me for I could feel safe with him, a freedom I could not afford if I were alone. We detoured again, caught in the spell of each other . . . and God.

To the right were ancient stone steps leading up a forested hill. Overgrown with moss and buried in pine needles, they were spaced too far apart for stair-stepping, even for Nic's long, lanky legs. They demanded our respect.

We were drawn to them inexplicably and slowly and reverently. Walking two by two— but where? We didn't know. We walked. Nothing.

About then, I got tired from walking and weary from not being able to find the fountain. Blisters were forming on my little toe, but I was too keen on my intention to know that's what I was feeling. It felt like a pebble in my boot that I continually stopped to shake out.

Up the stairway and down the forested path, we were led in a circle back to our starting point on the main road. We laughed an exasperated laugh. What else could we do? A short ways farther, we came to a medieval circular tower. If I read my guidebook correctly, I could conclude that the fountain was nearby. No more direction or clues existed than that!

In my fatigue, I'd even forgotten *why* I was searching for the *Fonte da Vida*. I just wanted to quit. But Nic, more determined than me, sweet-talked me down another trail farther into the woods. Bolstered by his enthusiasm, I agreed, yet a moment of fear passed through me. *It's a steep climb to retrace our steps to our starting point, and we're both unsure that if we continue on this dirt track, it will lead us out of the forest and back to the road.*

Nic didn't know I lacked an internal compass. But it was getting late, and one of us had to decide.

Trusting that Nic's instincts were better than mine, I gave way to his direction and followed his lead to find the shortcut.

Still, my anxiety kept rising and silently I questioned my willingness to trust him. As I started to voice my doubt, my words of worry translated into "I trust you, Dr. Nic."

Then the road appeared. Once again our bond strengthened. Whew!

Chapter 7

"Why is finding the *Fonte da Vida* so difficult?" I pleaded to no one in particular.

Fatigue births philosophy—and it also births talking to oneself like this: "The fountain of life is within you. You are looking outside of yourself for something you carry within. The eternal fountain of Grace and Illumination and Wisdom is not found outside of you."

Satisfied with the fountain's message, I was ready to head straightaway to the hotel in *Barcelos*. Done! But Nic had more in him and was willing to continue the search. Reluctantly, I agreed to keep looking as long as we stayed on the main road and walked only in the direction of *Barcelos*.

Eventually, we arrived at a seemingly abandoned old church and convent. A steep short flight of stairs led to its entrance. By now, even Nic was tired, and one more stone step seemed too much.

I agreed to walk the flight ahead and report my findings while Nic stayed behind, wanting to be sure the trek was worth his dwindling energy.

I waved him up to join me. Together, we walked to the entrance of the church. Locked! Next, we walked to the convent door and hammered the huge door knocker. This was answered by a barking dog. By the sounds we heard, he was big. But no other sounds were heard. And with the locked door between us and the dog, we felt safe to explore a bit.

To the left of the church on the side of a work shed was a faucet—the kind I attach my garden hose to at home. "Is *this* the fountain?" I asked. "Is this *it?*" Pointing to a dirt-smudged brass plaque hidden by weeds, Nic whispered, "Yes, this is your *Fonte da Vida.*"

"Are you kidding me? This is it?"

**Any spiritual joy suddenly evaporated.
I was tired, discouraged, and ashamed
that I'd led Dr. Nic on a sham.**

I was also filled with guilt and regret that I didn't spend more time at the *Castela de Faria* in the enchanted forest. *I'm crazy.*

"Come on, Shima," Nic cajoled. "Turn on the faucet and dip your hands in the cool water. It will feel good. Let's take our boots off. Here, let me help. Who's to say it's not the fountain of life? You can't always trust appearances."

I noticed how we'd switched roles, now I was the doubting one. So I followed my prescribed plan. From my pack, I pulled the Peace Waters and lavender essential oil, and I blessed the fountain and both of us.

Next, I filled my small vial with this eternal elixir from the fountain of life. Then it came to me!

Aha! The fonte's gift is disguised in opposites.

I realized this water faucet was metered out and portion-controlled, not universal and ever-flowing as I had expected. Rather, it was a symbol that man believes he can turn God's gifts on and off. But this is not God's Truth. Grace and all of God's gifts are abundantly given and ever expansive. Thus the *Fonte da Vida* symbolizes a system that controls God's gifts and doles them out at will.

Fonte da Vida was not a place nor an allocation nor a faucet on the side of a shed. *It's the Grace within my own body. The fountain of life is within me. It's God-given, infinite, and eternal.*

I felt jubilant knowing Spirit runs through me as unlimited Grace, constantly moving to whatever, whomever, or wherever I am asked.

The Missing i-n-o-s

By six o'clock we'd been walking on the road eight hours. One blister had formed on my small right toe, yet we had many kilometers to go.

Back on the cobblestoned lane we followed its path to the outskirts of a village, where we rounded the corner and came upon a garden of irises. Everywhere! Purple petals were surrounded by the saturated green leaves and grass trembling in the breeze. The purple blasted through the gray afternoon.

Dr. Nic had been walking in front of me all day; we had kept a nice pace, a steady rhythm—one, two, one, two. But when he stopped in his tracks awed by so many flowers, it caused me to stumble forward. After helping me stand upright, he turned back to the iris field, his mouth hanging. This roadside garden shimmered as if electrified beneath the dome of gray above us. "It's almost too much, you know," I said, breathy and flushed after all the walking. We stood in the quiet taking in the color, breathing in the scent of green with the dark soil beneath it.

"Yep, this is just the thing," he began, raising his arms upward. "This! This is what I needed—what *we* needed." The rain picked up a little. It tapped at our faces, the dirt, and the leaves around us.

We had made it to the village *Barcelinos*.

"And we've made good time," I said, nearly shouting.

I spread open my arms, taking in the scope of this moment, the grandness of it.

"We have arrived!" I felt silly and light, and that felt good. The rain washed over the irises, over us—a simple gift of the seasons changing.

"I adore springtime," I said, talking more to myself than to Nic. Finally, after traveling thousands of miles from California, I felt strong and alive—truly alive. I looked to Dr. Nic who remained in his own reverie, a smile across his face. All the walking and talking between our dips into silence had bonded us nicely. I was grateful for our friendship.

"It's all so lush and vivid," he sighed, then turned to me. "Let's keep going into the town."

"Yes, let's." I jumped to catch up, then quickly marching alongside him. But my enthusiasm wilted when he looked to a sign and pointed out I had mistaken *Barcelinos* for our destination, *Barcelos*, another five kilometers away.

"I didn't notice those few letters, the i-n-o-s," I wanted to say something more. *How could I fix it?* I felt my cheeks heat up. Once again the exhaustion was overtaking me. "Huh, it's amazing how a few letters make all the difference."

"Like five kilometers difference," he teased.

"What is it with this language? Everything seems to sound the same? It's nearly all spelled the same, too," I pointed to the map. He just laughed, not wanting to crush me further, not interested in stating the obvious that, yes, a few letters *do* matter. Of course, it's the same in our native tongue. I imagined a poor villager, map in hand, navigating the streets of New York, mind boggled over words such as "their" and "there."

"Yeah, I imagine it would be hard learning English, paining over words like 'enough' and 'cough'."

"Yeah, next to words like 'gruff' and 'tough'," he teasingly pushed me.

But my error wasn't the least bit funny.

Five more kilometers ahead of us seemed like a prison sentence.

My physical and my emotional exhaustion was palpable. The tedious walking was having its way with both my body and my psyche. *I'd been such a fool. Could I walk five more kilometers in this rain?*

"We didn't make such good time after all," I said, dejected. Dr. Nic, lifting his chin with a laugh, waved off the remark. "It's no problem. We're here now. And this isn't so bad. I still have a little fire in me from our big lunch."

Bellies Full of Oranges

And then our *Barcelinos* angel appeared. A small woman, lithe and spry, probably deep into her eighth decade. She wore a kind of happiness on her face that was contagious. Her laugh lines tilted upward from eons of smiling, an eternity of accepting life on life's terms.

We traded a look as if she also wanted to take me in and offer me the joy she carried. She pointed to a lush tree in her garden, standing resolute behind a low stone wall and then to her apron bulging with sweet oranges, *naranjas*. Then she filled our arms with homegrown fruit from her own tree. She gave freely, nearly more than we could hold.

In that moment, Dr. Nic and I both felt compelled to kiss this beautiful grandmother. As I did, her work-worn fingers touched my cheek, causing me to lose my grip. My oranges tumbled to the ground. She then turned and held her skirt, motioning for us to wait, and ran to her shed returning with a plastic bag. I was crying.

How simple. A woman in her roadside garden is giving away fruit. Why does it cut so close? Why do I feel an aching so acutely? I tried to hold back but could not. "*Estou cansado, muito, muito cansado. I am tired, very, very tired, so very worn out.*" I wanted to excuse myself with this weary rationale, but my desire for love—for a mother's love—went beyond my capacity to contain.

Our eyes locked again. I felt certain she could see into me, certain that she forgave my poor use of her language, certain that she cared about me. Then I turned to Nic.

"Are you crying?" I mouthed.

He blinked and turned his face into the rain, wiping away the wet. He must have also longed for his mother's love, but he said nothing, his smile slapped silly on his face.

Then our grandmother, this angel, ambled back toward her *casa*, her gait angling slightly to the left, her age more apparent from a distance.

We knew the meaning of life was as simple as loving and being loved.

A stone wall ahead offered a place to savor our gifts. Dr. Nic, so enthused by the *Señhora* and her oranges, bit into one orange whole and spit out the rind, juice dripping through his fingers and flowing down his chin. I carefully peeled mine at first, but soon I was diving in, too, sucking and slurping, half chewing, half sipping.

"This is almost too sweet, otherworldly sweet," I said through chews of orange. "We've died and gone to orange heaven." Knowing the fruit would be heavy in our packs, we ate our fill, leaving only a few to tuck away for later. *We're tired. Better to carry the weight in our stomachs than our packs.*

Chapter 8

What had been a light sprinkle turned to heavy rain, the kind that obscured the setting sun, turning the sky into shades of dark slate. Thankfully, we made it to the outskirts of town before nightfall. *Barcelos* marked our first big city since departing *Porto*.

After ambling in the countryside, the noise and grit of an industrial highway hammered at me. "Are we there yet?" I called out to Nic, not caring that I sounded like a child.

"I'm guessing we have about one more hour." He was faring better than me. I prayed for a taxi—aloud. "Please, God! Bring me a cab! Now," I yelled out.

"I can't pray for a cab right now, Shima. I can't pray for what I don't need. I feel good."

Well, la-dee-da for you. I thought it but didn't dare say it.

"You're right. We can do this. I *can* do this." Our lucky meeting with the angel-grandmother—with her love and her oranges—had given him a new lease on life. "All that juicy sugar must be running through your veins, Nic. You're hopping along like a kid on pixie sticks."

As for me, although I took it in and ate the sweetness, the energy somehow didn't stick. We trudged on, my mind circling upward high into the night. I looked down on us and saw two Americans—strangely together in a foreign land—walking along, bellies full of orange, and I let the tears flow.

A New Backpack and Memories of Tanner

The next day I woke up to rain in my heart. In contrast, Nic awakened to sunshine, a mirage from yesterday's enchanting moments.

Up early, Nic had been wandering the sleeping city when he chanced upon a Boy Scout store and while still enraptured he saw the store as a sign that it was a time for a new backpack. After nearly a month on the *Camino,* he had slowly come to the realization that his day pack wasn't carrying its weight against the rigors of the road. He was finally ready to let go of a burden he didn't have to endure.

With the enthusiasm of a young scout, he hurried back to the hotel to enlist my help in selecting the perfect back pack.

The bell, clanging against the opening door, transported me back to San Diego and the day I met Tanner at Adventure 16.

He was clad in khaki, plaid and green, featherweight mountain boots and name-tag. So rugged and handsome, this clerk was the perfect model to sell the company's wares. Every man entering the store would aspire to be Tanner. His short, brown, perfectly cut hair and dark-rimmed glasses gave clues that he'd be equally poised in cosmopolitan San Diego with an ingénue by his side—a young thirtyish "hip" kind of guy, no swagger.

Quiet and confident, he greeted me with an air of wisdom in a bookish yet out-doorsy sort of way. He treated me as he would an avid alpiner, even though he could tell I was a Nordstrom kind of girl.

I greeted Tanner with a list in hand— boots, backpack, sleeping bag, everything necessary to live on the Camino. Visit by visit through tiny bits of small talk, common threads unraveled, and we ecame friends. One thread: we were both Montanans.

Over time, Tanner taught me a little at a time as trust bloomed between us. Boots first—how to fit—Gortex versus leather. "And if they get wet," he advised, "do as the salty pros do and sleep with them."

Tanner outfitted me with the best and the lightest. He showed me how to cinch up and pack tight. He talked in terms of liters, ounces, and fill until I was confident I could take the first step outside of his inside outdoor store—like a good teacher. I liked Tanner.

When the clang announced the next scout entering, we headed outside. But every few steps, Nic would stop to adjust, align, strap, and clamp. He just couldn't cozy up to his choice of packs. Finally unable to hold back my laughter at Nic hoisting this cub scout-sized pack, we backtracked to the store. Without Tanner's expertise this time, I helped fit Nic with a pack rightly sized for his towering six-foot frame.

Rain on Our Parade

That day, we saw a citywide carnival staged in the town square. Like the scene in *Funny Girl*, it seemed to hum, "Don't rain on my parade."

Sadly, the sodden colors and stilled carousel cast against the gray skies were gloomy, not gleeful. It reminded me of a clown who missed the mark by frightening, not frolicking. The previous night had been so different. Then, colored lights illuminated all of the playful children buoyed by balloons. They were swinging their hands in time with organ pipes that trilled with each turn of the Ferris wheel.

**But in the early morning gloom, the sugary
scene from the night before held no allure.**

On the outskirts of the square, we passed an open-air market peaked high with colorful fruits and vegetables. Trying to create a joyful promise of an afternoon picnic, I leveled the mounds of grapes, apples, dates, and almonds with my purchases. Then I enlisted Nic, who had ample room in his new oversized pack to carry them.

Sao Bento, Saint Benedict's Church next to the market, called me inside to express forgiveness, but the sight of a grim sepulcher only served as an ugly incriminator. *How many times do I deny myself simple joy?* With that thought, I hastily dropped a few coins in the box and departed Godspeed. On my way out, I stopped to bless myself in the Catholic tradition. *Hmmmm. The holy water font was dry.*

In the City's Maze

While we had dallied in the church, the storm had dwindled in force. Because we had planned a short journey today—only twelve kilometers to *Quintiaes*—this delay was good. So we skirted in and out of side streets and main streets seeking the yellow arrows that would lead us out of the busyness of passing cars, mopeds, bicycles, stop signs, street signs, and shop signs. We sought to get back to the peaceful pathway of the country lanes. *I'm happy to be with Dr. Nic, for this city maze would surely offer a replay of my walking in lost circles in Vila do Conde.*

We passed a city dweller, a street beggar who'd polished his profession and set his sights on us. Even in Portuguese, I could tell his pitch was perfect and we weren't his first pilgrims. He promised if I gave him a few euros, he would not use them to buy a drink—a sure sign that he would. I gave him one euro; he begged for two. Nic offered him fruit and nuts, but he wanted euros, not nuts, as he pointed to his decaying teeth.

We kept walking.

Further on to the next church, we met another sort—a deaf and dumb man, open mouthed and toothless, with smiling eyes.

I felt a sweet, sweet soul reaching out to hug me from this man's restricted body.

We embraced. He smiled, tongue protruding. I asked Dr. Nic, "Is it money he needs?" *For this person, I would gladly empty my purse.*

"No, not money; just love." So I hugged him again and walked on.

Coins for Sweets

Walk, walk, walk—arrow by arrow, kilometer after kilometer—to the next *café* where we ordered *café com leite* and added *pan* and *queso* to our stowed treats.

With one eye on me and the other on Nic, two young boys about aged five and seven played chase between a labyrinth of legs lined up at the bar. The *meninos* shied away from me, but the lure of *vente centavos por dulce*—coins for sweets—melted their uncertainty. They grabbed my coins and ran.

Another older *garoto*, perhaps twelve, stood off to the side, too polite to take his share. I coaxed him into telling me his name. "Jaro," he answered. I ask him how to say a few simple words and then, in a mix of English, Spanish, and Portuguese, I haltingly asked, "*Por que usted no escuela*? No school for you today?"

"Silly, odd foreign woman," he undoubtedly thought before he proclaimed, "*é Sábado*, "It's Saturday! There is no school on Saturday!" So I reverted to what we all could understand and, in good fun, smacked my palm to forehead. I smiled, he smiled, and then he accepted my gift of *cinquenta centavos*— fifty cents, twice more than the young ones in honor of his age. Smiles all around. *I love the children.*

Ceremonious Spot

Not long after, along the roadside we came upon the ancient spring named *Fonte Ferreirinha*. It was easy to imagine weary pilgrims during medieval times stopping in this spot for rest. Nothing seemed to have changed. Or perhaps their spirits still lingered to greet those who followed.

Fonte Ferreirinha proved to be a peaceful oasis where ferns fanned the embankment, giving the feel of Elementals living among the wild parsley and mint. The gurgling waters reminded me of Middle Earth Beings giggling. What a perfect place to unpack my sacred bundle and create a ceremony.

First, I gathered waters from the trickling stream to add to my Peace Waters collection, and then I virtuously inhaled the essential oil called Citrus Bliss. With my senses awakened, I invited Nic to choose one of the little cards each with a sacred geometric symbol I call Ascension Kis that I had printed just for these mystical moments. There are thirty-three Kis in the card collection symbolizing Peace, Love, Forgiveness, Majesty, and such. Nic chose Patience—experiencing each moment with divine purpose and in perfect timing. I picked Gratitude—Grace and appreciation for all of life.

Like skipping stones, we flicked the tiny cards into the waters and watched as the current carried our spiritual desires downstream. Then we stepped back into the reality of the *Camino* and continued walking. We entered into a peaceful rhythm that would keep us together on the *Camino* for as long as our souls could keep pace with each other.

The Flower of Life

A short distance farther was a small stone wall separating the dirt path from a farmer's field of blooming mustard—perfect for wayside dining. The plots were squared off by the stones the farmer had harvested. In one square was a loan sheep posted to the ground and attached to a six-foot chain. That was the extent of Mr. Chops' universe. But the farmer, in his kindness I suppose, moved the post from time to time, which created perfectly mowed circles spiraling into each other. *It all came down to this: the spiral, the vortex, the flower of life.*

A second glance took me further into the cosmos, and the sacred geometry began to resemble miniature crop circles. I glanced up toward Nic and saw him smiling. Then I looked up at the Milky Way—smiling, too!

Chapter 9

"Every two hours, take off your boots and socks. This will keep blisters at bay." The voice inside my head carried the tone of a know it all. Too late. "I told you so!"

I thought back to when I hinted at the possibility of taking this pilgrimage and testing my idea with family and friends. Once they accepted the incredulous with rolling eyes and shaking heads, each had grim forewarnings accompanied by their expert but untested advice. It was always theatrical, no matter who was in judgment.

That day, I was hearing my son's advice from afar. "Dry feet—no blisters."

In retrospect, I should have listened to my son who had never hiked—I mean *seriously* hiked like his mother. I actually didn't know what a blister felt like; I had mistaken it for a pebble in my boot. Then my ever-present bubbled little toe became like an annoying little sister I couldn't get rid of. I hadn't believed Dr. Nic when he told me his blisters had sidelined him for days. Suddenly I understood. First hand.

My blisters both hobbled and humbled me. I had no remedy except to wrap, tape, moleskin, and pad them with whatever was available. Then I had to fit my club foot into my boot and walk through the pain. There was no other way.

Realizing I have nine other toes and two heels that could still fall victim to "a pebble in the boot," I heeded Jimmy's long-distance advice. I removed my boots and socks.

A Feast Along the Way

Nic and I unwrapped the special foods we'd collected along the way—dense crusty bread, farm-made cheese, apples, and nuts—an epicurean spread royally equal to yesterday's fare served on linen with silver.

As we sat on the stone wall picnicking, a few *peregrinos* passed by. An Australian couple we had met yesterday in *Pedra Furada* recognized us and called out, "Hello, two Americans!" Before long, another pilgrim—a Dutch woman older than us—took a seat beside me. She picked up midsentence telling us her chronicles, not caring if we were listening. It seemed she was used to talking to herself. She told us (or herself) that this was her fifth *Camino*.

I empathized. Yes, the *Camino* is like that. It gets into your heart and soul and won't let go until you find yourself—or whatever you might be searching for. I suspected Mrs. Dutch will walk all twelve routes before she's done.

The rain gave us a reprieve and the day turned dry. Even so, I still wore my rain pants because I couldn't take them off. Sealed in my waterproof bubble, my leggings had become soaked with sweat. The outside chill wouldn't allow for bare legs so I opted for sweat over chills and walked on in my self-contained sauna.

Actually, we zombie-walked—like slow sleepwalking—more tiring than a steady gate. I got hot, then cold, layer on, layer off. Nic's pack still demanded our attention, always needing adjustments. It was only a short four kilometers to the village of *Aborim,* but our slow pace got the best of us. We stopped at an outlying village church. And, as I'd come to expect, the church doors were locked—again!

Before we could unload our gear, we shifted into laughter—the tears running down our cheeks, rolled-over stomach-ache kind of laughter. The debacle of Nic's pack, my sweat pants, and our snail's pace had me on my back like an upside turtle who couldn't get righted. Nic's six feet doubled (maybe even tripled) over into a boy version of his tall self. Our laughter brought us so close to God, we could see Him everywhere.

In that moment, every nagging pain was released, replaced with a surge of energy to journey on.

An Innocent Request

"Can I hug you?" I was jolted from our torrent of laughter by Dr. Nic's innocent request. While laughing, I felt as close as two people could be in the moment.

I didn't judge my behavior as anything but appropriate. It was tender and affectionate and intimate and all things I know about love.

Yet his simple request for a hug, a harmless hug if he were still a stranger, had me swirling. Now he was more. And so was his hug.

I had to think. *Can he hug me? What does a hug mean? As a married woman, am I allowed to hug another man? Will this give Nic the wrong idea? What would Jim think? Will this change how we are with each other? I'm alone. I have to keep my guard up. I'm a married woman. I have to honor my marriage. I can't give the wrong idea.* On and on and on—all in a second's timeframe.

I sometimes use Jim as my defender whenever I get the feeling of sexual innuendo—not by Nic who hasn't crossed that line—but with others. I pull the "husband" card and cast Jim as my protector. *I can't have it both ways if I needed to play that card down the road. But there's no down the road now. We're in the moment.*

So we hugged. And our friendship deepened at this moment on the *Camino*. It was created in the intimate sharing of who we are in a place where nothing else exists—in the mirror of each other.

There was nowhere else for me to look and nothing else to reflect on—except who I truly am.

Yet it was complicated by a more difficult image too look at—who I was portraying myself to be. *There is nothing to attach to. I am in the present where the past has no relevance and there is no future. There is no escaping the truth of my self-realization.*

I felt Nic's melancholy weeping through his laughter. Or was it mine? Hilarity is hysteria, love is loss, and tears are tears, happy or sad. I spiraled in the oneness of sameness. I was losing my grip. I had to keep walking, but I can never get away from my feelings. They walked inside me.

We were getting close to my night's destination at *Casa dos Assentos* in *Quintiaes*. That was where we would say our good-byes. Nic planned to continue to the *albergue* nine kilometers away, while I stayed behind. I knew he was feeling the pull of our separation—not separating from me but from our constant and real companion, Spirit.

Our Separate Ways

After our hug, there wasn't much to say. Calm prevailed between us as we walked alone in our thoughts to *Aborim* where the *Camino* would split into our separate ways. I was trying to be strong but thoughts of being alone without him left me teetering. I wore my unease like an overcoat, and Nic could sense it.

"I'll walk you to your guest house." Nic offered. "It's not far, and there's plenty of daylight for me to make it to the *albergue* before dark."

"Really? Are you sure?" My need to feel safe with Nic by my side tugged like a puppy pulling at his master's pants.

Casas dos Assentos was off the yellow-arrowed *Camino*, which forced us to stop at the nearest *café* for directions and yet another *café com leite*.

Adjoining the train station, the *café* bustled with out-of-towners in transit. Away from the city and deep in the country, foreigners were few with English rarely heard or spoken. The country dwellers' earthy dialect was so gritty and guttural, even Dr. Nic couldn't comprehend their offers to help, further compounding our feelings of uncertainty.

I turned to my guidebook, but even the author must have been tired at this juncture. He didn't write much, and his few directions were vague and halting. The only thing I could garner was to follow an asphalt road.

When Nic headed down a cobblestone road, I dug in my boots and insisted we turn around. Since we'd been lost in the woods, we had made an unspoken pact that Nic would lead the way. In that moment, my decisiveness surprised and confused him. He didn't know I'd already gone solo in my mind.

It's one thing to observe the cosmos in the swirl of a porcelain sink; it's quite another to be in it, lost in space and alone.

Last Few Hours

No matter how well we had planned our day, the last kilometers required lots of grit to muscle through. The sun broke for a short while, but I felt cold and damp from my rain-soaked sweat pants. We were both tired, yet Nic was determined to walk into the dusk and bed down wherever he landed. Once he even slept on a firehouse floor, he'd told me. Without me whining by his side demanding a bed, bath, and home-cooked meal, he would go back to his macho digs. In fact, had it not been for his blisters and pains, he would have never allowed himself the luxury of *Quinta Sao Miguel* where we met.

**What gifts the *Camino* offers,
even the gift of blisters.**

Chapter 10

I learned that a special village celebration, a Bishop's feast, Saint Martin's Day, was being planned for the next day. Carnival music blared from over-amped speakers announcing the coming festivities. The sound oozed from the village church and smothered the hillsides, sending every bird, rabbit, and rodent into hiding. The message had an odd, trance-like cadence. "It sounds like mind control," I joked before I, too, got caught in its spell.

We marched to its rhythm until we arrived at the gate of *Casas dos Assentos.*

This old mansion made of faded pink stucco was a neglected manor too big to heat or maintain. Disguised as a sanctuary for weary *peregrinos,* I questioned if the rooms were fit for the high fee charged. Walking inside, I was simultaneously greeted and dismissed by a pointed finger in the direction of my room. The cold, damp mold transported me to the foul winter in *Estoril* when I was just twenty-two—too young to know better. If it weren't for being in the throes of Jim's love, I would never have survived that long-ago winter of homesickness and cold in Portugal. In the end, nothing could warm me, so I returned to Mom and Dad and what I thought was home in Billings, Montana. There, I discovered I was even more distraught without Jim—cold, mold, and all. Still, nothing could warm me.

**No amount of airing out could purge
these spores. They engulfed me.
They are the residents here,
and I am the unwelcome visitor.**

And now this. What have I done to repeat this sadness? What more must I learn? I held my breath, praying for stamina to withstand my memories and cross the threshold.

Yet, I was too tired and too unwilling to go another step. The *Casa* had to do.

Settling In

By the time we arrived, about six o'clock, Nic had decided to spend the night, too. "No reason to journey on. We've put in an honorable day," he reconciled. "Honorable!?" Snort. "M-m-making—" sniff, chortle, "time—" I choked out "at one kilometer an hour?" I felt my asthma setting in, but it was my relief that smothered me. We laughed into each other.

To our surprise and delight, our friends Klaus and Renata were sitting by the pool in a patch of waning sun. Perhaps in the heat of summer, this scene would appeal. Now it only sent shivers. In an effort to fore-warn us, they complained that the blaring music in town had been unending—as if we couldn't hear it. "The same song over and over since we arrived!" they declared in the same eerie cadence as the beat. It had unnerved them—and me—as I recalled my flip com-ment about mind control.

Then we all laughed in that frustrating, accepting sort of way. It's not pilgrim-like to give way to an-ger. Yes, we bolstered each other that way, keeping our tempers intact.

Pilgrims tend to armor themselves in courtesy with an unwritten agreement not to complain about our aches and pains, our tiredness and coldness. And aloneness.

But I did not play the pilgrims' game well. I whined. It felt good to speak out about my feelings, releasing the pressure of my emotional blisters like those on my feet.

I welcomed alone time before dinner, free of my pack and boots, the anticipation of a hot bath and a good meal kept my spirits buoyed. Thoughts of a hot bath and washing away the day's dust always en-couraged me onward when the last kilometer seemed impossible. We each have our mantra to prompt us toward our reward at the end of each day. Some think of a glass of wine, a sumptuous dinner, or the simple pleasure of staying still. Mine was Peace Waters—warm, healing, soothing, rejuvenating waters. Hot baths have long been my luxury. Besides my precious journal, my essential oils and toiletries were the heaviest of my belongings. I carried their weight specifically for this time each day.

My small room with its dark wood paneling and threadbare carpet was furnished with an antique washbasin and iron bed. It felt cold, dark, musty, *and* moldy. I turned the steam heater to high—nothing—plainly shut off at its source. So I moved to the bathroom to pour a tub in the sparkling white marble bathroom—clean, modern, and so out of place in this ancient castle. But its appearance was deceptive. *This renovated bathroom must be requisite for ratings in the guide books.*

The tub filled icy cold. I drained and refilled it. (It would not be the first time my lefts and rights, clockwise and counters, hots and colds were reversed.) This time the water poured out lukewarm—enough to clear the dust off the day's weary walk but far from hot enough to soothe my soul. Refreshed but not in the way I imagined, I hurriedly dressed to seal in any remaining body heat.

Remnants of a Better Time

In the dining room, I rejoined Nic and met Klaus and Renata and the same young German couple who shared the dining room at *Casa Sao Miguel.* To the young lovers, we were invisible even though we'd crossed paths twice and shared a meal. Yet I knew the feeling of their all-consuming love. In an emotional flash, I saw Jim as clearly as if he were beside me. I stared longingly. I stared too long. His absence pierced my heart.

Each couple sat at a separate table. We were acquaintances yet too unfamiliar to share a family meal. I was grateful for Nic's sharing my table and my aloneness. Still, the absence of a fuller sense of camaraderie added emptiness to a room that was already cold and lifeless. We huddled and shivered in silence as we awaited our first course.

I looked around the room and envisioned a better time of warmth and cheer and laughter filling this old house. But not this day. The heavy brocade curtains, evident of a time of wealth, hung by their threads. The hearth that once warmed this giant mansion with roaring fires when wood was abundant gaped opened like the entrance to a dark cave. Old curiosities collected on family trips and portraits of family forefathers gathered dust on mahogany shelves. The chandelier was dark with the remaining daylight casting an eerie glow through leaded window panes.

If I were to go any further, I knew this look into the past would sadden my soul, so I abruptly snapped back to the present. Surmising what went before—reflecting the pain and loss for this family—softened the harshness of what I saw in the surroundings.

**The *Camino* teaches surrender and allowance
over and again.**

Like a Grimm Tale

A young woman who looked older than her years served us. She carried the burdens of her lot heavy on her back and it showed. We learned she lived in small quarters with her mother and other members of her family off in one wing of the mansion. Her lodging most likely was just enough to pay her wages and not take profits from the matron. I imagined its cramped quarters were not enough to create a comforting home.

I sensed the woman's fear of the dominion, invisible yet present. Her timid smile and unsure gestures made it seem like she was being watched by a wicked witch shadowing her.

**Everything about this place
seemed to tell a Grimm tale.**

The soup arrived, portioned out in pre-determined quantities by the unseen authority of the innkeeper. But the soup was cold and watery—so unlike the traditional rich *sopa de legumes* of pureed vegetables, kale, and olive oil I had anticipated. I ate rice and vegetables because I equated food to warmth and taste, although it did neither. Still, the food filled my empty stomach. I passed time with others and for this I felt grateful. We huddled and shivered until our common misery united us. For the first time, we openly shared who we were, where we lived, and what brought us here together.

I don't remember the particulars of dinner, only the ugly reckoning at the end. When we received the final bill it did not reflect the pre-arranged price for our room and meal. I felt deceived and wouldn't back down in the face of this injustice with my fellow pilgrims bearing witness.

I was sorry to have to go through this enslaved young woman to reach the house authoritarian, but my sense of justice had been pricked. More than that, every promise of warmth and comfort had been breached. I declared I would only pay what was agreed and no more. And only the matron of the house held the power to resolve this dispute.

In the few Portuguese words I knew, I demanded to speak to the one in command to rectify this inequity. Nic, who's usually right there to fill in the right word, was silent. The young woman directed me to the owner's daughter Julia. Although early in the night, Julia was "in her cups." She, too, was equally enslaved and tried to dissuade me with all the excuses that have worked with others. Living under the thumb of her mother, through blood and wits, she'd learned to pacify both mother and guests.

Still, I insisted on speaking to her mother—the true authority—and Julia's fear of bringing this woman into our conflict got results.

Finally, we agreed on a price. It was hard for me to be the outspoken one saying what everyone was thinking. But rather than feeling courageous and justified, I felt ashamed for standing up to this tyrant. In the end, the personal price I paid was too high; I should have just paid the bill. Through the pain of Julia, the server, the guests, and my own, I saw this *casa*—this enslaved castle—for what it was.

It chilled me in a way the physical cold couldn't penetrate. Cold to the bone.

I dressed for bed wearing a wool cap, down jacket, wool socks, and cashmere shawl. Then I crawled into my sleeping bag underneath two heavy gray wool blankets. I burrowed under the covers to warm my nose, the only thing exposed, and I dozed off. Suddenly I was shocked awake by an earthquake. Turned out it was the roar of a train, but being awakened created a startled feeling just the same.

At midnight, the music ended and the fireworks began. Bang, bam, and boom without stop. This time I didn't mistake the explosions for earthquakes or trains. I burrowed deeper and tried to sleep, eager for dawn to arrive.

No rest tonight.

Trust My Intuition

I tossed and turned, my subconscious unwilling to give up, trying to convey an important message. Finally, at 1:27 a.m. the village dogs barked me awake to a myriad of thoughts.

I warned myself, *"In this place, energy had been severely misused. There are ruthless people on this trail. There are charlatans and thieves and gangsters even.*

There are disreputable people who will use me," I didn't think about this to scare me but rather to wake up and use my discernment.

**I had to trust my intuition
and watch what I say and to whom.**

I knew I'd be protected as long as I freely chose the path of God. Yet the question hung in the air: *I was choosing God, wasn't I?*

It had been six days since the beginning of my *Camino*. I had walked seventy-three kilometers.

I rose at dawn, intent on making the most of daylight. We had a long way to get to *Ponte de Lima*—more than twenty-five kilometers—with no optional layovers. I knew we'd be well served to start with a good breakfast.

The innkeeper, however, had cleverly learned to increase profits and avoid added wages by serving breakfast late in the morning at one seating time. No early breakfast for us! I suppose I couldn't fault her for wanting to make a profit, even if her schedule didn't fit my plans. So we agreed to meet promptly at eight and forego the early start for the sake of getting a hearty meal.

I should have known breakfast would be as dismal as dinner. But rather than scold myself, I grabbed a piece of bread and a slice of cheese while hollering to

Nic, "Are you coming?" My tone echoed across the room like that of an old friend, a sister even. Our fast bond had been based on a common goal.

The physical, emotional, and spiritual stamina that this journey required, pushing into a new horizon each day, begged unconditional support for each other.

As we bounded away from the *Casa*, I chose to leave my crankiness behind and slipped within the layers of thick fog saturating the road that morning. Searching for the silver lining, I found it hiding in a cloud of celestial reverence, a gift from God.

Chapter 11

The morning's all-consuming stillness was cool and ethereal. No room to carry both my emotional ache *and* the pain from my blisters. Then, as we climbed a slope, church bells pierced the silence. It was Sunday. Church. Before long, a slow stream of cars rumbled by with driver, wife, grandma, grandpa, aunt, brother, and *meninos* all buckled in and dressed for Mass. The cafes were closed, but the churches were unlocked and brimming with the commerce of God.

We turned a corner, the mist having burned off a little. Ahead of us we saw two pilgrims, a man and a woman, leaving from the pilgrims' *albergue*. When I'd first decided to journey the *Camino*, I had promised myself to only stay in the finest hotels, never an *albergue* (hostel) or *refugio* (refuge) for me. Having a hot bath and gourmet meal was requisite. I would even consider hiring portage to carry my backpack.

As my pilgrimage became real, though, I quickly realized my demands were unreasonable, even irrational.

So one by one, I surrendered each condition: I would carry my own backpack, I'd go alone if I couldn't find a willing partner, and I'd even consider guest houses instead of luxury hotels. But I dug my heels in when it came to sleeping bunk-style in a room with thirty strangers and group showers at an *albergue*. However, this couple's cheeriness and wide-awake smiles forced me to rethink my distrust of communal sleepovers.

The woman, a towering beauty with stylishly short dark hair, was quick to let us know she'd just returned from the London International Book Show. And as soon as she finished her little jaunt through two entire countries, she had plans to return to Johannesburg to celebrate her fortieth birthday. She had efficiently fit this *Camino* between London and her birthday celebration in Johannesburg.

Shea's *Camino*—and Mine

"My *Camino*," she called it. "It's my planned rite of passage where I hope to discover the meaning of my life!" she had declared.

I wondered how my story about my *Camino* sounded to others when I recounted my plans and reasons for this journey. Assessing her situation, I determined she lived her life on schedules mapped out with itineraries and to-do lists. But maybe I was wrong. Maybe I sensed a bit of myself in her schedules and her lists and her planned enlightenment deadline. I felt a nervous smile spread across my face. My stomach turned a little. Perhaps I was hungry and a few bites of bread and cheese weren't enough to steady me.

"My name is Shea," she announced.

"Reverend Thomas here," boomed her traveling companion, offering us his firm American handshake. He seemed a happy sort with a pink face and a gigantic backpack. That he was American came as no surprise—his oversized load and his equally oversized stature symbolized all things American.

Shea, the South African goddess, continued talking. The only element of her biography she failed to mention was her stunning beauty—tall and fit with the most magnificent bone structure this side of the Atlantic. I turned to Nic but he didn't even blink; he was apparently caught up in Shea's story. It seemed all pleasant but slightly annoying. I hadn't anticipated a day walking with Beauty and the American Preacher.

Shea's enchanting South African accent, I had decided, definitely added to her charm. I could feel the blood pumping in my veins. Why was I reacting so viscerally to this beautiful creature? Why did I notice the tilt of her eyes, the curve of her arm? When I learned she worked for a publishing firm in Johannesburg and had come from the International Book Show in London, a tinge of envy fluttered through me.

My God! Was I jealous? If I could have, I would have excused myself to go somewhere and gather my wits—to digest the feelings racing through me. But where could I hide? I was traipsing along a foreign road with strangers *trying to find myself*—at least, this is what I'd thought I was doing. Yes! I was walking *the Camino*—*my Camino*, I might add—frantic to find my way. Then comes this svelte, slithering siren, this perfectly put-together professional woman, working in a career I wanted to break in to.

This was no accident. Miss South African Beauty mirrored everything I was and wanted to be.

A flock of sparrows burst out from a tree up ahead. I watched them flying in unison, undulating back and forth, their wings bright against the sun. They moved as one. They *were* one, revealing how the whole was greater than the sum of the parts.

I kept pace with the others and steadied my breathing. *I, too, am an author. No, I wasn't attending an International Book Show. But I had written a thing or two in my day! And I am beautiful—with my long dark hair and with feathers! I may not be as tall as Shea, but I can affect a Southern California accent.*

I could feel her stare, so I glanced over. Shea was gazing at me quizzically, her mouth pinched shut. Dr. Nic, too, was looking at me—as if he was waiting for me to say something. Had I spoken aloud?

"Pardon?" she asked. "You were saying—?"

"Was I?" My thoughts raced to catch up. *Was I saying something?* I looked to Reverend Thomas, who wasn't paying attention to any of us. I felt hot, a little bit clammy. I needed food. "I'm just hungry. I think I'm a bit hungry. But—wow, the International Book

Show. That must have been really wonderful," I kept talking.

No one responded. We walked along as the birds fanned in and out of view.

"Are you okay?" Nic asked, stepping alongside, leaning in close. "You seem a little off this morning."

"No, no. I'm fine. Really. I could have used a little more breakfast."

He handed me some nuts. I felt them falling, little drops of sustenance, from his hand to mine. I was grateful.

Found My Pace

Shea slowed a bit and found her stride alongside Dr. Nic. It was time to give him up, so I slipped back a few paces and found my pace with Reverend Thomas. From there, I watched her arms swishing side to side. *She was a vision. After days on the trail she had remained polished, professional even—if that's possible on the Camino. I decided I genuinely liked her. And I liked her most for being like me—wonderful, fabulous me! ME!*

I laughed aloud at the thought.

"Now what's so funny, Miss Shima?" Nic asked, looking back at me. "You're mighty funny this morning."

"Everything's funny. My *Camino* is funny. Life is funny, skies are sunny," I sang out, raising my arms upward.

"That's the spirit," Reverend Thomas said.

Everyone laughed. It was one of those anxiety-relieving kinds of laughs. Everyone let go of their pent-up tension, shaking off the nervousness of new friendships. Then, again, perhaps I was the only one feeling the anxiety. Perhaps they were all kindly easing my burden.

Whatever the intentions, it worked. I forgave myself for my few moments of Shea envy. I looked over to this soon-to-be forty year-old woman, and smiled along with her, gliding along, a peaceful joy radiating from us. Walking alongside Dr. Nic, it seemed an easy pace was developing between them. *It had been only a day since I'd met him.* I chuckled again at the silliness of my fleeting envy.

The Methodist Preaching Hindu Reverend

"I hail from the redneck heartland of Oklahoma U-S-A!" Reverend Thomas began, startling me with his use of the word redneck (something I hadn't expected to hear from the mouth of a preacher). "I met Shea at the *albergue* a night ago, and we have been walking together ever since."

"Same with Dr. Nic and me," I said. "It's only been a day or so. Isn't it remarkable how the days last forever here? And the companionship feels like a lifetime in the making."

"I have followed a circuitous route," he continued. He picked up his pace, causing me to stumble to keep up. "I started in *Porto*," I answered, assuming we were talking about our pilgrimage.

"No, no, not my . . . I mean my journey in life. I was a Hindu in India, but with my light complexion, well, I just didn't fit in. I like their beliefs though. That I did like. So when that didn't work out, I returned to America. Today, I'm ministering to rednecks in a different sort of Indian country!" *Did he just say that? Again?!* He was huffing and puffing between his words.

"Oklahoma has the largest Indian population and the most reservations . . ." His voice trailed as he spoke. The weightiness of the word "reservation" hung in the air, its tie to poverty and prejudices a lump of blackness in the midst of his conversation. In between breaths, I could sense the enormity of his heart.

"I once made a pilgrimage on the Chief Joseph Trail," I chimed in. "I followed Chief Joseph and the Nez Perce. Do you know of it? After Chief Joseph's surrender in 1877, the government promised to return his people to their homeland in Wallowa, Oregon. But instead it exiled them to the Quapaw Agency in Oklahoma. There, half of his people died from disease. As a people, the Nez Perce never recovered. That's all I know of Oklahoma. I've never been."

"No need to go. Hard to believe I'm there myself, but I go where God guides me."

"Me, too." I could feel the lightness of my step. I liked this man. "I call it waiting for the tap on the shoulder. And here I am walking this road."

We were moving at yet a quicker pace, Nic and Shea still ahead of us. Talking fast, we were rushing to fill in the blanks and reveal the deepest aspects of our lives, our spirits, as if this were our last chance.

The *Camino* had a way of driving to the heart of every matter in an instant.

"A Hindu in India, a Methodist minister in Oklahoma, and here on the *Camino,*" he said. I wasn't sure if he was talking to me or just retracing his life's journey. "Can you believe it?" he asked.

"No—I mean—yes! Yes, it's all so amazing," I said, jumping up to speed. "And now here we are walking together in Portugal!"

"Yessiree," he said, nodding. He plodded along—not a slow plod by any stretch—but a sure-footed and well-paced walk as if he was meant for this journey in some meaningful way. He seemed to brim with contemplativeness. Basketball player big, I saw he was able to carry heavy loads. His blonde hair was tinged with strawberry, pink flushed across his pale cheeks. His eyes were masked by sunglasses, but I imagined sky blue irises beneath the glare.

I felt comforted by the presence of my new comrade, this American, and his sincere quest to follow the yellow arrows. Our conversation, following the chatter of Shea's and Nic's, gave me a moment to ponder the value of this journey for me. Hearing about his path gave me permission to honor what was in my heart, what was calling me. *This walk is worth every blister and every homesick pang of longing.*

Honoring One's Spirit

Reverend Thomas reminded me of the importance of honoring one's spirit. He also reminded me I was glad to have put a good deal of thought into traveling light, for he carried a huge backpack, easily fifty pounds or more—its girth even larger than its weight. It was overstuffed and overweight. I imagined he must have been prepared for every chance accident, any *what if.*

The four of us stopped for a snack along the way, the sun a high yellow ball in the sky. I noticed Dr. Nic stared as Reverend Thomas arduously dropped his pack from his shoulders. Shea slipped hers off with ease and pulled out a small bag of nuts and a bottle of water.

"Got a few bricks of gold up in that pack?" Nic called out to him, his shoulders shaking a little with laughter. He tossed a few almonds in his mouth.

"Yesirree. I'm headed for Fort Knox with my loot here," Reverend Thomas said, patting his precious cargo.

"Wrong country," Nic teased. Then he went for his pack, rifling around until he pulled out his bottle of water.

"He's a mule—on a secret delivery," Nic teased. Shea laughed, but I could tell she didn't quite understand.

"How are those dogs holding up, Doc?" Reverend Thomas called back to Nic, pointing to Nic's feet. "Looking a little tender over there, like you've been walking on needles. Are you gonna make it?" They both rested against a large rock, Nic snacking on dried fruit and Reverend Thomas eating an apple. It was true: Dr. Nic did seem to walk a little gingerly, his blisters not quite healed. And his pack seemed to get the best of him. Still, both of them had managed to keep pace with Goddess Shea and fabulous me. I sipped from my bottled water, content to observe my new mates. We finished our snacks, slipped our packs over our shoulders, and fell back into an easy pace, moving along the road.

Our shadows walking before us slowly disappeared, as the afternoon clouds secreted the sun, leaving the *Camino* once again shrouded in uncertainty.

Private Thoughts Seep Out

"So, you were raised a Catholic?" Reverend Thomas asked me, his voice booming in the clear air. *Had I mentioned that?* I couldn't recall. We'd been rambling across so many topics over the hours, I felt like I'd become a leaky faucet, all my private thoughts seeping out without restraint.

"Yes, I was a Catholic in childhood," I said. "And I married in the Church. My first marriage." *There I did it again. I didn't need to say "first" marriage but it was already out there.*

He slowed a bit, readjusting his pack, and then he went quiet. But it wasn't the silence of judgment, I could tell. It was the silence of respect. He must have known I regretted my admission of a first marriage—as a former Catholic and all.

"Being a reverend suits you," I commented.

"Why, thank you. I'll take that as a compliment." He huffed a little and then moved one more step, but his knees gave way. I turned toward him just when he stumbled and dropped to the ground.

"Are you okay?" I could feel him crumbling. "Reverend? Are you okay?" He had buckled under his own weight, and I could only stand witness to his girth and height as he faced his choice point. Would he continue carrying the pack (which I had deemed symbolically his cross) or would he let it go? He hunched over and pressed his palm against a tree, steadying himself.

"You know, I'm beginning to see how I must look." His face bright beneath the shadows of the trees. He lifted his glasses and rested them on his head. Then he blinked hard, readjusting to the light.

"I'm beginning to see I've been living in fear, living a life weighted down by utter preparedness. It's so American."

We laughed heartily at this admission. Then he paused and looked to the ground. I could see he was no longer laughing. Something more going on here, something private and painful. I stepped back and found my way to a clearing a few paces ahead of him.

"I've lived for the *what ifs*. I lived like a faithless wimp, carrying a veritable bomb shelter on my back! My backpack is a symbol of my life. I lug everything with me in readiness for what *could* go wrong. I'm dragged down by my fear of the future." He pulled the weight of his pack off his shoulder and dumped it beneath the tree.

"What if I let go right now, right this moment? What if I emptied my pack of Band-Aids and extra socks and bath towels and water purifier? How light would my burden be if I surrendered? What does freedom weigh? Would God show up if I had nothing?"

I looked away still listening, and I watched as Dr. Nic and Shea paused to check on us. I waved them on. "We'll catch up," I called out. Nic nodded, his stare lingering a moment longer to make sure we were okay. "We just need to readjust a few things." I watched the two of them talking, deciding what to do. "We'll circled back if you take too long," Nic called out, reassuring me that he wouldn't leave us.

Reverend Thomas kept talking. "I hold onto things, not wanting to let go of any *thing* for fear I might need it sometime. But the price I pay is heavy. Its weighty burden costs me. It's difficult for me to walk with this pack. And I'm the butt of jokes. Behind my laughter, that hurts," he confided, looking up to me. "My back ache is nothing compared to my heart ache."

I stood stone still holding onto my breath. But I couldn't control my tears, my emotions yet again running wild. *Help me, God. Help me help this kind soul. Give me the words to help him find his way.* Instead of saying anything, I took it as my cue to back away farther and give him space. I could still see Shea and Dr. Nic hovering at the top of the hill.

"You know what?" he began as he pushed himself off the ground. "You know what?" He repeated a little louder, brushing the dirt from his hands onto his pants.

"I'm ready, I'm darn ready to leave behind all the things I carry, and I'm prepared to walk the rest of the way free of my heavy load." He scoffed at is enormous pack. "I could want for nothing. I don't need an extra pair of shoes or the mosquito spray." He proceeded to pull out shoes and a can of spray from his pack. "There aren't any mosquitos here, anyway—are there? And these shoes on my feet are just fine."

Thomas looked over and caught my gaze, a glint of surprise flashing over his eyes. I looked away, busying myself with a scatter of pebbles along the side of the road. But Thomas hadn't been talking to me at all. Not at all. He was speaking to himself: The Higher Self of Thomas speaking to the fearful Thomas. The American Thomas had been lulled into the belief that if one had enough stuff, one could weather any storm. Just collect stuff, live in the hollow of a bomb shelter, survive in fear. And the more stuff one holds, the better prepared one will be.

**This of course flies in the face of faith,
pales in comparison to truly living life.
More than that, it suffocates freedom!**

I stood silent, witnessing his epiphany. I wanted to say something. I could relate, having had my share of false security in this life. And, as a witness, I grasped the moment of his breakthrough, his choice of faith over fear. The purpose of his *Camino,* stared at him as intently as I stared at the pebbles scattered on the ground.

Still, I remained silent, allowing him his moment of truth, of humility. Part of me wanted to rush to him and shout how grateful I was to have witnessed it. But now wasn't the time.

"You okay over there?" he finally called out.

"Am I? Yes, yes. I am," I said, standing up taller, pulling my gaze from the ground and into his direction.

A few kilometers later, we parted ways. I never saw Reverend Thomas again. But I was certain that the flush-faced Methodist preacher from Oklahoma had emptied his pack, lightened his load, and felt the peace that comes with faith.

Equally Yoked

After departing from Shea and Reverend Thomas late Sunday afternoon, Dr. Nic and I made our way to the hotel in *Ponte de Lima*. There, I flopped onto the white linen bedspread, relishing the modernity of my room, the hot water, the blond wood writing desk in the corner, the white-tiled shower and chrome fixtures. I was exhausted. Exhaustion on the *Camino* was unlike any other fatigue I'd experienced before or since.

Any respite, any rest, any moments of peace were tinged with the simple fact that the journey was far from over. There would be no way out but through.

Dr. Nic and I had agreed to meet in the dining room at seven. I had walked three days with him, an eternity on the *Camino*. This amount of time in my other life would have been fleeting, a blip on the screen. But on the *Camino*, three days of companionship was a veritable lifetime. Time slows enough to make room for lasting friendships to develop, to evolve deeply, fully. Hour after hour of witnessing leaves growing on trees, people working in the fields, blades of grass pushing up in between stones, Dr. Nic and I had experienced the slow pulse of life. We were witness to life happening all around us, connecting everything to everything else. Yes, we were forever bonded, bound and befriended by the *Camino*.

After we ordered dinner, we sat in the comfortable silence that comes with true friendship. He broke his bread into small bite-sized pieces; I'd grown accustomed to such idiosyncrasies. Indeed, I felt as if I'd always known him. Yes, I was ready to walk alone, but I knew I would miss my Dr. Nic.

"I'm going to miss you," I said.

He grinned and scooted his seat closer to the table to get comfortable, I guessed. "Me too, me too." He rubbed at the beard growth on his chin. "I'm going to shave in the morning—I swear I am." We both laughed. And then he began to talk seriously.

"You know, Shima, I have something to tell you . . ."

"Okay, of course. I'm all ears."

"You've been very nice and so candid, you know—," he tapped his finger on the table. It dawned on me he was feeling anxious.

"Are you nervous?"

"Shima—remember all the times I told you about my medical travels with the Christian groups?" I watched his lips moving, curling up with each word. He looked different all of the sudden, robotic, as if he were delivering a speech.

"How could I forget? Of course, yes, I remember. It was yesterday, silly."

"Remember how I explained that I had kept myself separate from the religious aspect of those trips and traveled solely to help as a doctor? Well—," he paused and looked toward the floor, causing me to look, too. It was a dark, polished wood.

"What I'm trying to say is that it wasn't entirely true."

"Oh?"

"Right. There are things about fundamentalist Christianity that I believe to be true."

I could feel my back stiffen. And it wasn't because of his fundamentalist leanings. Or was it? *To each his own—that is my motto.*

No—I was struck that he'd withheld his beliefs for the entirety of our 3-day forever friendship.

"Look," he kept talking, "it's not that I'm a fundamentalist. I'm not. But there are things about Christianity I agree with. You know?"

No, I didn't know. I didn't know what he meant—not at all—or what he was attempting to say. And so I remained silent.

"Well, aren't you going to say something? You always have something to say."

"What? What do you want me to say?" I asked. "Maybe I need a minute to digest what you've just said." I leaned back, unsure of everything. "That's what I have to say."

He stabbed his meat with his fork and shoved a bite the size of a small dog into his mouth. *Good. Chew on that. Gives me a minute to assimilate the fact that you've left out an important part of who you are and yet you know everything about me!*

We had talked about our respective notions of God and Jesus. Together we had swooned over the writings of Paulo Coelho and Carlos Castañeda, but any fundamentalist beliefs were left out. He had withheld all if it. In fact, when he spoke of his Christian missionary work as a traveling physician, he made a point of posturing himself apart from the fundamentalist group he traveled with. He'd been "joined in service, but not one of them," he had said.

It wouldn't have been a big deal if we had kept all of our conversations on things like the price of real estate, the importance of fruits and vegetables, or the growing concerns over climate change—but we hadn't. Almost all we talked about had been our spiritual beliefs.

"You see—" He started talking again, after he'd swallowed the Chihuahua. "Stacey—she's not a Christian, so how could I be with her? How could I truly *be* with her, you know, as man and wife? Christians should not marry non-Christians. You see what I'm saying?" He set down his fork. "They should be equally yoked." His declaration echoed through the restaurant, a definitive speech on good Christian marriage. I was spinning. And his word "yoke." *Yoke.* It provoked me. More than that, it shook me to my core, any fatigue overshadowed by its inherent meaning. *Yoke, shackled, enslaved.* My mind reeled.

"The yoke in marriage must be even." He plowed on as if guiding the oxen, spreading his palms out to emphasize this *evenness* he was trying to explain. "It could never work—never—not unless she was a Christian, too." He stuffed another bite of food into his mouth. It seemed this talk of marriage was making him ravenous. "And yet I love her. I do. This is my struggle."

He looked directly at me now.

The *Camino* had this way of bringing the truth to the surface.

I imagined his exhaustion must have stripped him of the image he'd been projecting. He could no longer hide his internal conflict: Love or doctrine? Follow his heart or do as his Christian authority dictated? This was *his Camino.*

"First of all, I'm unclear what you mean when you talk of a 'yoke,'" I said, wondering how I might proceed. My guard was up; a tinge of sadness fluttered through me. Suddenly, in our final evening, it became clear he'd hidden much from me, only revealing his doctor image, his pilgrim's persona.

"What do I mean when I bring up a 'yoke'?" he asked. "You know—a yoke: the harness that places animals side by side?" He grabbed at his shoulders, gesturing where his marriage yoke might be harnessed. "And, when yoked, the animals must move together in unison to accomplish their chore. It's biblical."

In my mind, I saw how birds fly side by side in unison with nothing binding them. They needed no harness, no yoke. *Birds move as one because of free will and out of love for the whole.* But I wasn't in the mood to bring up my perspective. I'd revealed far too much. My lips remained sealed.

Nic leaned in, his eyes squinting and scanning me. "In fact, in 2 Corinthians 6:14, the Bible says 'Do not be unequally yoked together with unbelievers.' This is how marriage should be." He sat back, apparently satisfied with his memorized Bible quote.

How did I miss this part of him? And how did this restricted belief system fit with our endless discussions on spirituality? And why withhold? He must have decided I would balk at his beliefs or judge them. And was I doing just that? Judging his beliefs?

"Look, don't you think it's important to choose a spouse of common faith?" he asked me, preparing for my rebuttal. But I wasn't concerned with marriage and common faith at the moment. No, I was mostly struck by the sense of betrayal I was feeling.

After all, I had bared my soul, revealed my heart and had held nothing back.

Then, in our last evening together, Nic was admitting he was more fundamentalist than he'd revealed during the entirety of our friendship.

Come to think of it, I was fine with his beliefs about marriage—of course. It was the fact that *he'd been hiding it from me* that stung. I imagined how Stacey might have been feeling. Stacey, the poor, non-Christian girl, dropped like a hot potato by her lover boy Nic for her lack of proper faith. (Okay, so maybe I was judging, but just a little.)

But could I give him my opinion without judgment, allowing him his beliefs without accepting them for myself? Wasn't that the essence of discernment? I needed to reassess everything—or at the least reevaluate the past three days with Dr. Nic.

Living in the Spirit of God

"To me the idea of God is all inclusive," I began. "If your choices exclude someone—anyone—then, to me, you are not living in the spirit of God."

"Well, yes, there's that," he said, leaning back on his chair.

As I spoke the words, the obvious judgment they carried came rushing out. Who was I to make such a declaration? *I hadn't even realized I'd held such judgment.*

I tried again. "All I know is that God is Love, unconditional Love. Religion is only a pathway to God and Love; it's a set of rules drawn up by men—men in power, I might add. If its doctrine is used as a point of separation, then wouldn't you consider it could be a misplaced doctrine—or at the very least a misinterpreted doctrine?" I paused, searching his eyes to see if I'd offended him in any way.

He lifted his napkin and dabbed each side of his mouth before dropping it onto his lap. "No, I get it," he said. "I hear what you're saying. I do. I really do."

"But this yoke . . ." I was finally finding my words. "Your statement that you need to be yoked in marriage—perhaps if both of you are of the same belief you will only be able to move linearly, in a straight line. What if you joined as the unique individuals you are? The yin and yang, the masculine and feminine?

"Perhaps your idea of what a yoke means is mystifying. What if you and Stacey were joined in marriage simply as two loving individuals and therefore complemented each other? Wouldn't that allow you to move in a spiral motion rather than in the straight, boring line of the yoke? Don't oxen wear yokes due to drudgery?"

I took a sip of my drink and shrugged. "It's just an idea—take it or leave it."

I stopped myself, wondering what my end game might be. Soon we'd be going our separate ways. But he had, after all, told me he loved Stacey. Wasn't that enough? "How can you go wrong if you love her?"

Nic shoveled another bite into his mouth, nodding politely at my perspective. I decided he had obviously been concerned that I would judge him, that I would disapprove. The thought stabbed at me; I felt I had let him down—or worse—let myself down. Yet he had let *me* down; there was that aspect to digest.

"What I'm wondering," I asked, looked directly at him unable to stop myself. "What I'm wondering is *what was it about me* that made you hold back?" A beat of silence. I wasn't looking for him to answer, not really; it was more a question to me. The betrayal I felt I'd have to sort out alone. I reminded myself that what I knew of this man was only my *perception* of him.

Then the sadness I felt in my heart rose higher, lodging in my throat.

"You okay?" he asked.

"Sure. I'm fine," I replied. "I guess I'm wondering if you chose this one rule of the yoke to justify your break up with Stacey?" I looked at him, checking to see if I'd upset him.

"What if you are unknowingly choosing edicts that suit you and discarding the rest?" He continued to chew his food, staring at me. *I had to stop talking, stop asking questions, stop judging. It was none of my business.*

I felt more troubled than I revealed. "Forget it," I finally said. "It's none of my business." But it somehow felt like my business. We had, after all, spent what seemed a lifetime walking together, spilling our guts—or rather I had spilled *my* spiritual guts. And he had held back. That made me want to hold back. But my mouth had run away—my emotions propelling me forward.

The worst of it was his admission about his faith, the Church, and his idea of a yoke in marriage. This all meant he never had felt safe with me. After all that walking and talking, step after step, trudging along the *Camino,* my *Camino,* our *Camino*—together.

**How could I have felt any other way
than to be open and honest?**

Many Paths to God

Yes, I had been discerning, but I also accepted the belief that there are many paths to God.

**Whatever belief system, religion, or school of
thought we follow, we have to realize it's only a
step on the spiritual path that we choose
to walk. No system is complete.**

My worldview and beliefs called for inclusiveness, not exclusiveness. I suppose they were hard-core in their own way, too, depending on who I shared them with.

In that moment, I had to make things right between us. "Look, I'm sorry if I made you feel as if you had to hold back," I said.

"Oh—no, not at all. This is my thing. I would have been the same with anyone. Really. I'm discreet when it comes to my religion, my beliefs. They're private matters, personal. It takes time for me to open up about that stuff."

Right. Exactly, I thought, for I also held my beliefs close, and I typically only shared them with those trustworthy enough to honor me. *But we had forged a bond, a measure of trust. That's why this stung so much. I'd held nothing back—until now.*

"Sure," I said. "Of course, I get it. You were guarded about your fundamentalist leanings. I get it." I nodded as if to show my understanding. But mostly it rankled me that I must have come across judgmental. It rankled me more that I had gushed about my own feelings.

Looking for Release

I sucked in the stifling air of the restaurant and then let out a sigh, trying to release the self-recrimination building inside me. *What exactly is my sense of myself and others? Wasn't I tolerant? Accepting? When would I shed my beliefs and be in the nothingness of non-judgment?*

I sighed again. This time it was audible—one of

those exasperated "I give up" kind of sighs. I hadn't meant to, but there it was hanging between us.

"Are you okay?"

"Yes. Yes, I was just thinking. It's nothing important."

Nic gave me a sideways glance, reminding me how well he'd come to know me. I wanted to leap from my seat and leave.

"You're sure everything's fine?"

"Yes, I'm sure," I lied—a white lie; after all, I wasn't obligated to share all my feelings. And I had to get over this incident. *Nic's beliefs are none of my business.* "All I can say is my practice is Love. Love all, allow all, and accept all. No matter what. This is my truth."

Then he started laughing. *Well, good, he was laughing. And why not.*

"So—I haven't thoroughly offended you?" he said, his big hand on his chest.

"No, not at all." I was still unclear what to think or say. "I'm just trying to take it all in."

I unfolded my napkin and tried another angle. "The question is, Nic, have I offended *you*? Because—well, it's just that I'd thought we were friends, and we'd been so honest, so open."

He looked toward the tiles on the ceiling this time. "Or shall I say, *I* have been so open and candid!"

"It wasn't you, Shima," he briefly clasped his hand over mine. "This has been my thing, my issue. And I'm sorry, too, if you feel slighted, if you feel as if I haven't been forthright." The waiter cleared our plates. "But—well, there it is. I've opened up and shared my beliefs."

121

"Of course," I said. But I wasn't as satisfied with this tell-all discussion as he seemed to be. We both shrugged, neither of us knowing what to say.

"It's fine, really," he offered.

"Well, good." The pang of sadness lingered inside me. My heart skipped in my chest.

The past three days with Dr. Nic, for me, had become colored by his withholding his true feelings until the bitter end. Meanwhile I had gushed out my heart and soul, my mouth yapping away for hours on end. I felt foolish.

"For what it's worth, I'd like to thank you," Nic said, interrupting my thoughts, clasping his hand again over mine.

"For what?"

"For understanding my feelings and my beliefs, for your acceptance of who I am. It means a great deal to me."

In that moment—and in response to his gratitude—I decided I couldn't ask for more.

What's Next?

At breakfast the next morning, our last meal together, I decided to learn more about him, especially since he'd said he would open up. His *Camino* was a walk to release old heart flames still smoldering. And when I thought of Dr. Nicandro and his yoke, it seemed that the passage he found in the Bible gave him evidence enough to walk away from Stacey. It was that simple.

"If I am to rid myself of my devils, I am afraid my angels will flee as well," Nic said, buttering his toast.

"Well, I say, have no fear. Face your demons and your angels will escort them away," I replied. But it didn't matter anymore. We were parting ways. And I was ready to walk alone. I'd had enough companionship.

I saw him briefly in the hallway—one last time—his arms easily swaying back and forth as he turned back toward me for one last hug. *"Buen Camino.* Be safe," he yelled, before walking out the lobby door.

"Take risks," I hollered back. "Especially in love!"

As he walked along the path in front of the hotel, I could hear his laughter until it faded into the morning air.

Chapter 12

Ahh—rest—it's a wonderful respite. I was only six days into it and already using the precious buffer days I was hording for the end. *It's okay for me to stay in a luxury hotel for two days. It's really okay.*

I had prepared carefully, mapping kilometers with capability; I'd studied, planned, and plotted. Yes, mentally and physically I could meet the *Camino's* challenge; I'd trained as if I were back in the days running 10ks and half-marathons. I had the faith, will power, and physical stamina to muscle through any obstacles, and so far, the weather, sore muscles, and blisters hadn't bested me.

What I hadn't planned for was the rebellion of my emotions. They staged a coup and overthrew me like a bad dictator. And they were entitled to—for they'd never seen the light of day. As a young tomboy, I'd mastered being tough, and later, when climbing the corporate ladder—controlled and tactical.

I'd worked hard, moving up the clerical ranks to management, yet even as an executive assistant I appeared powerful to our staff and customers. Behind the scenes, I was just my boss's pawn for play. My daily worth depended on the quality of my work, and I strived hard to prove worthy. In these days before computers and word processing, I typed on an IBM Selectric, the state-of-art kind with the automatic correction key. He would hand me letters scribbled in longhand and when I'd return the typed draft, he'd scrutinize it for errors. If he couldn't find any, he would change a sentence, ordering me to type it all over again. At first, this game was a challenge, then a competition, and later, just plain mean. The harder I tried and the fewer my mistakes, the more he'd scowl. He'd stand in front of me as I typed, hurrying me into mistakes, intimidating me into making an error until finally I would break into tears. At that point the game would be over—until the next letter. At last, when it was no longer fun for either of us and a promotion was at hand, he denied me by stating one sentence: "Your emotions are your nemesis." In this way, I had learned to equate feelings with failure.

Subconsciously—and ingeniously, I might add— I had designed a way to withhold my love and still gain approval by giving generously and open-handedly. But it only worked one way. I could never receive kindness in return. That would crumble my cover-up. For me, being unlovable wasn't nearly as painful as being loved.

On the *Camino*, I had no duties or commitments, no responsibilities or obligations to distract me from myself. I had no place to hide or run.

I was faced with me, all of me, and I was afraid. *What if I couldn't accept the truth of me? Then what?*

Like anything that has been locked in the dark then released, nothing could quench my emotions' thirst for freedom. Everything was out of my control, and I never knew how my feelings would surface or when. The smallest things took on giant proportions and what came gushing out shocked and embarrassed me. Nothing could stifle arousing their power. All I could do was surrender, surrender, and surrender again.

Thank God, I am alone. Ahhh—rest—a time to lull my emotions back under cover and into peace.

Discipline and Control

Clean clothes, washed in the bathroom sink hung drying on the shower door. I wasn't the first pilgrim who would have preferred air-drying my clothes on the balcony, but the placards inked in red threatened severe penalties for any infraction.

After eating bread and cheese and pastries with Dr. Nic it total abandon, feelings of guilt finally soured their pleasures. I resolved to eat only what was good for me—back to basics—fruit, green salads, and *sopa de legumes*. I bartered with myself to keep *café com expresso com leite* without restriction. My one daily treat. *Yes, discipline and control will corral my emotions.*

Fortnight Flea Market

With renewed purpose, I ventured out to explore *Ponte de Lima*, touted as the most beautiful city in Portugal. The *Rio Lima* undulated along tunnels of trees—oak, cork, and olive. Shaded shorelines blanketed in wildflowers and grasses were peopled by villagers enticed to rest in its reverie. The ancient Roman bridge *Ponte Medieval* arched the river's muddied spring waters and joined the busy southern town to its quieter northern quarter. I don't know when the walking bridge was originally constructed, but in 1368, I read that it was rebuilt by hand, stone by stone. Its sheer age and staying power seemed incredible to someone who lives in a 1968 master-planned community.

Each fortnight, the southern riverbank morphed into a flea market. There, the siren call from out-of-town vendors drew country folk secreted in the hillsides to *Ponte de Lima*. Packaged goods and produce, olives, nuts and honey, tools and hardware, lace and lingerie, flouncy dresses, children's toys, shoes, socks, and boots. The wares and novelties and off-limit items that couldn't be crafted from the land tempted the farmers to venture from their fields. The shoreline swelled with the coordinated chaos of tents, vans, boxes, and an endless parade of hawkers and barterers. *Timing, I smiled, imagining Dr. Nic buying new shoes that would carry him to the end of his Camino.*

Dr. Nic's Style

Unlike me or Reverend Thomas, Nic hadn't fussed over every aspect of his journey. Rather, he'd allowed it to unfold on its own and met its demands on command—in the moment. He didn't pain over every equipment choice or weigh every ounce. He did, however, superstitiously choose to walk in his worn-out favorite tennis shoes. They were way beyond their days, causing his feet to sacrifice for the sake of his dubious knee. Already he had been sidelined by blisters, and his knee probably wasn't doing well at all. When I witnessed him tear the cover off his guidebook to line his shoes, I was mortified, either by sheer pity or by the homelessness of it, or both. It roused the worst of my critical mother into action. I insisted he buy new shoes, not accepting his excuse there were no Foot Locker stores at the mall down the street. *After all, you're an adult, a doctor! You should know your limitations, or at the very least, should have planned better.* My ranting mother silently nagged on.

To tide him over, I emptied my stash of moleskin for a makeshift shoe liner. When the initial shock wore off seeing his tatters (or perhaps because he never complained), I stopped noticing his shoes. In fact, I hadn't given them another thought until meeting up with Reverend Thomas and Shea. They, too, distressed over his sorry sight. They openly prayed he'd arrive in *Ponte de Lima* on the third Tuesday of the month, market day. Yes, it was Dr. Nic's lucky day. *"Nic, I hope you stop at the market to buy new shoes!"*

Then I imagined him carefully lacing his new shoes, taking a few giant test strides, and as if unable to say good-bye to his old standbys, he'd pack them away next to his old backpack and carry on. Already I missed tripping alongside him with his new white shoes, his oversized backpack, his coverless guidebook. And his big, big smile.

Signs of Light Language

Slowly in rhythm with the flow, I ambled across the bridge to the peaceful gardens, *Jardims Tematicos*. Inside the gated entrance, a clipped hedge bordered the cobblestone labyrinth leading to different theme-designed gardens. I was drawn to a colonnade of four towering Greek columns. They supported a latticed roof snarled in woody rope and stippled with little nubs that promised spring. The portico created the feeling of an interior castle.

The garden was designed in a series of diminishing rectangles like a child's puzzle one stacked inside the other. Topiary of dormant rose bushes lined the perimeter of the outermost rectangle, setting the back-drop for wrought-iron benches in the next largest rect-angle. In front of the benches were perfectly squared mosaics designed from black granite and white quartz cobblestone. A shallow aquamarine pool completed the interior of the cascading puzzle.

I followed the garden's border lighting for a mo-ment on each bench, butterflying for the perfect settling point. When I finally calmed down to my surroundings, I was awestruck by the familiar. *The mo-saic designs were the same symbols in my book Ascension Kis—the ones channeled from spiritual realms described as Light language from the Pleiades.*

Here they were—
Grace, Majesty, and Oneness—as above, so below.
Universal designs in a Portuguese garden.

I spiraled in the oneness of it all. *The Truth. All is revealed. Nothing is withheld. We must simply say yes to receive. It's not about becoming more pure or transcend-ing yet another level of consciousness. All of life comes down to this; the microcosm within the macrocosm—the spiral, the vortex, the cosmos!*

I glanced into the reflecting pool and saw that I was smiling.

Buoyed by Spirit, I danced from the gardens to the adjoining church. A few Portuguese men held vigil outside, smoking and marking time until their wives inside would emerge to be chaperoned home.

These centurions lingered at every church entrance—as much a part of the church as the ceremonies inside.

I kept walking. Along the riverbank was a small shrine dedicated to Archangel Michael, *Capela do Anjo da Guarda Sao Miguel*. I took a sideways glimpse, peeked but didn't pray. That day, I had joyously received the gift of Divine Truth and felt content. And I wasn't about to repeat the same tough lesson I'd learned with Dr. Nic when I rushed from *Castelo de Faria* to *Fonte de Vida*.

This time, I would relish the God moment revealed at *Jardims Tematicos* and save Archangel Michael for tomorrow.

Quaking with Questions

Because of the late hour, the fortnight market was closing down when I retraced my steps back to my room. From a distance, the vendors packing their wares looked like colonies of ants making harvest. The river's edge was piled with trash; leftover boxes, wrappers, and discarded debris strewn for as far as I could see. The desecration was so overwhelming to my indoctrinated *Don't Be A Litterbug* that I couldn't grasp what I saw. It assaulted all my sensibilities. Yet, in a back-handed way, these merchants' messes made me proud to be a conscientious American and respecter of our Mother Earth.

In the aftermath of my shocked reaction, a resigned calmness settled in. I quaked with questions.

Who was I to judge defilement or impose standards of godliness? Who made me the arbiter of good and bad, clean or dirty, right or wrong? A few hours earlier, this trash had protectively boxed longed-for luxuries.

**In this mess, I saw myself and wondered
what litter was I hording within?
What long-decayed treasures did I cling to?**

What wildflowers and grasses of my essence were buried beneath lifetimes of debris?

Suddenly the wind picked up, widening the litter's berth. Paper and tissue flurried into a jumbled storm mirroring my thoughts carried on streams of consciousness. Blessing or polluting, it did not matter. I narrowed my eyes. I stared, searching for feelings, those familiar old judgments of aversion and revulsion. I wanted to see what I had been trained to see, but nothing would surface. *I am the landscape and this is how it looks. Not bad. Not good. Everything is okay.*

Tomorrow, the debris may be gone—or not. But I had culled through my own internal litter and without judgment discovered non-judgment was simply accepting things as they are; what is.

A Gift to Be Opened

I slept soundly. Two nights in the same clean, warm bed halted any dreams of phantom walking in search of yellow arrows. When I first opened my eyes, it took me a moment to appreciate that the rainbow in my room came from the sun's rays glinting off remnants of raindrops. I rested in the sunshine of it all, feeling content and grateful. In fact, I felt so at peace, I wondered how I'd ever felt anything less. I immersed myself in gratitude for the simplest things blanketed in happiness.

**For the first time in many days,
Light surrounded me inside and out. The day
ahead of me waited like a gift to be opened.**

On this day, I resolved to be a tourist, not a pilgrim, so I filled my knapsack with a purse full of things—sunglasses and lip balm, my journal and pen. If any item suggested *what if* or *just in case,* I left it behind with my boots and backpack. If I was thirsty, I would stop at a market or sit at a *café* and order from a menu. If I became tired, I'd return to my room for a nap. *Glorious gifts indeed!*

Chapter 13

My first quest: find *Estatueta uma Cantareira.* When I first read about the statue described in my guidebook, I knew she was something special. She was hard to find tucked away on a side street in a small alcove, but after lots of finger pointing and *"perdao, fala ingles*—excuse me, do you speak English?"I found her—the one who elusively summoned me to her side months ago and a continent away.

She stared straight ahead, her water jug atop her shoulder. I stared back wondering *Why am I having a moment with a centuries-old statue?* Or more critically, *Have I lost my mind having a moment with a statue? And why am I calling her "she" as if she were a living breathing being?*

Surrounding her were closed doors and barren stoops, none of which gave a clue to who lived behind them. She was simple and worn, so plain she could easily be overlooked. Still, when I gazed into her, I saw myself and a slideshow of faces clicking by one by one: Mother Mary, Kwan Yin, Lady Nada, Saint Teresa de Avila, Joan of Arc—all kindred sisters, alive and ascended, lighting my way.

I sensed how I stood taller, my feet rooted on the cobblestone fearing that if I didn't hold firmly to the ground, I would be consumed into the hologram. Like me, the special statue stood sturdy and strong, appearing comfortable as she carried heavy loads, both physically and spiritually.

Again, I saw me in her;
I knew her as I knew myself.

Aproned in dirt and grime, she gave the impression of neglect, yet she left no doubt that underneath her tarnish was a sublime sacredness. She knew her beauty within.

I sat at her feet and looked around for a gatekeeper, perhaps a bird or animal, to affirm what I felt was indeed blessed. Affirming this moment gave me an insight into the meaning of life and God. *Of course, this is a holy moment. I'm not one to imagine talking to statues; I can't just make this stuff up!*

The Stone Basin

At her feet was a stone basin fitted with a simple brass knob and faucet. I imagined *Estatueta* in person, one of the village housewives meeting over their morning chores—an inviting time that allowed for gossip and girl talk. While filling their jugs, they poured out their hearts to each other before duties to their husbands and children scattered them in different directions.

The faucet was corroded shut now, the basin filled with rainwater. I imagined these women—now reincarnated—living my life. They would purchase water in eco-friendly recyclable bottles as they met by the pool at the spa—and still they poured out their hearts and hopes to each other.

Symbolically, I sprinkled into the basin a few precious drops of Peace Waters gathered from streams on my sacred journeys. Next, I chose two Kis from the Ascension cards, Forgiveness and Manifestation. I placed them at her feet, asking for a release of any thoughts that might restrict my love.

**I prayed that my will and God's Will be one;
that my intentions—and all I think, feel,
and create—be pure and purposeful.**

In that moment, I envisioned a future memory: The vision of authority without control, of power without force, of joy and equality in the workplace, of feminine and masculine in balance, of equality without superiority, of freedom of expression without fear of oppression, and of honor and respect for all tasks— even the simplest task of carrying a jug of water.

I imagined taking the jug from the maiden's shoulder to lighten her burden. She in turn slipped on my backpack, our likeness and load one and the same. We balanced each other perfectly. She Was Free. I am Free. I am Light. I am.

For a fleeting moment, I desired to smelt into her bronze being, but I then resisted this selfish want for lifeless union.

**Everything was happening symbolically
yet I knew on some vibrational level—
on some dimensional plane—every symbol
was as real as its material counterpart.**

Then I said good-bye and walked the short distance to the *Igreja da Misericordia,* the Church of Grace.

Rekindled Love for Churches

The scent of prayer and incense took my breath away and transported me to lifetimes of holy remembrance, rekindling my love for churches and places of worship.

In an alcove of the church to the right of the altar was the statue of *Señhora das Doras,* the Lady of Sorrows. Her colorful indigo gown gleamed out of place in the stone gray surroundings. She held seven golden swords crossed at her breast.

In my studies, I'd never met *Señhora das Doras,* and I didn't understand the meaning of her name nor the swords nor her brightly colored gown. But I recognized a kindred spirit and felt an uncanny closeness to her that I couldn't understand or even describe.

**I silently begged her to put down her swords
and hold me in their place.**

We share the same angelic companions, I intuited. *And we'll both readily fall on the seven swords for love, for forgiveness, for understanding, for mercy, for others, for enlightenment—for God.*

To the right of *Señhora das Doras* in the same alcove was Saint Teresa de Avila, my mystic friend and teacher after whom I try to fashion myself. I was quieted into peace. When I could no longer consume any more of their outpouring of love, I swallowed the lump in my throat, lit a votive candle, dropped a few coins, and hiccupped to the exit.

Rows of School Children

Outside the church walls, the morning sun hid behind the clouds, making it easier for my eyes to adjust to the subtle change in grays. I returned one more time to the statue of the woman carrying the jug. There, rows of school children were parading hand in hand in pairs. The children's ruddy cheeks livened the somber tones of their hand-me-down coats too big for their tiny frames. All were dressed in earthy browns except for one—a little girl near the front of the line outfitted top to toe in pink.

Their miniature heads, haloed in brown caps, poked through coat collars to create the cartoonish effect of little bobbing doll heads. I smiled and waved but received no response. In unison, the procession turned their attention from me to their teacher, who then turned to me, deemed me safe, and nodded. I nodded back. Then she nodded to her pupils who nodded along with us!

We were all tightly wound bobble heads anticipating the teacher's approval to let loose.

When she finally nodded "okay," the children unwound. Like spring-operated toys wiggling and giggling, they shouted *bom dia* (good day) to a funny foreign woman with feathers in her hair sitting alone at the base of an unimpressive statue.

The tiny pink tot pointed her gloved finger at the statue. Then using my eyes for access, she entered my heart. I experienced a slowed feeling of *everything* disappearing into a God moment. In that timeless space, I felt the sword of *Doras*, the Lady of Sorrows, pierce my heart.

The release of my grief, swift and immediate, poured out from my heart *and* seemingly the jug of *Estatueta*. All that remained in our vessels was love. I watched the shuffling children move forward as the little girl in pink held her gaze—first on me and then on the statue. She was twirling back and forth until finally she righted herself in line with the others. She passed by, leaving me with the wonder of a child's innocence and the sudden splatter of rain.

Back on the *Camino*

Although I felt restless to get back on the *Camino*, the unrelenting rain and fading daylight made it foolish to consider leaving town that afternoon. After my third lap around the bed in my room, I gave in to accepting my delay as yet another spiritual practice of patience. I drained the clock by folding, sorting, and stacking the belongings I'd recklessly strewn around my room; it seemed I needed to make my mark.

After two days it was time to fit my life back into my backpack, neat and tidy.

Once each item was stowed, I stared at the sterility of the room; it blankly glared back. *Why are you still here?* The question echoed in my head. *Who had slept here before me? Who would take my place tomorrow, leaving without a trace, making room for the next, and then the next?* Then it hit me. I hadn't yet secured a bed for the following night!

Tomorrow's destination, *Rubiaes,* was a tiny village. If I didn't act quickly my only option would be to sleep at an *alberque* bunk-style atop snoring strangers. I rushed to the front desk seeking Phillip's help. His fingers tapped across his computer as he simultaneously called ahead in search of a suitable room. Words flew back and forth in Portuguese. I nodded and grinned in rhythm to his inflections. Once he secured a room at a guesthouse in the hamlet of *Agualonga,* we locked eyes and smiled to his universally understood thumbs-up gesture. Lucky me! The owner just happened to be in *Ponte de Lima* and insisted he stop by to meet me—*most likely wanting to inspect me!*

who would be sharing his home. I silently reasoned that the synchronicity of our meeting had been perfectly orchestrated by Spirit.

I blessed the angels and thanked my guides for the miracle of it all. I had a room! Then when I remembered that a full day's walk was a mere fifteen-minute drive, the owner's visit didn't seem quite so miraculous. But I felt holy all the same as I awaited my new host's arrival.

Franco's Old-world Charm

When the elevator door opened, a cloud of cologne-scented air billowed into the lobby. A man burst from the bathroom, slicking back his perfectly coifed silver hair. He flinched—just a little—at the sight of me. Caught preening, he must have felt embarrassed. But with one smooth gesture, he had slipped his hand into mine, invading my space before I could stop him.

"*Boa noite.* Good evening," he said, his accent thick but understandable. "You must be the lovely American who will be my guest tomorrow night. Please, *Señhora,* allow me introduce myself.*"*

His hand gestures were elaborate, his slender fingers flitting about, his palms dipping in the air. "I am Franco, the proprietor of *Casa de Flores de Lavanda,* at your service.*"*

The only thing missing from his old-world charm was a cape and plumed hat fluttering behind his sweeping bow. He, in fact, *was* stylishly dressed, looking handsome in an angular sort of way due to his sharply shaped nose and heavily lidded, darting eyes. I was taken by his chivalry, smiling (dumbly) like a blushing maiden. That surprised me.

That's when I abandoned caution
and assumed the air of the royal highness
He had presumed me to be.

And with him as my loyal subject, I constructed the queenly idea of having him porter my pack to his guesthouse.

But then his darting eyes landed on me. They traveled across my face before they rolled up and down my body in one fast, calculated movement—as if he were (not so secretly) assessing me. And I let him. What else could I do? I was unprepared for the inspection that ended before I could object. I adjusted my feet and folded my arms, an awkward American pretzel at the mercy of this fabulous Franco.

"But look at you! You are so radiant—" He kept talking, then he grabbed my hands, lifting them high. He stepped back and patted my shoulder, a friendly pat as if from a brother or a neighbor, I reasoned. I hoped his interest was trustworthy enough. But the thought that he was keen to my vulnerability traveling alone hovered in the back of my mind.

Besides, I was still intent on portering my pack for the day.

"Kind *Senhor*, perhaps, *por favor*," I began talking.

"I was wondering if you could possibly take my belongings with you tonight? Without my pack, I could
walk tomorrow without the weight."

**The thought of walking free
of this heavy weight sounded delicious.
My stomach flipped with excitement.**

"It's the small things in life," I smiled. "So—is it
possible for you take my pack? I could arrive tomorrow and retrieve it when I see you there."

"Ah! *Si, si,* I can do that for you. No problem."

He stepped closer to me, smiling too big. Yet he
was courteous—in a pushy sort of way. "I will not
charge you for my service since you will be my guest."

My queen's eminence plummeted with the words
charge and *his services.*

"But right now, I'm very busy," he said, "on my
way to meet friends at the theater. You must hurry
and pack if I am to do this favor. I cannot be late." His
expression of self-importance slicked a sticky residue
over me.

"Obrigado. It will only take a minute to sort my
belongings. I'll be right back," I shouted over my
shoulder, heading for the elevator.

But there was no need to shout, for Franco had
turned and was by my side, running along with me,
elbow to elbow. *The idea of personal space is unknown
to him.* And with no time for me to object, he rushed
ahead to the elevator and began tapping the UP but-

ton. "It will be much faster if I assist you. Like I said, I am a busy man and do not have a spare minute." He tap, tap, tapped the button until the ding announced the door's opening.

Franco's presence had overpowered me, tamping down my silly notions of divine timing. The synchronicity I'd sensed minutes before had totally squashed. He was in control, pushing me, and I let him, part of me hovering above watching the scene unfold. Still, the prospect of walking without a backpack outweighed the unpleasant stickiness of Franco. And thinking it through, there was nothing to fear. *He isn't a stranger in the strictest sense of the word; he's the proprietor of the inn where I'd soon be sleeping. It isn't a big deal for him to enter my hotel room.*

I inserted the key card and opened my door.

**I hadn't been in a hotel room
with another man besides my Jim—ever!**

Trying to convince myself of Franco's good intentions, I recalled the help of the kindly taxi driver. *What if I reject him? Or the handsome man on the farm with the horse? And then of course there was my Dr. Nic.* Yes. Absolutely! I could accept the friendly service of Franco.

Yet he was still hovering close—so close I could see the glint of a gold molar when he talked, so close his cologne clung to my clothes, so close I could feel his breath on my arm as we both stepped over the threshold of the door. After I gathered what I needed for tomorrow's walk I pushed my backpack over to him. He grabbed it and turned to leave. I gave him a little nudge, eager for the relief I'd feel once he was on the other side.

"*Boa noite*. Enjoy the theater," I said more forcefully than I'd meant. I had become the pushy one.

But before the swinging door fell between us, his unscuffed Italian loafer blocked it open. "*Señhora*, perhaps you would rather not walk tomorrow?" He lifted his chin high as he spoke. "The weather is blustery, and there are many spiritual places near my village you will not find on the *Camino*. I will clear my calendar and pick you up midday. I can show you lovely sights and ancient ruins you can't find on your maps."

"Thank you. Really. Thank you, Franco," I stuttered, though the thought of wandering off the beaten path was enticing. "But no, I have not walked in two days. I'm looking forward to a lovely day outdoors. I'll see you at your guesthouse tomorrow afternoon," I smiled. "Please have my belongings waiting for me. *Boa noite.*"

I was determined to take control and bid this fast-talking man *um abraco*—a hug good-bye.

Chapter 14

After Franco left, I tucked away the few items I had pulled from my pack and then headed for the front desk. It was set. I would walk freely for one day—with nothing to weigh me down! *Ah! On the Camino it's the small things that make all the difference.*

Waiting in the lobby, I sensed something go "plunk" beside me, a heaviness in the air created from the mix of earthy sweat. Pilgrims. There was no denying the familiar bottomed-out smell of weariness Dr. Nic and I had walked in with—that dry-mouthed, throbbing-foot, tired stench after a long day's walk. A hot shower had washed me clean for now, but it hadn't cleared my recall of the pilgrim's scent. I was reminded that my clean body, like a mirage, would soon again be layered with dust after a few miles on the road. Soon enough, I'd be smelly and thirsty and tired again—an integral part of the *Camino* I'd finally come to accept.

Two of them, a man and a woman, stood waiting behind me at the desk. Their weariness hung heavy on them. I assessed they must have just completed the longest leg of the Portuguese *Camino* from *Arborim* where there's no option but to tough it out in one day.

I could tell they were a couple by the way she dropped her pack at his feet and leaned on him, taking his last remaining energy for her own as only a wife or lover can do.

In that moment, I yearned for Jim to be here and share my weariness. I wanted to be a tired couple, too, but I didn't have a husband to hang on to. It had only been this morning since I said good-bye to Nic and already I missed him. One more day and I might have leaned on *him*.

When Jim said "no," I had consciously chosen to walk without him. Alone. But why? I was angry at my foolishness, my lack of foresight. I didn't *have* to make this journey except for the lofty thought that I was being guided by my Higher Self. However, that notion seemed silly as I stood alone in the lobby with no Jim by my side. I didn't feel one bit high and holy.

Enough with the self-flagellation! I screamed inside my head, turning the anger away from myself. Now I was mad at Jim—not that Jim would have come. He clearly told me he wasn't the least bit interested. Yet again, he was the wise one, and I was burning mad now. *He should have talked me out of it.* But look at this woman, this pilgrim, who managed to persuade her husband to come along and support her. He didn't look interested at all.

I'm a Pilgrim, Too!

I knew I needed to grab hold of myself and rise above

this pathetic wave of self-pity or I would surely come undone in my aloneness. I also knew I couldn't afford to come undone, to fall apart among strangers.

"Will you be paying by credit card, *Señhora?*" Phillip asked, peering up from the blue glow of his computer screen.

"Pardon? Oh, yes. *Si. Si.*"

Then the couple smiled and nodded at me. I felt a sense of familiarity, a camaraderie toward them. They were pilgrims, too. And this pilgrim thing was no small feat. *Jim should have come. He is the fool—not me. He could have been sharing this once-in-a-lifetime journey with me.*

Meeting these two—these fellow pilgrims— was just what I needed. I gestured to them, explaining as best I could that I, too, was a pilgrim.

Yes, I was doing everything but dance the hokey-pokey at the discovery of our common bond. That's when the man politely stilled my animations in perfect English, tinged by a lilting accent.

"Good evening. I am Vittorio, and this is my wife, Donatella."

"Ah! Great. Well, hello. I'm Shima. Shima from California," I thrust out my hand, eager to make friends.

"We're from Italy, and I am accompanying my wife on her pilgrimage," Vittorio announced as he shook my hand. "The *Camino* is something Donatella has longed to do and I am here to escort her."

So I was correct: the husband was walking the *Camino* for the wife. It was *her* thing—not his. *How nice of him.* I pushed down my ache for Jim (or was it anger?) and looked to Donetella. She was stunning in that wide tilting-eyed, full-lipped Sophia Loren kind of way. Vittorio was no fool to come as her chaperone, knowing that Donetella would be easy prey. Franco came to mind. If she'd come here alone, I imagined him pouncing on poor Donetella like he'd pounced me.

I secretly wished Jim had thought about me as Donetella's husband regarded her. But I hadn't given him the option. I had been bull headed; I'd set my pilgrimage plans with or without his blessing.

Next Stop: *Casa de Flores de Lavanda*

"My holiday from work allows me only two weeks," Vittorio continued, "so we're determined to complete her pilgrimage in that time." There! He said it! *Her* pilgrimage. "Tonight we stay at *InLima* and then tomorrow evening at *Casa de Flores de Lavanda.*"

"Me, too. I'll be staying at *Casa de Flores de Lavanda* tomorrow night, too," I nearly shouted, happy to learn they'd be with me for tonight *and* tomorrow night. When I said, "Two nights we'll be together," they only nodded. "And, oh! I just met the proprietor of the *Casa*, Franco. He was here. He offered to pick up my belongings and deliver them to his guesthouse. I'll be walking tomorrow without my pack. Wouldn't you love to walk free of that pack after such a long day today? I could call him for you!"

It hit me that I probably was talking way too fast. Were they having difficulty understanding me, especially with English as their second language?

**Still, I felt exuberant and enthusiastic.
I was big. I was American. And that was enough
to get Donetella's attention.**

Then Donetella stood up on her own weight for the first time, showing her full presence. "No, no, that is not the way for us." She looked to her husband for confirmation. I, too, looked to Vittorio. I was considering he might agree with me, since he wasn't a pilgrim but a chaperone to Donetella. Vittorio merely shrugged.

"We're following the *Camino* in the way of true pilgrims," she said, "and we'll carry our own weight. It would not be in keeping with the strict code of the *Pilgrims Way*." Her statement, ended any further discussion.

The Pilgrim's Way

The Pilgrim's Way. It sounded official and exclusive with its strict codes. The fact that she was a *true pilgrim* sullied me. The guilt of unloading my pack with Franco caused me to question my plans. *Am I less of a pilgrim for seeking comfort over her perceived idea of authenticity?* Memories of the fortuitous meeting with Franco, as annoying as he was, vanished. The thorn of doubt and guilt slivered its way into my consciousness.

Meeting the Italian couple left me sleepless. I questioned everything. I doubted my reasons for walking, for leaving home, for worrying Jim, and for asking him to wait for me while I fulfilled my selfish wish to walk the *Camino*.

**I questioned my validity as a pilgrim—
a true pilgrim.**

Then I worried over what life would be like after I returned home. *Will Jim finally snap?* I'd asked far too much of him this time.

That night, I lay in bed and watched the skies move from the inky black of midnight to the early pale of dawn. *Is this yet another one of my runaways in a lifetime of runaways?* I knew one thing for certain: This was not at all the springtime journey of joy and awakening I had imagined. My expectations of the trip had been so far off the mark, it was laughable. I had become my own tormentor. I was to blame. I'd gone as far as I could to find myself, and it still hadn't been far enough. Portugal or the Milky Way, it would *never* be far enough.

Then I regretted I hadn't left yesterday afternoon as I'd wanted. Had I done so, I reasoned, I'd still be happy in the head. Had I left, there'd be no Vittorio or Donatella to draw me into doubt. But with twenty kilometers and no stop-over in between, I realized there simply weren't enough daylight hours—and I wasn't foolish enough to walk in the dark.

Chapter 15

Sunlight hit the walls of my room, but it soon darkened because of the rain. I flipped on all the lights, took one last steamy shower, and dressed for the day as the rain drummed at the window. I searched the room for my rain pants. And then Franco's voice popped into my head: *Hurry, I am a very busy man,* he had said. *You must not keep me waiting.*

In my haste (stirred by his pushiness), I'd failed to pull out my rain pants! Darn. Darn it all. A simple yet serious mistake. Without them, there was nothing to do but wait out the spewing liquid shrapnel powered by the low gusts of wind. Today, Franco's offer to pick me up felt like a blessing, so I made the call.

In the breakfast nook, a small hollowed-out room adjacent to the lobby, I ran into Vittorio again. My bright American voice flooded the morning quiet. "Hey—Vittorio! Good morning. This rain is severe, yeah? The worst I've seen since I departed *Porto.*"

"Yes," he said, sitting at the table. "Donatella was kept awake by the rattling windows most of the night. And I—," Vittorio continued.

But I cut him off. "We—" I said and then paused.

We? When did I become a "we"? My mouth was once again moving fast ahead of my thoughts like a slippery fish. I took a breath and tried again. "What I meant was that *we*—all of us pilgrims walking today—will be soaked to the bone within minutes if *we* head outside. Last night when I met the innkeeper where *we* will be staying tonight, he offered to pick me up and drive me to *Agualonga*."

I sipped my coffee, eyeing him, waiting for his affirmative look. "So you and Donetella are welcome to join me. Franco says he'll even take us on a countryside excursion and show us the historical sites off the *Camino.*"

Realizing I was desperate for company, for approval, and for not having to travel alone with Franco, I pelted Vittorio with my desire to become a *we*. But that didn't happen.

"No. We will wait one hour. The rain should lift, and we'll be fine. No. We will walk the *Pilgrim's Way.*"

And there it was again: *The Pilgrim's Way*. I wanted to gag.

If not the Pilgrim's Way, what am I doing?

No "We" After All

Rejected again, I kicked myself for reaching out not once but twice. Vittorio's and Donatella's pilgrimage dared my purpose. *Is my way the way of the cheater? The slacker?* Then I regretted calling Franco rather than toughing it out as a real pilgrim. But he had my rain pants! Should I tell Vittorio, pleading with him? I'd say, "Hey, you don't understand! The man has my rain pants. I can't walk in *The Pilgrim's Way* without my rain pants."

Rattled by Vittorio's and Donetella's superiority in keeping with the strict rules, I threw my hands into the air. *Isn't walking all this way enough?*

But no matter how much I desired their companionship or how alone I felt, I knew I had to quit trying to fit into their paradigm. I wouldn't fall into a medieval lifetime pattern of self-punishment when flagellation was the way to get closer to God. Instead, I finished my coffee while thinking about how difficult old beliefs were to break. "The past dies hard," I said to the waiter. He only grinned and cleared my plate. *If I am to accept their beliefs for want of their approval, I would lose my truth, and that just wouldn't do. No way.* So with thoughts of *my Camino* and my idea of *my* God, I returned to my room.

There was no *we* after all. I was alone.

The Flamboyant Franco

By noon, the deluge had lifted. I said good-bye to my *InLima* family—Phillip, Iria, Rita and Natalia—and turned to greet the flamboyant Franco. He was as dapper as ever that afternoon. It was obvious he'd taken great care in dressing, and for some reason, this made me all the more uncomfortable. He wore a '70s-style wide-striped red-and-blue soccer shirt that I would have tossed if I'd found it in Jim's closet. His blue jeans, a bit too short, showed off his red crew socks. Red, it seemed, was his signature color. Completing his outfit, his soccer-style tennis shoes replaced his Italian loafers. His hair was the same—silver and perfectly coifed—and the smell of his cologne still preceded him.

He rushed to open the passenger-side door for me. His well-meaning chivalry weakened my sense of independence, which made me feel uncomfortable. But there I was, stepping inside his Range Rover, which was not as well-kept as his person. Papers and napkins littered the floor, forgotten boxes and bags of once-important items cluttered the back seat along with a lone can of yellow spray paint. While attempting to brush aside my unease, I brushed the film of dust that covered the upholstery. Then I hopped in.

Something percolated just below the surface of my consciousness, a rumble that began in my stomach and shot through me, tingling up through the top of my head.

Caution. Well, duh! Here I sat: a lone woman, a foreign woman, riding shotgun in a vehicle with a stranger. I was *that* girl. I envisioned the news reports back home: *American Woman Found in a Ditch Next to Long-Forgotten Sacred Site.* Before I'd left California, I'd given myself permission to be spontaneous, meet new people, go off the traditional path if invited. *I guess this is it.*

I buckled up. And then this message came barreling into my thoughts: *Be mindful. Use discernment in your spirit of adventure. Things are not always as they appear. You are handing over your freedom to Mr. Slick here, veering off the beaten path of the Camino.* I watched Franco primp, eyeing himself in the rearview mirror, smoothing back his already smooth hair. Not to state the obvious, but holy cow! *I have stepped into this stranger's car.*

He started the engine. And before I could bust out the door, we were in motion, driving away from the hotel.

Overreacting?

I pulled out my guidebook, my mind still racing between thoughts of fear and self-recrimination followed by the competing voice of rationalization. He was my host for the night, after all! Maybe I was overreacting.

I glanced over; his body was rather slight, the size of a horse jockey, and his feet no larger than mine. *I can probably take him down if I have to.*

I flipped through my guide book, landing on page sixty-three. "Let's go here," I said, holding it up for him to see, pointing to *Fonte Tres Bicas*. Page sixty-three indicated I'd walked a third of the way! This small fact boosted my spirits, but I didn't tell him that. He wasn't a pilgrim and would hardly understand. "*Por favor*, can you take me to *Fonte Tres Bicas?*" I asked. "It's a small stream where clear water flows into three stone-carved channels along a countryside lane. It's close to the village of *Revolta*. Here—" I pointed it out on the map.

"*Si, si, Senhora.* Yes! I know *Revolta*. It is near." Franco drove along, a pleasant grin pinned on his face.

I decided he was probably harmless, pushy but harmless.

"Did you know the *fonte* is a sacred vortex?" I asked him.

Franco tilted his head, a quizzical stare complicating his thin smile. I continued, "Yep, a vortex. I read about it. Apparently, there are gifts offered to us from a triune of energies—you know, the Holy Trinity?" He leaned back, pushing onto the steering wheel, pursing his lips, a quick furrow across his brow. *He doesn't have a clue what I'm talking about! And whatever I might say surely would be lost in translation. Well, I'm perfectly fine with it.*

Because I hadn't talked to anyone for a while, I yakked away, eager to experience the *Fonte Tres Bicas*. Not caring whether he was listening, I rambled, happy to hear the sound of my own voice. Until he slammed on the brakes.

He then jumped out of the car and crossed the road. I unbuckled and followed behind. We quickly arrived at the fountain. I stood silently in its presence—*the one and only Fonte Tres Bicas*. I felt dizzy, ungrounded even. That made sense. *This is, in fact, a sacred place—*

a breathtaking, once-in-a lifetime moment I had pon-dered and plotted to see for months.

I stood in the midst of it all and then glanced briefly toward Franco. He was leaning against a rock, staring into the water. I dipped down, finding a place to sit while pushing aside any feelings of light-headedness and, for a time, thoughts of Franco. I carried on with my spiritual play: praying, singing, and collecting a vial of the sacred water.

When I finally looked up from the stream, I could see I wasn't the only one feeling touched this place. Franco, too, appeared taken with its energy.

He gazed at me lovingly (too lovingly, if I were a betting woman). *Connecting to Spirit can be ecstatic. Especially if connecting to the divine is new, it could eas-ily be misunderstood for carnal feeling.*

Franco stepped closer, gazing into my eyes. I knew then I was indeed the object of his desires. After quickly gathering my things, I rushed to the far side of the fountain. "Wow, it looks like the weather's go-ing to hold up nicely today," I said in a neutral voice. "Look! The clouds are clearing up ahead." I pointed into the distance.

"*Si*, yes. It is a perfect day—rain or shine." He stepped closer. I knew he was a chatty sort who spoke English quite well and enjoyed showing it off. He kept talking, either to connect with me or to ease the obvious tension that ran like a feral cat between us.

"I see your *visage*," he cooed.

Was he referring to my aura? "My *visage*? You see my visage. What do you mean? Wait—don't tell me. I don't want to know."

"Your eyes. It's your eyes. There's something about you I can't identify."

"That's because we've only just met. Remember? You don't really know me. And I'm a mere guest and will be gone before you know it." Although I laughed, there was no funny bone tingling in my body.

"Your eyes are the windows to the soul—"

"Yes. Right—," I cut him off. "Windows to the soul."

Before he came closer, I sent a short, silent prayer to God and the Angels, and with no better choice, jumped back into the Rover.

Chapter 16

Back in the car, Franco steered up a winding mountain road, focusing on the twists and turns, and soon we came to a promontory called *Monte de Sao Romao*. It had been raining for days; the ground was sodden and so dangerously saturated that it threatened mudslides. I noticed the road had no guard rails.

Around the bend, my fears dropped (just a little) at the sight of a bridge arching over *Rio Ave* like a beacon, graceful and wide, spanning from east to west.

It was a sign! It had to be.
And a sign was what I needed, for it occurred
to me I had nothing left to hang on to.

In fact, this Portuguese bridge was identical to one near our home. Jim and I fondly referred to it as our gatekeeper. I'd driven beneath it hundreds of times. But unlike its secluded Portuguese twin, our bridge arched over eight freeway lanes of unrelenting California traffic. Whenever Jim and I passed beneath it, we nearly always saw a hawk, sometimes two of them, soaring above. This would prompt us into a prayer of gratitude for God and Mother Gaia.

This Portuguese twin bridge has to be a sign, a good one. It just has to be. And then I saw it: a hawk soaring in the sky directly in my sight line.

The gratitude and sense of being protected shivered through my body.

Thank you, I repeated silently as the hawk swooped upward before dipping into the valley below.

Ancient City

When Franco and I arrived atop *Monte de Sao Romao* and reached the ruins of *Citania de Briteiros,* the winds had kicked up, roaring in my ears. The drive and the bridge and the quiet had relaxed me. I stepped into the ruins of this ancient city dating to the Bronze Age five thousand years before. Recently unearthed by teams of archeologists, it had become a designated historical site.

I walked through the ruins examining how archeologists had reconstructed some of the round stone structures and had left others outlined in excavated stones for the visitors' imagination. Roughly a hundred family dwellings were grouped in circles and organized in a grid pattern.

My hair flying and my jacket flapping in the wind, I stepped up to a circular stone house connected to a paved courtyard. It accessed a larger circular structure, presumed to be a community gathering house. Evidence remained on the hillside of conduits likely built to carry water from the spring uphill to fountains and bathhouses below.

I hurriedly took all of it in, the good tourist, eager to snap my photos and rush back to the warmth of the car.

The Handsome Stone

To the side of the village was an intricately carved stone almost three meters square. The minute I saw it, I was inextricably drawn to it. The cold no longer mattered. I looked up to see Franco mouthing over the howling wind, "It is the *Pedra Formosa*, 'the handsome stone,' and part of a burial chamber."

Unlike the other ruins, the *Pedra Formosa* stood impervious to the passage of time. Around the beginning of 1000 BC, the families who called *Citania de Briteiros* home abruptly disappeared. No one knows why. Things disappeared. Poof. A civilization once vibrant, alive. Gone.

I glanced over at Franco, his hair spun up into devilish, pointy tufts on his head, his eyes wild in the sunlight. I could see gusts of wind barrel through the ruins in between us. A chill ran through me, my eyes gritty and burning, my vision blurred.

Franco and the wind fused together in my experience.

Both had been exhilarating at first, slapping me alive.

But at this point, peeling me away from the situation seemed nearly impossible. *No way out except to allow him to drive me back to town.* So I gripped my jacket, pulling it around my waist, running toward Franco's vehicle. The chaos made it difficult for me to catch my breath. I sucked in air and then exhaled, yet I still felt depleted of oxygen.

"I'm right behind you," he hollered, coming up alongside me. "You look beautiful, no?" he said. "Your messy hair—so cute."

I stiffened and turned away. The thought to forego his vehicle and walk back to known territory—or better yet, run back—crossed my mind. *After walking for days and across an entire country, I can walk away now.*

No Clue How to Get Back

Then I looked up ahead and realized I hadn't the slightest clue how to get back. I hadn't paid attention on the way up to the ruins and would surely get lost. Plus I had no water, and all of my belongings were at Franco's. So I hopped into the Rover with no better plan. Franco stood beside me uncomfortably close, and without warning, he kissed my lips, his mouth pressed against mine. Stunned, I found myself responding in kind, pursing my lips against his for a brief yet extremely awkward moment.

He'd kissed me! And I'd kissed him back. Inadvertently, I had kissed him back—like a knee-jerk reaction when someone says "thank you" and I say "you're welcome." It happened so fast that I wondered if I'd imagined it. I wiped my mouth, then buckled my seatbelt. *Safety first.* These words ran across my brain in a frantic rush as the seat belt buckle clicked into place. I used to say this phrase every time I'd buckle my young son's seat belt. And here I was buckling up in this madman's vehicle.

All Tangled Up

As Franco jumped into his seat, I watched him, highly conscious of his every move. He had ambled around the front of the hood, a thin smile plastered to his face, like nothing had happened. Then he turned on the engine and began backing out, leaving his seatbelt buckle dangling. It clanked against the window, appearing to be broken.

"Is that broken?" I asked, pointing to his seat belt and surprised by the sound of my shrill voice, shaky and cracking.

He swiveled around and yanked on it. "Oh, no— not broken. It's just tangled, see?" He pulled it one more time, chuckling, before turning onto the road.

"It's like you," he said, his eyes fixed toward the windshield. "It's tangled, like you—all tangled up." He laughed a little.

I guessed he was expecting me to protest, but I held back. I wasn't about to fall into another trapped conversation with Franco.

**I only knew I needed to make it down
the mountain and away from him.**

"I need to get back now," I said. "I'm done with sightseeing." I was stammering and shaking. "But, thank you. I want to go back now—please."

"Well, as you can see, we are driving back." He looked calm and self-assured. "But—you're nervous? Why so nervous?" He dropped his hands away from the wheel, twirling and twisting them in the air. "You're all tangled! Tangled and nervous." He let out a barking laugh.

"Is it about us—about a man and woman alone?" He reached over, patting the tops of my knees. I looked down. I clasped my hands tightly, leaning on my crossed legs. *Yes, I am all tangled up.*

"It's all right," he backed off. "We're going back." He turned a corner that led to the narrow main road. We drove along in silence, the Rover lurching over every bump, the side of the cliff to my right, jagged and steep. Cumulus clouds stacked up ahead.

"More rain coming," he said. This mindless chatter made me all the more uneasy, knowing that behind these words his mind was cleverly planning his next move—a pause in charming me into complicity.

I pulled out my lip balm and lathered my lips, staring out, my eyes tracing a long row of pine trees. Then Franco broke the silence.

"I remember my first love. I was the tangled one that time."

What's that supposed to mean? His voice boomed inside the cab, too loud. I held my tongue, afraid to say a word. We veered around a sharp turn, causing me to jerk and sway toward his direction.

"I remember it well," he started again. I could tell he was working every angle, trying to pull me into another one of his tricky conversations—as if I would dare say something about my first love or love in general.

But I wasn't about to budge. *Just take me back to town.* I kept repeating this plea inside my head. My cheeks were hot, my lips dry. I pulled out my lip balm again and then asked, "Do you have any water?" I looked to the floorboard before turning around to scan the backseat. All I could see were the same piles of old mail and trash.

"No. But we can stop for a drink—"

"No," I said sharply. "I'm fine. No need to stop. Just keep going."

Taking Charge

"My wife, she's a good wife," he said.

"That's nice," I responded coldly.

"But sometimes—you know—we've been married many, many years now, and a man's needs are different from a woman's . . . "

Are you serious? I focused on my breathing. *Where is he going with this?* "Well," I said, feeling the need to take charge of this runaway conversation. "Well—that sounds like a private matter and certainly nothing for me to know about."

"She was a good lover at first. When we were courting," he said, obviously uninterested in taking my cue to change the subject. As he was baring his soul, I could barely breathe. I thought of Jim sitting at home. Because it was evening in San Diego, he was probably reading the newspaper and definitely worrying about me—as he should. I was someone to worry about! *Running off to a foreign land to do a walkabout is bad enough. Jumping into this Casanova's car is absolute insanity. Dear God, protect me, keep me safe.*

"You okay?" Franco asked.

"Yes, yes," I stammered. "I was praying—that's all. The road's bumpy and steep here." I peered out. The puddled ruts were as wide as manholes. *No one knows where I am or who I'm with. If I am not in danger from Franco's untoward motives, nature isn't offering me any safety either.* One thing was for sure, though.

Franco had unleashed his baser self, leaving behind the charismatic innkeeper at the ruins. I saw a side of his ego I'd happily drop-kick off the next cliff.

The fact that I willingly accepted his invitation still baffled me. How unlike my typical overly cautious nature. *Are we playing out some karmic relationship? Obviously!*

Confusion Reigned

From the moment I'd been in Franco's presence—more like under his spell—confusion had reigned. But I had to gather my wits and snap out of this dream. I'd arrived at this point of my own free will. I knew that by taking responsibility for it and then taking charge was my only hope. And I knew I must get down this mountain and out of his car. *I just want Jim by my side.*

I pressed my body to the window, turning away from my captor and the situation. The elevation was winding down as we passed several farmhouses. Behind a thick glade, I spotted a tall stone house—more of a castle, really, with its tall angled roof and gargoyles, its arched entrance and windows adorned by black shutters. A small garden carpeted either side of the front entrance. It looked like a fairy tale castle laced with small white flowers and an iron gate.

"Who lives there?" I blurted out.

The fairy tale castle had been built from rocks mined from the ground it stood on with no right angles, no squares. Everything appeared topsy-turvy, created without plans or design. Rooftop angles intersected triangles and then swirled into cupolas. The shock of its oddness took my mind off Franco.

"Ah, this place is—this person is not good. He uses energy. He calls himself a healer and takes people's money. He is bad. He promises cures for things with his craft," Franco explained.

He's a spiritual healer! The thought fascinated me.

"Pull in, pull in. I want to meet him." But Franco drove past. "Please," I said. "Turn around and see if he's home."

"No! Did you not hear me? The man who lives there is no good. He's a bad man, an impostor." My request clearly unnerved Franco more than it should have. It was a clue I was not easy prey for his romantic shenanigans.

The Charlatan

Why on earth would I listen to Franco! Who was he (of all people) to judge another?

**If he thought the man living in the castle
was an impostor, I became all the more certain
the man was a spiritual healer,
an energy worker, maybe a reiki master—
and someone I'd like to meet.**

I said, "Let me be the judge of that. I have no concern about him using energy. We all use energy, for that matter." My attention turned head on toward Franco, my revived self-control working its way through me. I sat up straight.

"Turn around," I repeated.

"No! He is evil. How do you say *charlatao*?"

"Charlatan?"

"*Si, si!* He is a *charlatao*."

Franco refused to stop, reminding me I truly was at his mercy. I leaned back as I relinquished my desire to visit the castle, but I couldn't catch a full breath, and my stomach churned. *It's better not to provoke Franco than demand meeting the so-called "charlatao," whom I sensed would be a kindred spirit.* Then I tried convincing myself Franco was a local who probably knew better than I did. Yet something told me to hang on—and that my gut instincts were right on.

"You see, my dear, you need to listen to me and do what I say. And I say we are not stopping at the castle," he said. Franco was the charlatao.

Chapter 17

My imagination took off. Silently, I screamed out for Franco to stop. *Please, stop!* I imagined tearing myself from his vehicle and running to the castle, pounding on its giant door. And for whatever time I was allotted, I would enjoy a visit with a soul like me, someone who could ease my distress.

Of course, with every moment, the wheels of Franco's vehicle sped farther and farther away from the castle, and Franco had no way of comprehending my silent plea. I corkscrewed into my seat and imagined the healer as a kind old man sitting on his porch.

Then, when we rolled into town, I begged feeling car sick. "I'm not feeling well."

"Oh? Let me help you," Franco said, his voice sounding genuinely concerned, reminding me how easily he'd ensnared me. "We're almost at the *Casa*," he promised. "Is it your stomach? Your head? My wife has many remedies . . . "

"No, no. Just take me to the inn. I'll care for myself." Franco drove in silence, pulling to a slow stop at the side of the *Casa. I'll still be under his roof but safely out of his car.*

Holding My Breath

Settled in my room and away from the wind and Franco, I felt the air silent and still. That's when I realized how much I'd been holding back my breath. I raised the wood-shuttered windows and gulped for more.

My lungs worked greedily as I sucked in as much oxygen from the room as they could hold.

I looked around at the room, my home for the night, crammed full with a mix of used furniture. But the clean details of the windowpanes, the floorboards, and sleek ceiling tiles marked the design of an architect with an eye for quality.

The bed, too small for two, was dressed in a grandma's quilt and embroidered pillows. Ivory-colored crocheted doilies covered the dresser and dripped over the edges of the nightstand. Needlepoint protected the arms of a green wingback chair. Still conscious of each breath, I sat in the chair, taking in this tribute to an insufferable life of needlecraft. *It feels good to be away from Franco.*

I sighed audibly, my fingers rolling over the needlework of a loose doily. I imagined the thousands of woman-hours it must have taken to complete only one of these. *This wedding cake of a room was the kind my mother used to swoon over.* I noticed the clean lines of the wood door, its latch a fine polished brass, and I imagined the architect would have wretched over the thick film of lace and ruffles—a sticky frosting over his modern design.

The room had been decorated for a lady and was no place for a man—no place for Jim. I somehow found comfort in this. Jim wouldn't have been at home here; he would have scoffed about it.

**I hoped this was a sign
I was meant to be here alone.**

My dirt-colored pack, a lump on the floor, looked like I was a hobo in a teahouse. *I don't want to be here, either.*

A Mindful Ritual This Night

Breathing a few more cleansing breaths, I began to undress, an activity that had become a mindless ritual since my trip started. The same set of clothes, on and off each day, in the same order. Some nights, I wouldn't undress at all, flopping into my sleeping bag fully clothed. Other nights, if the room was clean and warm, I'd peel away every bit of stale fabric and bare it all. Franco was out of sight and I was grateful that *Casa de Flores de Lavanda* at least offered a clean, private space. Off came my blue wool sweater (rated 250 for warmth, according to Tanner at the hiking store); off came the next layer, my purple sweater (rated 150), followed by my pink, long-sleeved under layer, a silky item I'd chosen for its beauty. My clothes fell into dirty piles on the loomed wool rug.

I laughed at how like my mother I appeared in this moment. She would have loved the doilies. In contrast, I had gone out of my way to find the most stylish hiking clothes money could buy. I'd purposely scoured shops to find a flouncy skirt and leggings instead of opting for hiking cargoes. Again, fashion ranked equal to form.

Last Rays of Sunshine

Dressed in my leggings and a camisole, I grabbed my beauty satchel and made my way toward the bathroom, the guestroom door clicking shut behind me. The last rays of sunshine had fallen in a hatched pattern between the blinds, the hallway steeped in a foggy brew leaking from underneath the bathroom door. The scent of Dial soap, Old Spice, and the ever-present mold of Portugal hurled me into memories of earlier years—the defiant girl whose mouth was washed out with soap, Grandpa and his intoxicating Old Spice telling me stories of bunnies in dens and trolls under bridges, and the young woman deeply in love braving the cold damp winter in Portugal for the sake of Jim's affection.

Waiting for my turn in the bathroom, I stood in the hall ensconced in a cloud of steam,. Like molecules swirling in the air, tiny droplets of water lit up against the last rays of the day, a galaxy of spiraling mist.

I imagined every cell of my being moving with each particle, uniting with the whole, creating who I am.

And in that moment, I loved God deeply for lifting me out of the delusion I'd stepped into when I'd met Franco. The molecules and steam and spiral became symbols—revealing all that makes me strong and devoted and impassioned and changeable and doubtful and afraid—and lovable. *All these things I am.*

Close Encounter

Holding back a flood of steam, the bathroom door suddenly swung open, startling me out of my thoughts. From within the soup of steam, the shape of a man emerged. He was easily two-and-a-half times my size and wrapped in a paper-thin blue-striped towel that strained across his thick girth. He stood within inches of my face, silent and close—so close I could have raised up on my toes and kissed him. *What was it with men so close to me today!*

I scrambled backwards, edging my way along the wall and to the threshold of the bathroom. "Excuse, me," I said. "Pardon me, I'm sorry . . . "

And with a bright smile, he replied, "No worries, my dear. There's plenty of hot water for you. See you at dinner." And he was gone, disappearing through a door at the far end of the hall.

I took a huge breath and stepped into the bathroom, smelling the man's toiletries and scent clinging to everything. I reminded myself I had asked for this. *Being a pilgrim meant sharing rooms and showers and giving up any semblance of privacy.*

In *my* book of rules, I was indeed a *true* pilgrim.

Our Polished Host

Franco busied himself for dinner until, one by one, we each entered the spacious downstairs living room furnished with a rocking chair, recliner, and couch. All had matching pillows and upholstery similar to the decor of my room. A bookcase lining the far wall was stacked with board games and grocery-store paperbacks printed in English. A bar-style counter separated the service kitchen from the rest of the room. It was stocked with help-yourself utensils, cups and glasses, tea and coffee, and a microwave for the late-night snackers and early risers. Adjoining the living room and separating the kitchen was the large family-style dining table with a place set for each of us.

Once we'd finally assembled, Franco commanded our attention with a booming *Boa noite!* What a polished host! His greeting was perfected with the same sweeping bow he had used on me at *InLima.*

"Tonight, I will be your host, sommelier, and server. At my *Casa,* you are *my* guests, and you will enjoy the most delicious dinner prepared by my lovely wife, Zezenia. A home-cooked meal that has never tasted so good, served with the finest Portuguese wines you won't find outside of my countryside."

The shadowy "giant" I'd met outside the bathroom had just stepped into the living room. As he was happily nodding his approval of Franco's speech, I couldn't guess what the others were thinking, but looking around, I decided I might be the only one in the bunch who could see through Franco's bravado.

"*Por favor*—dear people. Please make yourself comfortable," Franco said, pointing in the direction of the couch. But rather than settle into forced intimacy, we all remained on our feet grinning foolishly back and forth at each other. We waited for someone to speak, tell a joke, make small talk—anything to shatter the awkwardness of our first meeting.

Franco's flair and cordiality made me wonder if the events of the afternoon had ever happened.

Maybe I'd imagined it. And then I saw him lean in and swat Zezenia on the behind, reminding me what a jerk he truly was. *This was the same Zezenia he had lamented over, the woman who no longer made love in a manner that suited Franco's needs.* My stomach turned at the thought. He was as smooth and uncouth as ever while showing off his slickness to the other pilgrims that night.

Breaking Bread

Finally, when no one sat down in the living room, Franco signaled us to take our seats at the dinner table. With bread and wine and water to distract us, we eased into the deliciousness of our meal. My tension from the day's excursion had softened after the shower, and I felt safe from Franco's advances in the company of others. Aside from Vittorio and Donatella, whom I'd met last night, the other houseguests were David

Carter, a retired investment and commodities trader (now gentleman farmer), with his wife Sal—a lovely South African couple. David and I had already established familiarity in our shared bathroom. Sal, a former therapist who now tended to goats and grandchildren, led the conversation with ease.

Happily, I was able to put aside my earlier reservations about Vittorio and Donatella as I learned more about who they were. I couldn't help but genuinely like them. Donatella sat quietly eating bread and sipping wine as she listened intently to the conversation. I couldn't help but be drawn to her, a woman as sweet and serene as she was beautiful.

Vittorio, a vice president of a global corporation, shared his piercing views of U.S. commerce and politics backed by his incisive business sense. He commented on Americans' raw reaction to the recent oil spill in the Gulf, which was a clue for me to remain silent on my own feelings for this environmental disaster. Unlike our first meeting, this time I felt comfortable in my own skin as we compared our corporate experiences.

I reminded myself that, much like Vittorio, I was more than a pilgrim. I easily fit into the business world, the spiritual world, or any world for that matter.

Once we all got acquainted, our inhibitions quickly fell away, and we all dove into Zezenia's excellent meal. We also marveled over our similarities in choosing this journey, yet reveled in our different backgrounds.

"The path of the *Camino* leads each pilgrim on his or her own unique journey," someone said . . . "Yes! I continued completing their thought . . . "each seeking a personal quest."

"Isn't that like the adage, there are many paths and all lead to God?" I asked. "Interesting how this one path carries many to God in myriad ways."

**I am beginning to honor my *Camino*
and my place on this journey.**

Chapter 18

To my delight, everyone spoke English except Donatella, although her smiles and nods assured me she understood all she needed to know.

As the conversation livened up, the ever-annoying Franco disregarded his position as the silent waiter and became more talkative than before. He soon carried on a monologue that left little room for others' conversation. Not wanting to be rude, we politely remained silent until the moment he would stop to catch his breath or attend to his serving duties. Then we'd steer the conversation to our experiences on the *Camino*. By the sideways stares back and forth from David, Sal, and Vittorio, I was not alone in my distaste for Franco's gigantic ego.

During Franco's pauses, David and Sal broke in and told us they had previously walked the *Camino de Santiago Frances.* This was their first venture on the *Camino Portugues,* and they were disappointed that, so far, the churches along the *Camino Portugues* were locked. *Exactly my experience.*

"Since this is your first *Camino,* you may not realize," David began, "that because the churches are locked, you will not receive the *Pilgrim's Certificate* when you arrive in *Santiago.*"

"What?" I asked, trying to comprehend what he was saying.

Frankly, I hadn't set out on this journey to win a piece of paper with a gold seal on it. But this was news to me.

"It's true," Sal said before sipping her wine, her South African accent musical and lilting. "When you arrive in *Santiago,* you must present your pilgrim's passport at the *Casa do Dean* to receive the coveted *Compostela*—the Certificate of Completion. If the Dean determines that the majority of your stamps are from cafes and inns, you will be viewed by his authority as a lesser pilgrim."

"A lesser pilgrim?" Donatella and I said in a slur of both English and Italian.

A Lesser Pilgrim

From this discussion, I learned that the category of *Compostela* is based on whether a pilgrim's stamps come from churches or cafes. There are two classifications: The *Pilgrim's* Certificate is granted to those deemed a true pilgrim, and the other—the *Pilgrimage* Certificate—is for travelers who have received the majority of their passport stamps from bars and cafes. You're only considered a *true* pilgrim if your passport is stamped by a church.

"Now that's plain crazy," I replied. "Who do they think they are deciding *who* is a worthy pilgrim?" I was shocked that once again the Catholic Church was laying its critical stamp of disapproval on me. "So, you're saying I'm viewed by the authorities as a lesser pilgrim because I stopped at cafes and not churches and chapels?"

"Yes, that's essentially what I'm saying," Sal continued. "You'll receive only a *Pilgrimage* Certificate, not the more coveted *Pilgrim's* Certificate, and so will we. And it's, of course, through no fault of our own. *No one* has had much access to the churches."

Sal and Donatella continued the tirade I'd started. So I sat back, slumping into my chair, lost in my own thoughts. *Here I go again. Why do I even care? I have no intention of going to Santiago for a stupid certificate. Why should I care about the coveted Compostela?* But I could sense the prickle up my arms, a feeling of being left out, of being less than, a *lesser* pilgrim. My feet ached in my boots, reminding me of the miles I had walked that would never be seen as worthy by my Church. However, I knew God was and will always be omnipresent and omniscient. God is not confined to any one religion.

What is wrong with me? Here I go again with the ego stuff, caring about stupid certificates and belonging. I've seen the Catholic Church for what it is.

I scooted my chair closer to the table, shaking off my creeping insecurities. The soothing words "I am a Child of God" repeated inside my muddled head.

My Inner Battle

The inequity and judgment of the Catholic Church had once again gotten the best of me. And I couldn't seem to stop myself; my inner battle to shut up wasn't winning. It was due to the abandonment I'd experienced by the Church I had once identified as my source and connection to God. This still pained me. *This moment was a lifetime in the making when—once and for all—I could dispel the lie that I was outcast from God. Here it was, my golden moment.*

"It's not our fault the churches are locked. We have no choice. I'm walking *The Pilgrim's Way*," Donatella said, speaking haltingly in English as if she were only consoling herself. I could see tears popping into her eyes. This was *her* faith. The Catholic Church was her only path to God, her religion, her end all, her Way. The reality of what she'd just learned deflated the last bit of energy she held. I could feel her body wither beside mine.

"Yes, had we known this, we would have never chosen to walk the *Camino Portugues,*" David said. "It *is* a travesty."

Outraged, we sat in silence staring at our unfinished soup, reeling in the somber reality of our crashed *Camino*. I felt damned again. Discriminated by the

Catholic Church that had locked the doors to its worshippers, and then labeled them lesser pilgrims. *Too much to bear.*

No Escaping the Reawakening

My emotional pain of being excluded from the Church was oppressively smothering me, and I wasn't about to allow it to surface. Not at Franco's table and not in front of my new friends. But there was no escaping its re-emergence like a sleeping monster inside of me nudged awake—all because of a pilgrim's passport being stamped by bars and not churches. Its rules cut close and deep enough to hit the bone. I sat mute hoping no one would notice my insides crumbling, dying.

My exclusion from the Church had been a big part of who I was; it had shaped my identity for more than forty years. The untruth of it all.

I had to brace myself, wondering if I could hold back the dam of sorrow long enough to finish dinner. For now, I could only call upon the God presence within me. *The Church did not have judgment over me. I only needed to practice this belief. Practice. Believe.*

I left the meal graciously thanking my hosts, the thought of Franco as a threat was long gone. His presence, in fact, appeared comical. Tipsy, he was still as chatty and filled with bravado as ever. Then I walked out into the brisk night air searching for the Milky

Way. The sky that evening was a blue black, the moon hidden behind the tall trees, the stars blanketing the velvety blackness. The scene gave me solace, peace of mind. *That's why I have come here.*

I knew what I'd been told that night about stamps and pilgrims was true—and I was fine with it. In fact, I had already decided I would not travel to *Santiago* to collect the prized *Compostela*. In that moment, I let go of the old ego need to please, the old ego need to win, the old ego need to belong and be part of something. I didn't have to show the world I was worthy.

**To win the Church's heart was not my mission.
To win my own heart was all that mattered.**

I slept well that night.

Chapter 19

The sun kissed me out of a deep sleep, and before I had reached full consciousness, I felt like a Julie Andrews character humming the "Sound of Music." *Nothing like a brisk night walk and a hard sleep to knock sense into a pilgrim.*

Outside my window, the day appeared crisp and bright. Any signs of rain, any fog or clouds, had disappeared. I gazed out the window, rubbing the sleep from my eyes to see if I'd been transported to Austria. I was still in the embrace of *Agualonga,* of course, which wasn't too bad after all, especially with Franco at bay.

So I picked up the pace, packing for my departure and feeling my purpose return with a vengeance. Maybe it was a genuine breakthrough, a letting go of the decades-long agony of being excommunicated by the Catholic Church. As a young girl all I wanted was a life with God in the convent. But then I discovered boys, married too young, and after an inevitable divorce, the Catholic Church never forgave me. It had denounced my marriage of more than thirty years to my true love, Jim, and forbid me the Eucharist.

I awoke knowing the Church's shackle of denouncement was broken. I was free!

Feeling light and empowered, I decided to risk walking that day without rain gear. *I felt as if I could scale a mountain if I so chose.* I planned to forego breakfast and find a nice *café* farther down the road. On this heavenly day, I was determined to soak in every bit of sunshine, knowing that clouds and rain in Portugal could drift in quickly.

A Somber and Reserved Franco

When I stepped into the front room at the inn, Franco was coming in from the kitchen, his eyes downcast, his shoulders slightly slumped. Somber and reserved. I was secretly glad about that. I guessed it was because of too much wine or perhaps another side to his ever-spinning bi-polar personality. Of course, Zezenia's watchful eye was no match for his silly brand of shenanigans. Raven-haired and of slight build, her golden brown eyes darted around checking on her biscuits and keeping eye on her guests. She had seemed to flow smoothly with the activity despite Franco's crassness. I suspect she had an inkling her husband was often up to no good.

At that point, I settled my bill and gave Franco my pilgrim's passport to stamp.

"You're not staying for breakfast?" he practically shouted.

"Can you keep it down?" I whispered.

"But why? Why you are not staying?" he protested. "We have beautiful food for you—already prepared. Don't be foolish." He was loud and close enough that I could smell the tobacco on his breath.

"I've already made plans." I smoothed my hands over my pack.

Zezenia walked in, her hair tied back in a braid. "What's this? *Señhora?* You must leave us so soon?" She was gentler than him in showing her dismay. Nonetheless, I felt pressure to stay as she gave a sweet pout and then turned around, heading back into the kitchen.

Franco, though, was unrelenting. He livened up his push to persuade me to stay, jumping into action with plans to arrange one last meeting at tonight's hotel, even offering to porter my pack to *Valenca*. Still not getting a "yes" from me, he promised to save me a room on my return from *Finisterre*, even offering to pick me up at the train station.

"Franco—stop, please," I demanded. "I appreciate everything, really. I do. But I'm leaving." I could feel the presence of other guests moving about in the dining room. Finally, I had managed to fend off his advances.

This time, I felt armed and ready for his overbearing ways. And this time, I held him at bay.

Gratitude

As I walked outside of the office to the pathway leading to the gate, Zezenia rushed out speaking fast and
in Portuguese. I turned to see what was causing all
the commotion. Nearly out of breath, her arms flail-
ing around me, she came toward me fast, kissing my
cheeks and grabbing both of my hands. Then she
opened her hands, leaving the contents of a satin bag
in my palms. The sweet and familiar scent of lavender
billowed up in the air between of us. Our eyes locked,
and I sensed she was trying to tell me something.

"Thank you," she said again and again. I could tell
she was grateful for my trust. I knew then she was well
aware of Franco's advances toward me and, more important, my stand to keep him away. In that moment,
we shared affection for one another, a love surrounded
in lavender that contrasted with his ugly betrayal. Also
in that moment, my heart broke open for Zezenia and
hardened toward Franco. *I have to sort it out later. I can
only hope he will find a way to honor her.*

Following Zezenia's directions to town and reeking
from her lavender, I found my way through the gate.
Yet I couldn't escape the downpour of emotion I'd
been holding onto for days. Even the sky responded.
The clouds had drifted in and rain fell in big drops,
wetting my cheeks and the path in front of me.

Passed the Initiation

After walking across a wooden bridge, I found my way to the open road. I spotted a yellow arrow up ahead, my beacon showing me the way. Moving at a brisk pace—left, right, left, right—my limbs loosened now that I was outside breathing fresh air. My spirits lifted. The lingering puffiness around my eyes that comes after a good cry didn't bother me.

As I moved closer to the nearest yellow arrow, it was clear it had been freshly painted. The can of yellow spray paint in Franco's backseat clutter surfaced in my thoughts. He had stopped to clear the weeds hiding the arrow that had surely caused many missed turns for passing pilgrims like me. My heart softened toward him, knowing firsthand the relief a yellow arrow can offer a pilgrim.

For the first time in ten days, I was on my own. No Dr. Nic, no porter, no taxi, no Franco (thank goodness). Only me—all alone—following the yellow arrows. I had passed the initiation of being lost and trusted the rest of my way would be well marked.

Missing!

I was only a few kilometers down the road when I discovered my Pilgrim's passport missing. First I felt my breast pocket, then stopped to rifle through my pack, my back pockets, the insides of my jacket. In desperation, I even checked my socks. Nowhere.

Had Franco not returned my Pilgrim's passport after he stamped it? Was that on purpose? It had to be. His subtle distractions and his desire to meet me at my next stop in *Valenca*—and his desire for me to return to *Casa de Flores de Lavanda* on my return—all of it had thrown me off. *What have I done to bring on this drama? What lessons are in it for me to learn? Why would he want to taunt me? Or keep me?*

From the start, I had guarded my *credencial de peregrino* with my U.S. passport, cash, and credit cards next to my heart in a satin pouch. I constantly checked, rechecked, and checked again to make certain they were safely on my person. This was *one* aspect of self-containment I had maintained—a mindful practice to keep things together. It couldn't have been of my own doing, I concluded. Then I searched the inside of my breast pocket again. Confirmed. My pilgrim's passport truly was missing. My stomach dropped.

My open-heartedness, no, my gullibility is no match for Franco's manipulations.

I picked up the pace, hoping to get to the nearest *café* so I could call him and retrieve it. After more than an hour's walk (only a ten-minute drive), I arrived at *Café Ponte Nova*. I still did not have cell phone service, so I implored the *café* owner to hook up her fax line and help me connect to Franco. *Franco! More Franco nonsense! Like gum on my shoe, I can't seem to get rid of him.*

My body was hot both from the walk and the anger burning inside me. I dialed and Franco answered on the first ring. "I need my passport," I blurted out. "I'm sure you have it. You're the last person to have held it. You need to drive to the *café* in *Ponte Nova*. now!"

"I'm on my way, *Señhora*," he said. As smooth in his delivery as ever, he didn't even attempt a protest. This infuriated me even more.

When he walked in with my passport in hand, he offered to drive me to the next hotel as if we were old friends. I plucked the document from his grasp and barked, "Sure, like that'll happen." I said it with a fake laugh. He, of course, didn't understand my joke. In fact, I believe that, for a second, he thought he'd once again hooked me in.

"So—you need a ride, then?" he asked, his wild eyes showing too much white. *Crazy eyes.*

"No—I was joking. It's an American thing." Then I stuffed my passport inside my pocket. "It was a joke. And it doesn't matter."

About then, the *café* owner, who had stepped away to serve a lone patron a drink, returned. "You are well, *Señhora?*" she asked me, motioning toward her fax. "Do you need to make more calls?"

Franco stood between us, his dumb red socks peeking from beneath his pants.

"Thank you, no. I'm quite well now," I nodded and left the two of them standing at the front of the *café*.

Chapter 20

Finally, I was in my element, alone on the *Camino* to pray, inhale the menthol-sharp scent of eucalyptus, and step in rhythm to birdsong, all in the presence of God. This was the kind of day I had envisioned, the *Camino* experience I had dreamed of, the oneness with all I had longed for.

On this day, I could soar to the heavens as easily as tread on Earth. I was ecstatic in knowing that it was all God asked of me—ever.

As the day wore on, my path crisscrossed with Vittorio and Donatella and with David and Sal, but mostly I was alone with my mala beads and my thoughts. Everyone had seemingly put aside last night's disappointments and, like me, simply felt content to be walking in sunshine.

When I stopped for coffee at the *café* in *Fontoura Fuente*, I saw Donatella sitting off in the corner rubbing her knee, her pant leg raised. Vittorio stood at the counter. I sensed they were at an impasse and followed his grimace in the direction of Donatella, then I sat down next to her.

Pointing to her knee and waving her hand in a gesture, it was clear she wanted me to think her knee injury was "nothing." But I knew it was "something" and needed treating. Her devotion to her pilgrimage had pushed her and, I could see, she was not about to surrender. Her first-aid supplies were limited and, until they reached a pharmacy in *Valenca,* few remedies were available in the countryside.

Vittorio seemed helpless to comfort his wife, which was creating his own kind of pain. *The* Camino *never lets up, whether you are on it for yourself or for others. No hiding from what it stirs within.*

I slid off my pack and shuffled through the pockets until I uncovered my buried first-aid kit. Thank goodness I had prepared for every situation, supplying my kit with Western pharmaceuticals, Chinese, holistic medicines, and herbal concoctions. So far on this pilgrimage, I'd only reached into it for Nic's sorry shoes and my blisters. For Donatella, I pulled out homeopathic pain relief ointment and handed it to her, showing her how to massage it into her swollen joint. Then I searched for the more substantial pain relievers and handed her four capsules, just in case, for later. She tried to hand the tube of ointment back to me but I insisted she keep it, instructing her to continually massage it into her knee at every rest stop. Then we silently shared a *café com expresso com leite* and said our good-byes for the last time.

I hoped our encounter had alleviated her knee pain. If nothing else, it nourished my soul and I felt alive.

In that moment, my feelings of inadequacy vanished. I was in service, a true pilgrim, walking the Pilgrim's Way.

As I left the village, a host of sparrows broke from the trees and began following me. Earthy smoke billowed from the entrance of a tiny *casita*. Charcoal-grilled *comida:* It was a familiar fragrance, a pungent aroma that roused memories of Jim and me thirty-seven years ago when we discovered Portugal and Morocco—and each other. The memories fell over me like a comforting cloak. *My past life has become so intertwined with this journey, there no longer seemed a separation from then and now, from here and there. Jim's presence at my side was palpable.*

I smiled inside, truly knowing there is no time and space.

Toughened Up

Moving deeper into the quiet, I hadn't noticed the shift in weather until a band of thick clouds drifted overhead, shuttering the sun and causing me to shiver. The temperature plummeted from cool to cold. Dampness gave way to a wet that soaked me to the bone. At times such as this, I had learned to slow down and have patience with the weather while adjusting my clothing. But every time I flung off my pack and then put it on again, my shoulder complained. Eventually, I decided it was easier to persevere through the fluctuations. Yes,

I had learned it was best to muscle through; I had toughened up. Traveling a continent far away from my home, slogging through countless miles, sleeping in lumpy beds, fighting off Franco—all of these things—and I had learned to toughen up.

The thought made me laugh out loud.
"Is that it, God?" I yelled into the cold air.
No one answered.

The mist that had hung close to the ground all morning gave way to hard rain, which quickly turned to hail. I was soaked on the outside but dry underneath. The stinging shards didn't harm me, but they pierced my peace of mind. It was fear and anxiety that managed to cut through my protective gear.

I had only a kilometer or two to go before reaching *Hotel Lara,* but as soon as I made it to the outskirts of *Valenca*—a big, bustling town by village standards—I stopped at the first roadside restaurant. The last kilometer proved difficult no matter how well I gauged my endurance; it just *was.*

With its white linen tablecloths and shining silverware, this restaurant seemed out of place on the busy industrial highway, a mainline for diesel trucks freighting gravel from the pits. There, once I'd unbuckled my backpack and boots and finished my order of *sopa de legumes,* I asked my waiter to fetch a taxi for the short ride to *Hotel Lara.* A snap decision, I know, but I decided I deserved the luxury.

However, once I stood on the stoop of *Hotel Lara,* I felt no relief after the short taxi ride. Instead, I second-guessed my weak resolve. Maybe I was using my pronouncement as a "non-traditional" pilgrim as an excuse. But I was, after all, soaking wet. And I had walked nearly twenty kilometers that day. It was smart of me to know my limits. Anyway, who was counting my every step? Me! I was the only one. I was the only one holding myself accountable. I was my own judge and jury. What on earth did I have to prove? I'd made it to my destination for the night. Wasn't that enough? Surely the medieval pilgrims wouldn't have walked alongside donkeys if there'd been taxis! *Of course, I knew not to raise this question to a true pilgrim.*

"Modern" Hotel

The more I tried convincing myself everything was okay, the worse I felt. So with no more excuses and nowhere else to go, I entered the lobby. The polished mahogany floors and updated furnishings weren't enough to conceal its elderly bones. The lobby swallowed me up, my footsteps echoing as I moved toward the vacant front desk. No other guests were in sight. In my mind, I could see the self-described "modern hotel" advertising that had lured me here. In fact, I chose *Hotel Lara* for the word "modern," which I quickly surmised was a ploy. The only "modern" device I could see was the landline telephone incessantly ringing on the counter, a dusty marble slab chipped at its edges.

The phone rang again. *Two agonizing days since I had talked to Jim!*

Finally, a towering man dressed in a navy rayon suit with a slick patina due to wear, grabbed the phone and began a rapid-fire conversation. As I stood directly across from him, his height seemed to dissolve, his authority paltry. An echo of the sound of a woman laughing came from around the corner. It let me know at least *one* other guest graced the place.

Then the man welcomed me in perfect English. "Good afternoon, *Señhora*. I can see by your damp appearance our lingering rains so late in spring caught you unaware. You are a pilgrim on the *Camino de Portugues*, yes?" Standing before him wet and wrinkled in my clunky boots and with no suitcase, clearly I was a pilgrim. And I could tell by his sneer he wasn't impressed by this pilgrim.

I nodded, not in the mood to speak more than the necessities to this gentleman.

"Well, you have come to the right place," the clerk, Rodrigo, continued. "Our clean and modern *Hotel Lara* will provide you a hot shower and a night of comfort and rest before you continue your pilgrimage in the morning."

Behind his words, I could tell he had already checked me in *and* out. *Just another pesky guest to deal with.* For him—for both of us—the less interaction for the next twenty-four hours the better. Indeed, Rodrigo left me with the feeling I should be grateful for *not* having to speak. But before I could reply, he had dismissed me by efficiently handing me my folio and key card while pointing toward a grand spiral staircase.

His canned show of courtesy was as polished as the brass trim, the waxed floors, and his worn rayon suit.

An Invitation

I quickly hoisted my pack and withdrew to the second floor and Room 209, finally safe and alone inside after a sunny, then windy, then hailed-on day. I craved being inside the confinement of four walls, but no sooner had I unlaced my boots than the bedside phone rang. *It had to be Rodrigo calling to apologize for his abrupt manner. Who else knew I was in this room?*

"*Boa tarde,* hello?"

"Hello, Shima?" a woman's voice called out. *No one knows I am here? Who knows my name?* Caught off guard, several seconds passed before I could reply.

"Shima? Shima is this you? Have I caught you at a bad time? This is Sal, Sal Carter. You remember, David and Sal Carter from last night?"

"Yes, yes, of course I remember. I just wasn't expecting a call. How did you know I was here?"

"Funny thing, we saw you walking up the stairs just moments ago—David and I. We arrived over an hour ago, a bit before you. And by the looks of you, we must have just missed a downpour. Lucky for us we missed the worst of it."

How did they arrive before me? I was ahead of them walking, and I took a taxi the last kilometer!

"What a coincidence we are staying at the same hotel. Please join us for dinner. Nothing fancy."

Fancy? Let's see, should I wear my hiking boots with or without socks? What is she talking about? Fancy.

"We'll make it an early evening if it makes you more comfortable. No obligation, but we'd enjoy your company. And you know, too much time alone can be wearing on a person." She paused. "We insist. Being by yourself and all. I don't know. It might be fun to join us. There are so many things we've yet to discuss. Best not to leave on a sour note after last night's disappointment about the pilgrims' credentials and all." *The psychologist in her is trying to make it okay after too much reality last night.*

"David and I can meet you in half an hour in the lobby," she concluded. Before I could reply, Sal clicked off.

I sat by the phone wondering if I'd lost all ability to talk or, more to the point, make any decisions on my own, no matter how small. I hastily freshened up, postponed calling Jim from the coveted landline, and sashayed down the grand staircase—one more suitable for a ballroom than a businessman's hotel—wearing my boots with *clean* socks.

Restaurant Dead Zone

Early evening dining left us few options. The Portuguese rarely eat their evening meal before nine or ten o'clock, and the better restaurants closed after midday service for the afternoon *sesta,* typically reopening at eight. We found ourselves in the *sesta* dead zone, after lunch and before dinner. We circled the block in search of a nice eating place (but not fancy) until our tired feet finally forced us to settle on a *café* still open from the afternoon.

The fact it was open hinted at its mediocrity; the linoleum floors confirmed it, along with its well-worn Formica table-tops and aluminum chairs. But the ambiance didn't bother David and Sal, and I since I had lost my voice when I'd agreed to come along, I couldn't object now. So we took our seats among a few remaining locals who lined the bar beneath a loud TV and fluorescent lights.

Our meal was quick and simple with David's only objection being the poor quality of the wine. We couldn't recreate the spirited conversation from last night and when small talk became unbearable and enough time had passed to be polite, I excused myself. *In David's and Sal's presence, I feel alone, uncoupled. I miss Jim terribly.*

Yes, Sal was right. Time alone can be wearing on a person.

Chapter 21

The day started out rusty. It was early morning when I awakened to rain slashing at my window. The thought of another day in the cold and wet left me perplexed. How would I spend my day?

Frankly, I was lonely. And sad. My room provided sufficient shelter but wasn't conducive to the kind of comfort I longed for. I couldn't truly name what I longed for, but I knew this place wasn't it. The air inside was thick and dense as if thoughts and emotions from previous guests lingered between the walls and made me restless. My energy matched the heavy outside air. *I have let Hotel Lara's damp energy and Mother Earth's attempt to hold onto winter get the best of me.*

The anxiety and uncertainty of travel was wearing on me like a low-grade fever. I had lost my ecstatic visions of skipping down cobblestoned streets, dancing with birds and butterflies, and soaring with Spirit. In fact, those images taunted me. I felt foolish even *considering* that was the *Camino* I had envisioned. *If I can just persevere to Finisterre, all would be well.*

But still, I questioned my stamina to withstand the cold and wet and aloneness—my frigid aloneness.

Everything seemed foreign; I couldn't see beyond my self-created misery. Although eager to keep going, my rain-intensified fickle emotions stalled me. I had woken up tired of being wet, tired of being in the outdoors, tired of the cold and damp outdoors. *I want sun, just a ray, to jumpstart my solar-powered body.*

The sound of the constant rain rattled through me. I couldn't stick to a plan or even make one for that matter. The *Camino*, from the start it seemed, had me in its grip and made my plans for me. Stay. Don't stay.

**I'd thought, I'll walk enough to make
my way out of this bad weather!
But the rain followed me like a stray dog.**

I knew it was three kilometers to Spain—a short distance by any measure—yet for this pilgrim, Spain's culture was worlds apart from the Portuguese way of life. Before I made the unknown cultural transition, I desired to stay in Portugal a bit longer. I'd come to know a sincere kindness of heart in the Portuguese people and felt reluctant to let that go. I'd discovered a truth and light radiating from the aged country that couldn't be extinguished by lack or limitation. My gifts of allowance and acceptance had been hard earned, profound.

So there I sat in my sparse room trying to make a plan for the day. In my mind, all the days had run into each other, no different one from the other when all I could see was gray.

A Train Ride into Spain

I checked the schedule and learned a train would depart at ten a.m. from *Valenca* in Portugal and cross the country's border en route to *Redondela*, Spain. If I could muster the energy for the short ten-minute walk to the train station, then I could travel relatively dry to *Redondela*. From there, it appeared to be a manageable seven-kilometer walk to *Arcade* in Spain.

In *Arcade*, I saw I had many overnight options, but I chose *Hotel Isape* from its photo and description as the quietest hotel in *Arcade*. Quiet. Alone and quiet. I enlisted Rodrigo's help to call ahead and make a reservation.

With a plan formed and a clear direction, I headed to the *Hotel Lara's* third floor for complimentary breakfast. In a sad attempt to globalize the food, they had substituted the beautiful European custom of *queso* and meats, *pan* and pastries, and fresh-squeezed *naranjas* for the Americanized version of the day's first meal—individual boxed Cheerios and Corn Flakes, canned peaches, and white toast—the kind of fare found in a 1950s roadside motel in the U-S-of-A! Even the rich coffee, watered down to appeal to Americans—a thoughtful gesture meant to make tourists feel at home—made me feel all the more estranged. Once I looked outside of my soggy disposition, I noticed a rainbow arched across the red tiled roof. Yes! A sign! It had to be a sign. Mother Earth was enticing me to lift my spirits. I gaped out the window, mesmerized by the rainbow. *Pass on the breakfast.* I knew my soul needed nourishing more than my body—and the rainbow provided exactly that.

Off I went, arriving at the train station soaked to the bone.

Passport Has Its Privilege

I'd crossed the border from Portugal to Spain without fanfare except for the uniformed border police who boarded the train wielding guns and holsters. Otherwise, I wouldn't have known I was traversing into a new country.

The policemen set about examining travelers' passports with a military seriousness that caused me to snap shut and sit tall in my seat. As passports were flashed, though, I became aware of my favored American status, the benefit my citizenship afforded me, for many of my fellow travelers were pulled aside. More often than not, they weren't treated gently. *Is this based on the color of their passport? Of course.*

After I showed my passport and before slipping it back inside my silk pouch, I felt the gold embossed emblem stare back at me and pondered the falseness of borders, labels, and emblems. *In truth, we are all connected. We are one, the microcosm of the macrocosm, foolishly divided by invisible lines.* Then an officer passed by me one last time. Staring above his eyes, I shot a polite American smile to his furrowed forehead and mumbled the American slang of *"buenas dias"* *"Buenas Dias, Senora,"* He silently nodded back, officially welcoming me to Spain.

Finally, Sunshine!

When I stumbled off the railway platform, my eyes were momentarily blinded by the sun. Sunshine! Like a confused groundhog, I stood blinking and waited for my eyes to adjust to the unfamiliar glare. My vision returned and basic shapes emerged: squared cobblestones beneath my feet, a rectangular bench emptied of passengers who'd departed only moments before, silhouettes of humans pacing in tracks of their own. The sunshine made me choke into tears. *Sun. Its warmth is all I had needed.*

Inside the train depot, I saw that most of the tables and chairs were unoccupied. However, I noticed off in a corner nearly concealed under a pile of books a young woman sat absorbed on her laptop. Lucky me! Surely she's a college student who could speak *some* English.

"*Bom dia.* Uh, *Buenas dias . . .* hello! Can you help me? Do you speak English?" Interminable seconds passed before she glanced up from the glow of her screen, her fingers still tapping away.

"Yes, of course," she finally offered. Her appearance gave no doubt I had left the conservative countryside of Portugal and entered the more liberal and modern country of Spain. I imagined her dressing that morning, meticulously choosing each item while feeling hip and self-assured. Her open jacket, tailored and black leather, revealed a t-shirt declaring her allegiance to someone or something. *A rock band, perhaps?* The jacket barely skimmed the top of her black pencil skirt paired with knee-high leather boots, also black. *Black and chic. Sharp and coifed.* She'd tucked her long brunette hair into a beehive, the retro trend du jour. Rows of colored studs and hoops encircled one of her ears. Her dark brown eyes peered out behind boxy '50s-style glasses.

Yes, I see who you are. That's I wanted to tell her. Can you see me? I'm chic and cool, too. Look at my feathers!

Before she could turn back to her computer screen, I set my guidebook down next to her on the table. *"Por favor.* I'm walking to the town center of *Redondela.* Can you show me the way?"

As I stammered, I so wanted to explain away my pitiful appearance. I wanted her to know that even though I was a generation older, I too was hip and chic and cool. I wanted her to see *me.* This revelation shocked me as I realized that I *cared*—that I wanted her to at least see *me* as someone worthy of her time.

"You see," I prattled, senselessly sweeping my hands from head to toe as if refashioning my appearance into the shape of chicness. "I'm an American, a pilgrim on the *Camino de Santiago,* and I've just entered Spain."

She halted the spillage of too many more words by grabbing my guidebook and began studying the map inside. "Yes, here is the way," she pointed. And then slowly as if speaking to a young child (or more likely an old woman), she traced where I was on the map and indicated the route I'd take to get to the city. She delivered her words with great measure as if it were difficult for me to comprehend the simplest of directions—even in English. Then she went so far as to have me repeat her advice.

I took it gladly, happy for the kind help. And my rainbow. I gladly took that, too. Yes! *My way is made straight with the help of such angels.* And with the sunshine on my back and feathers in my hair, I started my search for the yellow arrows.

Chapter 22

Redondela was a mess of people and traffic, clattering restaurant noise, clapping of heels on cobblestones. The centuries' old buildings lining the narrow, curving streets amplified the noise and crowds. I guessed that pilgrims before me must have experienced the same distractions, for the yellow arrows appeared every few steps, stacked on top of each other. This nearly caused more distraction, but it offered a bit of comfort amid the chaos. I thanked those unknown guardian painters highlighting the way.

Once I'd made it through the gauntlet of the city and found myself back on country lanes, I finally let down my guard. How dreamily I walked, an indulgence after so much watchfulness.

**Walking was my way of grounding;
it always had been. It connected me to
the Source and to nature and to truth.**

If I walked long enough, I could almost always walk my worries away. Perhaps that's why I chose to walk the *Camino. If I just walk long and far enough I'd come home to myself and find peace. Home.* This thought made me smile. Maybe it would be as simple as that. But what was ever simple about anything I'd done?

Then as I made my way around one of the countless bends on the dirt trail, I saw what looked like a trash heap. *How unusual for the Camino to be strewn with litter.* As I got closer I realized instead it was a makeshift memorial.

Letting Go

With *Santiago* fewer than 90 kilometers away, signs of approaching were visible. I could see how pilgrims—attention fixed on their journey's end—began letting go of possessions they'd no longer need. At one time, these left-behind remnants were tacked to a wooden cross, but with the weight of their discarded symbols of pain and sorrow, the cross had collapsed.

Every discarded boot, water bottle, scarf, talisman, and token left on the broken-down cross represented a pilgrim's desire for forgiveness, approval, or worthiness. As I took in this tender sight, I knew in my heart that begging for forgiveness or proving oneself worthy was not how God wished us to spend our precious time on Earth. *In the same way these cast-off items mar the landscape, do our misguided beliefs mar our souls?*

Perhaps bearing the cross represents one way of absolution and atonement, but is there another way? If we awaken to who we truly are, do we realize the joy and peace and harmony we desire? *In truth, we are sons and daughters of God—perfect. It's impossible to be anything else.*

A Pilgrim's Shell

Strewn among the discards were scallop shells. A pilgrim's scallop shell is native to the shores of *Galicia* and, historically, the shell served proof the pilgrim had completed their pilgrimage to *Finisterre*. It also served as the perfect vessel for food and water. During medieval times when pilgrims presented their shells at churches, castles, and abbeys, they could expect to receive as much rice or porridge as one shell would hold, thus ensuring their nourishment.

At that moment, the meaning of discarding one's precious pilgrim's shell came flooding into my consciousness. I received this clear message:

To discard my shell means I have come to the realization of God as the Source of my supply. It is no longer necessary to rely on others or jobs or situations to bring me safety, security, supply, or companionship. Those on the Camino who retraced the medieval way of the cross through flagellation and punishment are given the opening to realize that all aspects of life can ascend into higher consciousness. Finite law can be altered with changing times, and spontaneous creation can occur in a holy instant.

There is another way to see reality and bring Truth and Love into our hearts. There is a new way to walk. Walking the Camino requires that we leave behind what no longer serves our highest good. We redefine our reality as

Light Beings, both inwardly and outwardly. Reluctantly or willingly, we can accept that laws constantly change to match our vibration.

Life is joy meant to be celebrated.

Through the Grace of the Holy Spirit, I found what I was seeking within—God's sufficiency and His Love. He would never leave me.

I took a moment to let all of this to sink in, then I blessed myself and blessed those like me who had passed this way. Sometimes the burden can be heavy. It was for me when I chose to accept separation and the duality of a third-dimensional reality rather than the Oneness of God.

Yes, I got the message, but I kept my shell—for now.

A Mother's Caution—and Love

All my life I have been protected and guided by Spiritual Guardians. I know this. Archangel Michael, Lord Sananda, Joan of Arc and my Guardian Angel. I have many unnamed Guides as well. It's an intuitive feeling of being watched over allowing free will to explore life, yet remaining safe from serious harm. I knew this journey would be no different. I'd be guided and protected by Spiritual Guardians who may or may not appear in physical form.

**The Portuguese mother who gave us oranges
and spoke directly to my heart
surely embodied my Spiritual Guardian.**

In the next village, I passed a weathered old Spanish woman, her face tunneled with lines. She was sweeping the street in front of her stoop. Then she paused from her chore and eyed me, completely taking me in. I, too, was as absorbed with her. Together, we entered into a space out of time, out of dimension. The air was gauzy and thin, everything around us dissolved—she with her broom and I with my pack. We acknowledged each other, our eyes meeting in a sea of kindness. We had recognized each other from another world.

She said, "*Son caminar solo?*" I didn't understand these words, so she reverted to sign language, pointing to my pack. "*Peregrino? Solo?*"

"*Si, si.*"

At this, she became animated, even agitated, and strung words together so quickly, I felt pushed back by the gush—back from our space of no time. My awareness of Spain and the street became palpable. She warned me not to walk at night, cautioned me of dangers from marauders, warned me of things unknown. "*No está seguro!*" ("It's not safe.")

I tried calming her. "God protects me. Don't worry. All will be well."

We continued yapping over each other in our native tongues, but it didn't matter; we had come to understand each other beyond words and worlds. I told her again I was walking with God. "*Con Dios!*" This clearly wasn't enough, so she warned me again. Stepping closer to me, she dropped her broom and held me in her arms, my body crumbling beneath the weight of her love. A mother's hug.

I cried. She cried. And after a time, she collected her broom while I walked away heaving with sobs. A good cry. I had been especially touched by old women, first the Portuguese matriarch who shared her oranges outside of *Barcelos* and now this Spanish mother in *Redondela*. Both spoke directly to me with caution and love from the Divine Mother.

My emotions fell open around me, exposed like a diary left on a desk for all to see. I was passionately sensitive but knew opening up was part of the process. *I am being stripped, dumping old memories, old lifetimes, old karma with every tear and blistered step.* In my own way, just like the others, I had left my belongings on the fallen-down cross. Perhaps I did it differently than others, but in the end, it was all the same. Compassion entered my heart, a deep well of compassion, a soothing sensation that warmed me like a mother's hug.

I missed my mom.

Alone Again—Nipping at my Heels

Even having experienced a deep sense of self-love and compassion, my aloneness followed me like a bothersome dog nipping at my heels. It required my constant attention to keep it from consuming me. The more I struggled for it to go away, the longer it lingered.

Trying new tactics, I donned my rose-colored glasses—the ones I'd inherited from my dad—and my new age idea to "love it with kindness." The continual *aloneness* I could handle; it was the *lonesomeness* that was breaking my spirit.

I tried ignoring my feelings, keeping them at bay so they wouldn't lead me to the brink of insanity and take over my entire being. But feelings of aloneness pestered me, never letting me forget I'd made the choice to be alone. Still, I couldn't escape the thoughts about being alone that filled my mind. And I had no one to blame.

Why did I choose to walk away from my husband and home and the things I loved? Alone—step, step, step—alone—step, step, step. This was not the mantra I wished to pray. I held to the conviction that if I accepted being alone and surrendered to its presence, it would smother me until I broke and acquiesced to its victory. It could be the end of me. *Alone wins! Shima, you are alone! Aloneness won!*

And so I fought it.

Finally, it proved a worthy foe and forced me into the depth of my being where I found my *self* and the companionship of *me.* All alone, I sang, I prayed, I talked to myself, and I laughed out loud. The crazy lady of the *Camino!*

**I discovered my own company and learned
to love me in a real way, flaws and all.**

Walking made my world both huge and small at the same time—huge in the vastness of how long it took to walk one kilometer but small in my ability to go only where I could step next. This is it. *And I want to share it with anyone—with everyone. What a fantastic revelation!*

Truly, that's all there was of the world—the next step. And I was fewer than two kilometers from my day's destination, *Hotel Isape* in *Arcade*.

Chapter 23

It would have been only two or three kilometers to respite, but my lessons of discernment bade their time, for in my eagerness to take the next step I yet again found myself lost.

Lost! Surely this wasn't a pop quiz for my lesson to accept "being lost." I'd passed that. No, this was different, deeper. This was a lesson in how to always choose Light, even over the virtues of what appear as Love and Compassion.

Discerning Dark from Light is my blind spot. I have a gift of seeing God in everyone and overlook the possibility that ego is not always aligned with one's Higher Self. It gets me in trouble. A lot! Jim has usually been by my side to protect me from my lack of discernment, and I've come to rely on his judgment. Here, I was alone with only my wits and intuition to decipher good from the denser, darker aspects of man.

I'd passed the broken cross and taken heed from the wizened Spanish matron. I was just putting in time and distance until I arrived at the next village, *Centro*. There at a bus stop, I noticed a man sitting under the shelter, crumpled over on the bench, his face hidden from view. His appearance instinctively repelled me and a grip of fear passed through me. I ignored its warning. To the contrary, I reprimanded my feelings for being heartless. *Perhaps he is homeless after having fallen on bad luck. Who am I to judge? A bit more time on the Camino and I could look like he does!*

Shadow Man

At first blush, I had judged this man on appearance. Or was there something more "shadowed" to his energy than his tattered jacket and worn shoes? I squinted and looked closer. *It wouldn't be the first time I mistook Ascended Master Lord Maitreya for a homeless beggar.*

After a few more steps, I reconsidered my initial reaction. He may in fact *be* Lord Maitreya. So, determined not to let appearances fool me this time, I retraced my steps to the bus stop.

"Hola." My voice sounded meek. I paused only for a second and then picked up my pace, one fast step at a time. But even after I'd turned on the compassion full throttle, his sideways glance startled me into a shiver—a quiver so sudden and piercing it could only have originated from the depths of my consciousness, bypassing any logical explanation. Unnerved by the encounter, I picked up my pace even more, my breathing heavy in the cool air. A few feet up the road—I hadn't seen that road the first time—I missed the yellow arrow. I headed up a steep hill away from the city.

After enough time when no yellow arrows appeared, I knew I was lost. Finally, I found a spot along the roadside, not sure which way to go, contemplating if I should continue up the steep road or backtrack down. I couldn't face retracing my steps if I'd made the wrong choice, so I sat. I simply sat.

The sky behind me was the color of milk—high clouds but no rain. I rifled through my pack in search of nuts to eat. Then I heard a scraping sound. Two farm hands, their heads poking around a shed, were eyeing me. The dirt on their hands and soiled knees told me all I needed to know that we were comrades in our common love of tending to the land. I stood up like a lit fuse and ran toward them, no thinking involved. Language was no help; they didn't understand a word I was saying. But after much gesturing, they pointed me down the hill, each patting his right leg.

I took this as a signal that I should turn right at the next intersecting lane. Down the hill. Turn right. Got it.

Off the Path and On the Path

Poor judgment and lack of discernment had taken me off my path. But it turned out to be only a two-kilometer mistake, although a mistake nonetheless. It could have been ever so much more! All that time, my heart cried out for Jim. My Higher Self kept pushing me, encouraging me: "Carry on, Shima." And this is when I learned my discernment lesson: *Not everyone I meet is pure of heart.*

Some people on any path would have delighted in dissuading or discouraging or detouring me. (Franco came to mind.) Sitting lost on that hill reminded me I must remain ever cautious. My intuition had given me the first warning. And when I ignored it, my Spiritual Guide stepped in with a shiver.

Indeed, my course was watched closely by many beings of many dimensions both Light and Dark. Although I felt protected, the ascended masters cannot cross my free will. That was, and still is, true. Caution over dark energies remains a practice that requires diligence, discernment. *Those who guide us do not wish for harm to come our way, but they will never interfere with free will.*

Chapter 24

The room at *Hotel Isape* at least afforded me a view. Forget its lumpy mattress; don't bother sitting on its spindly side chair; ignore the wobbly table lamp. From my picturesque window, a view of a verdant and stately garden led up to the ancient and lovely steepled church, *Iglesia de Santiago de Arcade* laced in ivy. Beyond that, the *Rio Verdugo* flowed lazily into the *Ria de Vigo*. It was as pretty as a fairytale picture book.

The hotel, which had captured me in its grip when I first found it, was deserted. It seemed I was its only guest, but in Spain, one never knew. If I listened carefully, I suspected I might hear snoring in the rooms around me, for the Spanish live by night and rest by day. Later, when the stars make their journey across the inky night sky, Spain's people slowly resurface for the nightly ritual of food and wine. I arrived on a Friday night at the *Isape*, so I'd expected an especially lively display of humanity.

**Don't the singing, laughing, and revelry
continue into the wee hours?
So far, all was silent.**

Stale Cookies

I wandered down the stairwell and sat at the *café* for a snack. Nothing except coffee. A standoff ensued between the gruff innkeeper and me. Food. *How hard is it to drum up a snack for a weary traveler?* He acted is if it were an act of God, his scowl revealing his disdain for my request. So I sat on a stool in misery until he eventually pulled out some stale cookies packaged in cellophane. He then dropped one in front of me, and I watched it crumble into pieces on the table. So hungry, I gobbled it fast and offered to buy three. Since I'd passed on the Cheerios that morning expecting a meal down the road, I'd only eaten one measly apple all day. One apple!

He threw two more cookies my way. Literally. Tossing them onto the table, crumbs falling about, bouncing onto my sweater. He wouldn't take my money. *Fine by me.* I smiled sweetly and retreated through the abandoned halls of the *Isape.*

When I returned to my Spartan room and assessed my journey, I deemed this day the most troubling of all. Of course, I'd thought the same thing many other days. But still, in crossing from Portugal into Spain, nothing could have prepared me for the cultural differences I'd experienced so far. At least the sun was shining outside, but I was too tired and cold to go out—not to mention I was still recovering from an unpleasant exchange with the cookie monster. When all I'd asked for was a bite of food and a little heat, he refused to understand me. Instead, he scolded me, even shaking his pudgy finger as if I were a nuisance for even being there.

I clicked my door shut and retreated into my rather chilly but paid-for room, too afraid to ask for any more comfort. No five-star rating here.

A Lone and Frozen Guest

I imagined the hotel heat had been off for so long that, even if the innkeeper ignited it, it wouldn't be enough to pull the chill from within the cement walls. The cold had clearly nested inside and set up camp. Hot water, not surprisingly, was also scarce.

So I turned on all the faucets—the sink, bidet, and tub. I let it gush, hoping it would only be a matter of time the hot steam would course through the hotel's old pipes, pumping up from the basement to the second floor. But the water ran cold, ceaselessly cold, so I finally gave in and sponged off in an icy spit-bath, sulking in my wool cap. After that, I wriggled quickly into my down jacket and napped in my bag on a twin bed, the lone and frozen guest in Room 206. I felt like a statue lying stiff from the cold, my breath visible in the stale air. My stay at this disreputable hotel where the cookie monster was dishonest and disrespectful and inhospitable proved to be a replay of the enslaved castle *Casas dos Assentos*, only worse. This time, I was without Dr. Nic.

After enough sulking, I decided to make this an opportunity for a God service. I poked around for a place in my heart to reflect love for the innkeeper. Then pressing my eyes shut, I lay back on the bed and visualized the cookie monster, his stubby fingers, his cold heart. I seared a hot coal of God's love into his soul. *He needs warming up, after all.*

More Than a Beautiful Walk

It had been three days since I left *Ponte de Lima* and the last time I had deeply connected to Spirit. There, God was plainly in sight: Light language mosaicked in cobblestone at *Jardims Tematicos,* Archangel Michael at *Capela do Anjo da Guarda Sao Miguel* consecrating my journey, making my way safe and True. And the women—*Esstatueta uma Cantareira,* Joan of Arc, Teresa de Avila—and me—all offering to fall on the seven swords of *Señhora das Doras* for the Love of God, for forgiveness and mercy, for understanding and enlightenment, for the little girl in pink, and for each other.

Since these events, my daily walk along the *Camino,* though beautiful, was barren of the higher dimensions that buoyed me. The exceptions were the occasional birdsong and the fields of yellow flowers. But, I concluded, the journey was merely a beautiful walk, one that didn't require traveling thousands of miles to another continent to experience.

Still, I was clear in my God work and why I was there. My *Camino* had been lifetimes in the making. It meant meeting all aspects of me—those Dark selves I couldn't face and the ones I judged unworthy of my Light. This was my journey into Oneness. I set out to prove that one's spiritual path did not have to be difficult. (Easy for me to theorize while at home in front of my computer.)

I was wrong. My steps *were* painful. Yes, in its purest sense, suffering is *not* a part of Christ consciousness, but my emotions didn't care about Christ. They wanted to argue with *what is* and try to change and control everything. Instead, the way to God required my dedicated, unwavering faith and commitment to face of all forms of adversity. And it was hard. It was a singular path—Home to Oneness and God—and I had to go it alone.

My preparations and initiations had been piercing and intense, but the spiritual journey was proving even more difficult than I'd ever thought. *Perhaps what Matthew meant when he wrote "Many are called but few are chosen" (22:14), he really meant to say, "All are called but **few** choose."*

In my heart, I had no choice except to say *yes* to the *Camino*.

A Hypocrite

I was ready to get down to the work. I'd started my Camino intending to walk the ascended path of Christ with compassion for all and free of judgment—to accept and allow anything and everything and everyone. By design, I created this self-test. However, the sporadic spiritual highs weren't of the frequency that kept me afloat in the higher consciousness of my God Presence. I was wavering. More than that, I was tested by the forces of Dark—and Light.

I was immersed in the density of the third dimension and trying to make the most of it, but it was wearing on my soul. I was tired.

There I was, espousing my lofty notions of how to live on Earth without suffering as a necessary path to God. *Suffering is not the way to God. Rather, it's choosing joy and bliss is the path to enlightenment.* I was a hypocrite. As I pondered my journey, the discomforts, the strange characters along the way, and the thoughts screamed out in my head: *But I am suffering! I am suffering . . . and by choice I suffer!*

Then I reminded myself that suffering was not my purpose. *Only I am the creator of my reality.* However, if it was Thy Will preparing me for union with God, I would accept it without question. So I repeated this mantra, "Thy Will not my will" over and over, thinking that when I'd had enough of the suffering, I would find alternatives. *Have I had enough? Have I been wrong all along? Or is the suffering a matter of perspective? What if I find the joy and bliss along with the blisters, the lost days and aloneness, the Francos, and the cookie monsters of the Camino? After all,* it's not what happens to us but how we *perceive* what happens to us.

Do I really have to do this? The Camino *has beckoned me home to myself. Yes, I really have to.*

Chapter 25

And yet more challenges arrived. Clearly, I hadn't had enough, and suffering played a powerful role on this journey.

##*# Verizon

Yes, the walk was lovely, the birds, the trees, the endless sky, moving from a clear jeweled blue to a cold milk white.

Yes, my stamina was high, my bones strong, my feet accustomed as much as they could be to the dawn-to-dusk beating I gave them. Yes, my blisters pained me with each step, my right Achilles screaming out each day after ten kilometers. I was managing all of this on this endless narrow road that wandered to the horizon, more often than not shrouded in a curtain of rain. Yes, the weather was a trickster—rainy and cold—not the springtime I'd envisioned. Indeed, the disparity between what I *wanted* and *expected* contrasted with what I actually *experienced*—like night and day. *Here is my lesson, and there's no escaping its pain.*

Truthfully, I couldn't bring myself to accept or even fathom how or why I'd voluntarily placed myself in this situation. *I have no one else to blame. Only me; only Me. I take responsibility, fully and completely. I am suffering.* But even my surrender to these thoughts didn't soothe my discomfort. I'd squandered all my positive enthusiasm, my optimistic heart. Feeling angry, I directed it to my cell phone.

I'd been ten days without using a cell phone, and I declared I couldn't take it another second. But like the other obstacles I'd faced, I refused to accept this fact—that this was *just the way it was*. Desperate for connection, I also refused to suffer alone any longer. I needed a phone to share my misery, to vent, to complain, to cry and be listened to.

This journey was fast becoming my unraveling.

I scanned my hotel room for the landline to call Jim. I pecked and searched, knowing it must be there. But I couldn't find a phone anywhere, not tucked in the closet or the desk drawer, not under the bed or in the bathroom.

I mustered the last of my energy to walk the two flights down to the reception area and demand a phone. No one was at the desk, so I returned to the *café* and faced the cookie monster once again. He insisted there was a phone in my room, that I was simply not seeing it (that is, too stupid to see it, I imagined him thinking). He made it quite clear it was due to my inability to speak Spanish. "Yes, of course, that's the problem. My Spanish!" I snorted, hoping he couldn't understand me either. He barked back—something in Spanish—intimidating me into believing he was somehow right. And so I spun around and climbed the two flights of stairs back to my room to search again. The cold made my blood run slow and each step felt like one too many after so many hours on the trail. But no phone.

I returned once again to speak to the monster, but he wouldn't bother with me. He flashed his palm at me as if I were an intolerable nuisance, a pain in the behind, a stupid American tourist. "I just want to make a phone call," I stammered again. Then his wife blustered in and her quick examination of me—rolling her eyes up and down—made it clear she would take care of the situation. Like talking with her husband, the wife and I rallied round and round, barking foreign words at each other, getting nowhere—until finally I wore them both down. In their exasperation, they followed me to my room intending to point out there was indeed a phone right beside the bed. The gist of their verbal battering in Spanish went something like this: "You stupid American woman—who shouldn't be walking alone or traveling at all in our country—how could you not see the phone?"

"Because it's not there. HA!" I yelled, marching into the phoneless room.

When they saw for themselves the phone was indeed missing, they erupted into more Spanish slurs.

They scurried to pull one from a vacant room, surely causing a repeat performance for the next unwary guests who found themselves trapped there for a night. While they were in my room, I pointed again to the cold radiator. *Why not? I might as well try.* They fiddled with the knobs just as I had and told me to wait one hour. And then they left.

Connected to Jim

With a landline, I was able to connect to Jim. Jim! A familiar voice, the *most* familiar voice. My love, my husband, my friend. Poor Jim. Poor, innocent Jim, for he was the first recipient of my fuming anger, my insistence that he get our cell phone service provider on a three-way conference call to rectify my lack of cell coverage. The chilly tone in my voice must have been enough for him, because with little else said, he quickly complied.

"Got it, Shima." He was all business.

After a few beeps and clicks, we were connected with a Verizon representative. Before leaving the States, I'd found a plan that seemed to be the best choice. But so far, it had provided abysmal service—which meant *no* service because I hadn't been able to dial out for ten days. After a few minutes of explaining and some pecking around by the representative, we discovered that when Verizon set up the phone for my trip, the simple process of activating the SIM card—whatever that meant—had been overlooked.

"You mean the little card that activates my service?! That wasn't turned on?"

Within minutes, this ginormous oversight was corrected. At the point when the Verizon rep had nothing more to say except "Ma'am, how do you rate my service?" I hung up on him—and on Jim.

I wasted no time in speed dialing whoever would answer my call, reaching out for whatever I couldn't find in myself. But there was no one to call, no one who would understand what I was going through except Jim. And I felt too ashamed to call him back after what I'd just put him through. *Tell me again, please. Why am I doing this? I am cold, wet, and stuck in time in a place devoid of the spiritual resonance I usually can summon. I am lost. Not physically lost—I mastered that lesson at Vila do Conde.*

I am spiritually lost in Spain.

Flurry of Texts

With my SIM card active and my cell coverage fully operational, I received a flurry of texts that had piled up after more than a week of inactivity. They blipped in one after another. As I scrolled down, a message from Jim immediately caught my eye. It was a text dated precisely on the day and hour of my dubious excursion with Franco *and* the day I witnessed two hawks soaring over the Gatekeeper Bridge.

Sent from IPhone
From: Jim Kelly
Date: April 25, 2012 2:55:50 PM MDT
To: Shima Shanti
Subject: Your Gatekeeper Bridge.
"Just passed under and two hawks are soaring over-
head to greet me. I connected immediately with your
essence!"
Jim Kelly

I sat on the bed, reading and rereading Jim's text: *"Just passed under and two hawks are soaring overhead to greet me. I connected immediately with your essence!"* I rushed to my pack, my eyes stinging with tears, and pulled out my journal. As I suspected, Jim had sent the text *on the day and at the hour* when I'd been in view of the hawks gliding along the Gatekeeper Bridge in Portugal. *The message is loud and clear; we are united.*

The bridge between us had always been short though the distance may at times have been far. We were together in the synchronicity of the bridge and the hawks, forever merged in Oneness transcending space. *Aha!*

I plucked my cell from the bedside table and frantically dialed home. Jim picked up on the first ring. He'd been waiting. I thanked him for helping me with my cell phone, my SIM card, and my raging fury, which in truth had amounted to a mountain of fear. I blessed him for sending the text ten days ago.

"The hawks! The bridge!" I said, crying out. "I saw it too. I saw two hawks at my bridge *here*. We witnessed the hawks in flight together, and we were continents away! Isn't that wonderful?"

"Of course. And, yes, it is wonderful. *And* it makes perfect sense."

Finally, I begged his forgiveness for hanging up. But there was nothing to forgive, he explained. Jim was my rock, my home. He understood that, in those moments alone in my Spartan room an ocean away, fighting for food with the cookie monster and frantically needing my phone to work, I was not in my right mind to speak or talk or think. He understood.

Guidance from Archangel Michael

Next, I dialed my friend Ahriah and, from a continent away, her guidance from the Ascended Masters soothed my soul as she reminded me of my connection to God, my Self, and my higher purpose. With Ahriah as his channeled messenger, Archangel Michael lovingly warned me of pending danger should I stray from caution. These were not astral energies, he explained, but the powerful rulers and lords of the underworld, referred to as Archons in my studies of the *Pistis Sophia*. These very real rivals were attempting to thwart my journey. They were making it known they would take all measures to protect the status quo— the universal belief of mankind that tells us we live in a universe that's separate and apart from God. If we would stop believing in this hypnotic illusion, all discord, every temptation and sin, every lack and disease would disappear. Its only power is humanity's acceptance of this lie, an untruth that has existed from the beginning of time. It's only real because of the near-universal belief in it.

The Archons' allegiance to keep mankind mesmerized is as fierce as my devotion to God, love, and the expansion of Light. I have to stay single-pointed, conscious, and present to quell their power.

I felt no fear in Michael's warning, knowing he was by my side and only a thought away if I could simply remember to call on him. I knew that my purpose in this lifetime would not be readily accepted nor rarely understood. There were real opponents to my one purpose, both in the physical and non-physical realms. I began to ask specifics about these dangers but then abruptly stopped. *Better not to know.*

When I said good-bye to Ahriah,
I felt bathed in love and stronger for it.

Dinner Delight

It was after nine o'clock at night when I finally said my good-byes. No sooner had I hung up, the landline jangled, startling me back into the four walls of my room. It was the cookie monster demanding to know why I wasn't at dinner. Talking to Jim and Ahriah had numbed my hunger, and I had forgotten all about my measly apple and cookie crumbs. I was confused and caught off guard. *First he has rebuked me for pleading for a snack; now he scolds me for missing dinner.*

Like an abused child made to feel guilty for not being thankful of meager offerings, I slammed down the phone, flung open the door, and flew down the stairs afraid to rile him further. The cookie monster had hooked me through intimidation and control. He triggered something small inside me, and my issues and insecurities around authority surfaced. I was late for dinner and didn't want to upset the monster.

Down the stairs to the right of the bar was a large dining room enclosed in walls constructed half of glass and half of wood. This created the odd feeling of being inside a terrarium eerily watched from the outside. Rows of unoccupied tables dressed in white linen lined the perimeter. The center of the room was empty. Then I saw two lone diners off to one side. Klaus and Renata from *Quinta Sao Miguel!* What a longed-for welcome sight!

I could never imagine the surprises that awaited me at every turn—at just the right moment! And even though they were halfway through their meal, they invited me to join them.

"How nice. And, yes, thank you."

Their small gesture of kindness took on immense proportions in the aftermath of my scolding. Their familiar faces warmed my soul. My energy was bolstered in their presence.

Klaus and Renata, both retired physicians, were of healthy, hardy German stock. Being in their company, my self-pity dissolved like sugar in hot tea, impossible for it to maintain its hold in the reality of my new friends' vibrancy. *Amazing how the presence of goodness can ignite a flame inside!*

Set before Renata was fresh *linguado*, which immediately transported me back to *Caiscais* in Portugal decades ago with Jim. We were so young and so in love, and we had shared this delicacy netted daily from the sea. Memories of that loving time—and reuniting with Klaus and Renata—were sure signs that things were taking a turn for the better. A good omen? I'd take it. I, too, ordered the *linguado*. With each bite, my madness lessened and my heart softened. I returned to my room nourished both physically and emotionally.

Chapter 26

I was done walking. I had died to my former self. That's what the *Camino* had done. It had forced me to surrender every conscious thought that no longer served my divine purpose. So far, it had been a walk filled with preparations, obliterations, and initiations.

I felt certain in my preparedness for what awaited me in *Finisterre*, knowing I had nothing more to surrender. Like a worn-out book, the *Camino* was a path I could now put down. I had no need to turn its pages to the end; I already knew the ending. There was no surprise, no revelation, no reason to further debilitate my body.

Why walk a trail that no longer held spiritual resonance for me?

It was futile. Instead, I would make my way to *Finisterre* by train, bus, or car.

Finally, I felt strong enough to withstand my self-inflicted guilt for my decision to bypass *Santiago*—a traditional Pilgrim's destination. I had been warned twice by my Spiritual Guides (in case I didn't heed the first warning) of the harm that *Santiago* could instill on my etheric body. It would shatter my energy, tempting me with guilt and second guesses. *Santiago,* crowded with all its pious pilgrims, would force me to compare myself to others—a challenge I wasn't sure I could meet. *Could I accept myself for exactly who I am, so different than the others?*

I simply wasn't ready to put myself to another test. I could not look for approval from others. There would be no approval in *Santiago* for my following the Milky Way and not the prescribed Way of Saint James.

No More Suffering for the Sake of Suffering

I felt centered in my truth, prepared to withstand the incredulous reaction of those at home when they learned I'd bypassed the whole purpose of a pilgrim's journey—to *walk* to *Santiago.* The world was shifting; my way was a new way, a new time. *Suffering for the sake of suffering makes no sense.* That insight, that gift, came from the derelict at the bus stop mixed with my ability to discern the highest good—no matter the appearance, no matter the judgment. The suffering way was over.

I looked up to the window, a rectangle of blue sky framed by the ivy that grew outside. It was morning. I had survived. Only hours before, I had slipped inside my sleeping bag, fighting off the cold while being wedged within the walls of my paid-for room. It had been one hundred and seventy kilometers since I took my first step in *Porto* eleven days before. This journey—filled with cries and catharsis—had forced me to face and release all the obstacles blocking me from my God Presence.

For the first time, I arose feeling beautiful and relaxed. The sun blazed outside my window and inside my heart.

Peace in *Pontevedra*

There had been only two stopovers where I could let down my guard and just be: *Ponte de Lima* and here in *Pontevedra*. Both were different.

In *Ponte de Lima,* I was adjusting to the ongoing physical and mental exhaustion and the rigors of the road. It was a time to give my mind a rest from the constant diligence required to follow a map on foot in a foreign country. And it was a time for physical rejuvenation.

Because it was early in my journey, I'd not yet learned to cherish every moment. I expected that would always to be so. Innocently, I took things like companionship and fortitude for granted. Spirit was at my beck and call, and the comfort and security of Dr. Nic's friendship had not yet been stripped from me. I was battling the physical fatigue of twelve hours on my feet, the blisters, and sore muscles, yet those physical pains were nothing compared to the emotional wounding that followed.

At this point, I had gone beyond desecration; I had entered the space of blessings and celebration. There was no room for anything except smiles and cheer. I was at Peace.

On this new day—a new chapter for me—I made a new plan: I would settle at *Hotel Ruas* for two nights, maybe more, then take a train to *Padron,* bypass *Santiago,* and make my way to *Finisterre. Yes, so lovely how it's unfolding.*

**That's when I began to see how the
last two weeks' passage was required
to prepare me for the sacredness ahead.**

With renewed purpose, I was ready to make my way to beautiful *Pontevedra* where I'd spend time wandering the town, visiting shops, sacred sites, and gardens, and doing all things pleasing to my senses and soul. I chose a taxi over trekking, arriving at an early hour in *Pontevedra.*

Seagulls and Soap Suds

Once I'd checked into my room, I basked in its quaint, old-world beauty and its richness in history. Having dropped my pilgrim's walk the day before, I had transformed into being the tourist.

Hotel Ruas was square in the middle of the town center of *Cuidad Pontevedra.* Family and friends, lovers and mates, all walks of life gathered at the *praza.*

It hummed with life, everyone sashaying around its *cafés* and shops on this weekend holiday. The rain had vanished, ushering in spring fever. After so many rain-sodden days, the *praza* was tapping with music and chatter. Spirits soared high. Even the seagulls kept time to the beat.

My room was small and sparse, typically European. A rooftop window opened to a view of the sky—a blissfully blue sky. White gulls cawed their welcome as if greeting me. I set up my altar—Ascension Kis, crystals, oils, feathers, and tokens both from home and collected along the *Camino*. Gentle flute music played on my iPhone in rhythm with my heart.

I'd emptied my backpack and took my time settling in. For the first time in many days, I was living *outside* the confines of my pack. Before long, I'd found a place for every item, which expanded my soul into a space of sweet satisfaction. I handed off my laundry to hotel staff to be returned clean and folded to my door in an hour. One hour!

Then I stepped into the shower. Hot water—hot, hot water, immediate and powerful—poured over me. I stood beneath the cascade until I could absorb no more. It was my first hot, clean shower since *Ponte de Lima,* complete with the luxuries of body wash, shampoo, conditioner, and lotion. These were the details that only weeks before had been part of my everyday life that were now relegated to precious gifts.

I melted into my new surroundings, the fatigue of high alert lifted. Only then did I realize what a toll everything had taken on my body, mind, and spirit.

In this time and space, I would revive and rejuvenate. There was no better place to be.

Chapter 27

Rested and clean, I was ready to venture out. Sacred sites were calling me.

I strolled unencumbered around and around the circular lanes of *Rua de Cinco Ruas* searching for the *Cruceiro das Cinco Ruas,* a statue marking the center point where the five time-worn cobbled streets united. For me, the *Cruceiro* symbolized a mystical stargate.

My first impression gave clue I was in a dilapidated part of the ancient town where shops had been abandoned and gated with iron bars. Curling signboards and graffiti competed for attention. Standing in the seedy alleyway, my senses opened to fear. The lively shoppers and tourists who, moments before, were walking elbow to elbow with me were out of earshot.

"Oh, no, this can't be it," I said aloud. "So forlorn and neglected!"

**The ancient statue, *Cruceiro das Cinco Ruas,*
was surrounded by mythological creatures
and buried in filth.**

I stepped closer, pushing away a bit of grime from the arm of the statue. *Ah, but what do I know? Was I judging from third-dimensional appearances, unable to see the higher dimensions with my physical eyes?* I felt blocked from its spiritual connection.

As this thought crossed my mind, in perfect time a seagull landed atop the statue. He settled in, fanning his feathers, making sure I had not missed his arrival and his message. "This *is* it," I mused. "It is." The gull remained still, not moving an inch. I had misjudged the energy of the land beneath, once again basing it initially on appearance. *Its Spirit was veiled, perhaps for protection.*

I decided to return the next day to see if it would reveal its secrets then.

Next, I planned to visit *Santurario de las Apariciones,* the place where the Blessed Virgin Mary appeared again to Sister Lucia on December 10, 1925, eight years after her first appearance at Fatima. There I would immerse myself in the love of Mother Mary in preparation for what I considered to be the final, most enlightening stage of my journey to *Finisterre.* Like the *Cruceiro,* though, the Sanctuary was unwilling to reveal its gifts to me on this afternoon and remained out of sight. Perhaps tomorrow.

Peace and Renewal

As I wandered through the shadowy streets weaving my way from the alleyway back to the promenade, I was drawn to an ancient olive tree smack in the middle of the street. Less conscientious city officials might have cut it down, deeming it an obstruction to progress. Instead, it stood protected in the middle of the lane.

Instinctively, I sensed something special about the tree. I knew that the olive branch marked the sign of Peace, but this tree offered *more*. Its limbs reached out and grabbed hold of me like the seagull making sure I wouldn't miss its call. It had been painstakingly preserved for hundreds of years.

I faced the tree straight on as I would if I were meeting a person. *My time alone has honed my acumen for speaking to trees and animals as easily as I connect to people. Aloneness does that.* In the presence of my new friend-tree, whom I perceived to be feminine, I was immersed in Grace—the kind that makes your heart sing when you're first reunited with your beloved after a long time.

I sensed the feeling of being outside of myself, only me and the tree. Our surroundings faded away. I remained unmoved by the chatter of passersby, even the children running circles around its trunk. The tree and I were sharing all of our experiences and what we'd learned since we'd last met eons ago. She offered the gift of her lighthearted vibration, her longevity, and her life force.

Her energy pulsed through me, tingling down my limbs.

"Now I am truly losing my mind!" I laughed aloud, not caring if anyone saw or heard me. I let go of any remnants of fear and surrendered to it; I had no choice! I allowed this ancient beloved to overwhelm me with Love and Peace and everlasting Life.

The coo of a dove broke my reverie. *Too much! These symbols of Peace and the Holy Spirit—the Dove and the Olive Branch—had become real, no longer abstractions in my mind.* I consciously moved between dimensions. My mind whispered that I might be crazy; my Soul screamed to me, "Let it *Be*! Yes! This is what you seek, pray, and yearn—Oneness—home in your Heart."

In one blazing moment, the Holy Spirit descended, embodying me with Peace, Truth, and Everlasting Life. *This must be what Jesus felt when the Holy Spirit descended upon him with Saint John the Baptist in the desert.*

After that, I must have made my way back to the hotel, for I found myself awake and well rested the next morning in the comfort of my room. The darkness of the enslaved castle, the isolation at *Hotel Isape,* and everything else that had transpired between *Ponte de Lima* and here had shifted. *I am myself again. Transformed.*

Perfect Start to a Wondrous Day

The constant caw of seagulls outside my roof-top window kept me company while I prepared to discover the day's spiritual delights. They reminded me of yesterday's message at the statue of the five lanes when I doubted the stargate's location. Now, as I gathered my things into my daypack, I came nose to nose (separated only by the glass of the rooftop window) with Mr. and Mrs. Seagull gathering moss and plants for their nest. *How perfect for the day to start with lovebirds making a home for their new babes.* And in this simple, instinctual act I immediately connected to the love of the Divine Mother, strengthening my resolve to find the elusive *Santurario de las Apariciones.*

If we listen, a seagull truly can show us how to communicate with Nature Spirits. She can guide us to trust our senses and pay attention to nonverbal cues—good advice for what lies ahead. On this wondrous day, the seagull had shown me how to allow the rhythm of the wind to be my guiding pulse. I knew that seagulls often appear to prompt us into cleaning up our environment.

And wasn't that what I was called to do— clean up the eons of energetic debris heaped upon these natural spiritual vortexes and stargates?

Going forward, the seagulls would guide me.

Energy Beneath the Energy

It was early when I returned to the *Praza de Cinco Ruas.* The Spanish residents, who had dined and drank and danced late into the night, had yet to emerge on the streets. All was quiet; I was alone on the *praza.* The avenues had been washed clean and the sun glared, obliterating the grime—grime I'd come to appreciate and understand. All of a sudden, the grit from the day before didn't seem so offensive.

The universal quiet of Sunday morning and my solitary presence erased the forlorn feelings of the previous days.

I strolled the perimeter of the *praza,* taking note of the name of each of the five lanes: *la ruas do Baron, de San Nicolas, Paio Gomez Charino, Isabel II,* and *Princesa.* Then I ceremoniously took a seat on the base beneath the *Cruceiro das Cinco Ruas,* and I waited. *For what? A sign?* Suddenly, the seagulls called out, cawing in a chorus around my head. My Vogel crystal, the one I wore devotedly for protection and illumination, never left its place next to my heart. It cast prisms and rainbows of delight.

I sank into the energy beneath the energy, feeling the layering of it. Yet I couldn't *feel* the stargate. It occurred to me that more subtle awareness must be necessary. A buzzing fly, a chirping bird, and the ever-present seagulls' caws took me deeper into meditation. *Still no feeling.* For the moment, I stood up and walked away from this sanctified site, retracing my steps through the alleyways in search of the *Santuario de las Apariciones.*

Mother Mary appeared to Sister Lucia, one of the three children of Fatima at *Santuario de las Apariciones,* an out-of-the-way sacred site lesser known than the thoroughfare through Fatima and Lourdes; places where so many devotees had left behind their grief and pain.

**Here the energy remained immaculate
and pure, unspoiled by illusions of suffering.**

By comparison, this shrine was immaculate and held a highly calibrated energy. The *Santuario de las Apariciones* also held the promise that everyone will eventually open to receive the Divine Mother's Love. Until then, She waits eternally patiently.

Knowing this gave me a sense of faith, an assurance beyond hope.

Inside the Shrine

I entered the nondescript doorway, one of many lining the side street. If I were not guided, I would have easily missed the tiny brass placard. When I stepped into the vestibule, I welled up, a heaving sensation deep in my solar plexus and my throat chakra. I felt as if there was too much invisible air for my lungs to hold—like a balloon ready to pop.

I was alone. The door had shut, leaving me with just enough light to make out shapes—not exactly the inky dark of deep waters but otherworldly all the same.

**Compared to the cathedrals, temples,
and basilicas, this was a dollhouse, too tiny for big
people and especially too small for Americans.**

Once I adjusted to the sensual deprivation of sight and sound, I climbed a miniature circular staircase to the choir loft. It was nearly pitch black. Only the glowing candles on the altar below gave the impression of space and dimension. They did not reach the nave above. I blindly stumbled upon a stool and sat at what I thought was a desk. But when my feet bumped into pedals, I realized I was seated at the base of an organ.

Cherubs' Nest

From what I could tell, the size of the choir loft allowed room for only one of each: soprano, alto, tenor, baritone, and bass. The ceiling rose to six feet. (I knew this because I could touch it when reaching up on my tiptoes.) I imagined being part of this chorus for the simple privilege of having access to this cherubs' nest. It was like a secret loft, a sacred hiding place, and I delighted in being hidden in its dollhouse charm.

Candles illuminated a statue of Mother Mary below, and I envisioned her smiling at her children at play. I took a moment to rustle through my pack to find my IPhone with its flashlight app. It felt satisfying to have what I needed in the moment instead of carrying unnecessary things "just in case" or fearing "what if." I smiled as the memory of Reverend Thomas flashed across my mind and, with the glow of my phone, I began to write in my journal. Finally, when I'd had my fill of this holy playhouse, I stepped down the circular stairwell to pray at the altar.

Before entering the nave, I stopped at the holy water font to add its holy contents to the Peace Waters I'd collected from the streams and rivers along the Chief Joseph Trail and Lake Louise. When I filled the small vial, I noticed the water inside was cloudy, reminding me of how Masaru Emoto's water experiments visually revealed the effects human consciousness had on its molecular structure.

Holy Water symbolizes a renewal of baptism and a cleansing of sin. It complements the ritual of signing the cross when entering a church, offering the faithful protection against evil.

In effect, this font was a depository of pain and sin. It held the energy of a lost belief in the purity of our God-created human nature. Devoted parishioners walked through these doors and used these innocent waters to bless and profess themselves as unworthy sinners.

From the recesses of my mind, the little prayer I would recite as a young Catholic girl came bubbling forth. *By this holy water and by Your precious Blood, wash away all my sins, O Lord.* These words I used to describe myself shivered through me. Unworthy. Sinner. Suffering. This simple prayer served as a chasm separating me from myself and God.

The same tightness I'd experienced in my chest earlier returned. I felt bound, breathless, and corseted. Yet I took this chance to willingly break free from this lost prayer hidden in my subconscious, the belief that held me a sinner and unworthy of God's Love. That's when the ties that had corseted me broke free.

My chest expanded, the tightness lifted, and my tears flowed with the inhalation of each deep and satisfying breath. I could breathe!

The Peace Waters of Mother Earth—her streams and rivers, lakes and oceans—these are *my* holy waters, the ones that transport God's love through Mother Gaia.

Chapter 28

I left the font behind and proceeded to the altar. The chapel was simple, impeccably clean, with hardwood floors and paneled walls polished to a sheen honed by love. Lemon-scented furniture polish layered over the holiness of incense.

In procession, pew by pew, I paraded to the sanctuary and the statue of Mother Mary. With each step, I consciously consecrated myself into Divine Love. Row by row, my straight and narrow steps softened into free-floating dance.

It was Mary, not Jesus, at the focus of the altar. The cross with her Son affixed to it hung unusually out of place to Mary's right. The altar flowers still glistened in morning's dew, so fresh. They weren't the kind purchased from a florist. Rather, they were passionately picked from someone's garden—white roses, baby's breath, and pink daisies. Unobserved in Mary's holy playhouse, I felt free to act out my pious ceremonies without fear of criticism or comment. I prayed for all mothers and their daughters and sons to surrender their misunderstandings, to come home into Love once again. I especially prayed for my son, Jimmy, that he could realize my love for him despite my missteps.

**Then I asked Mary to be my conduit
to the Treasury of Light so I could realize
the Divine Mother's Wisdom.**

And when I was consumed in Grace and could hold no more, I danced back down the aisle to where I'd first entered.

Loving Sounds

To the left of the entrance was a wide and winding marble staircase. Oddly, I hadn't seen it before. The sound of children's voices carried me up the steps. Hidden behind closed doors, I could hear but not see choir boys and girls scaling octaves under the tutelage of their director, most likely preparing for Sunday Mass. Soft golden sunlight diffused by stained glass shimmered off the plaster walls. Mother Mary shone everywhere.

**In the sound of the children's voices,
I heard only Love.**

It took me a moment to adjust to the outdoor glare and clamor of life waking up to a Sunday morning. I walked back to where I began at *Cinca Ruas*, made myself comfortable on an abandoned stoop a few feet from the cross, and began to journal. I hoped to preserve the swaddling of Mary's love in my words.

The clatter of a large group numbering in the fifties stopped at the cross and pulled my attention from my page. The tour guide positioned herself directly in front of me while assembling the group around her. When she had their attention, she broke into her foreign monologue describing the cross's historical importance. Even in Spanish, I could tell she was unaware of its Spiritual significance.

I flashed forward to a future time and saw myself as the tour director, speaking English to my group of soul journeyers and sharing the mysticism of this sacred stargate. On this day, however, the tourists were not visiting for my reasons. But I knew that, someday, this sacred portal would be revealed in its glory, and what a story will be told!

Tightness to Lightness

Thankfully, my *tightness* of heart had become a *lightness* of heart. One small letter—"t" to "l"—pointed to perfection. I smiled, remembering when the transposition of one letter first occurred at *Megaltico do Fulom* as the "earthly tomb" transformed into the "Universal womb." And here, in the expansion of Love, "tight" had become "Light."

How marvelous is the power of language, its layers of consciousness, the secrets and symbols it holds. How easily language could be transformed in a holy instant.

In a prayerful mood, I walked to the basilica called *Santa Maria la Mayor*. In the Catholic religion, a basilica is larger and more important than a church but not quite a cathedral. Only the pope has the authority to designate a church a basilica and convey to it special ceremonial privileges. I was humbled by its grandeur.

This Elizabethan Gothic structure was built in the sixteenth century and designated a basilica by Pope John XXIII in 1962. Its architectural magnificence is unrivaled anywhere in the world. Pilgrims especially are drawn to the statue of the Christ of Safe Journeys to pray for protection during their pilgrimages. Here, my hopes to receive a *credencial de peregrinos* soared. So far, not one church stamp had been available to me since my first day in *Porto*. The churches had been locked, vacant, or even worse, refusing refuge to those seeking God.

It was Sunday, a time when all the faithful should be openly welcomed to join in the Mass. But when I attempted to enter *Santa Maria la Mayor*, I was turned away. A church volunteer held sentry at this doorway and next to him stood a sign in English that said, "No Visitors—Mass in Session." In medieval days, this volunteer would have wielded a Centurion's sword, and punishment for disobedience would have been swift and harsh.

So far, every church on my pilgrimage had not been the welcoming open door I'd imagined. In this case, an entrance fee in a currency I couldn't pay was required. My pilgrim's status labeled me a curious onlooker, not a devoted parishioner, not worthy to share in communion with Christ. I expected the House of God to be a welcoming place and free to all. I imagined reverence and worship, choirs and song, incense wafting inside.

But I wouldn't know if what I imagined was true, for I wasn't allowed to enter. In front of the closed doors with the volunteer parishioner as my witness, I slumped, drowning in the deep well of being forsaken.

In the name of God, under the rules and authority of a church sustained by granite and wealth I was denied entrance again.

Then I reminded myself of the purpose for my pilgrimage. And even though my journey followed the *Camino de Santiago,* it was actually the Milky Way that charted my way. My *credencials* were stamps of nature: the leaves, flowers and feathers I pasted in my journal, the rocks, branches, and waters I carried in my satchel. My route was stamped by the *cafés* peopled with smiles and *holas.* These were my *credencial de peregrinos.*

What happened after that I don't recall. I just trusted to be in the right place at the right time, to feel the tap on my shoulder and answer God's call. Looking back on that day, I remembered most the Grace and Love of Mother Mary at the *Santuario de Apariciones.* That's what I have held dearest to my heart ever since.

Chapter 29

Back from my morning excursion, I settled into my room where I was struck with a longing for Jim. A flash of heat spread across my cheeks. I could feel his absence most in the good moments when I was rested. When involved with the challenges of survival, I was okay. It was during the sweetness of the day that I longed for Jim's presence, to share, laugh, and experience the good moments. It would be foolish and wishful thinking to rely on him thousands of miles away in times of worry. And whenever he'd entered my thoughts during the trying times, rather than miss him, I tended to curse him. *Easier to blame him than me for my trials.*

But in those peaceful moments when the waves weren't crashing, when I wasn't fighting to keep my lips above water, I'd get beached. I cried until the tide receded. My self-pity consumed me until my stomach rolled with hunger. *Food would soothe me. Yes, food.* I'd learned from Jim that food can soothe the heart, and so in my own companionship, I headed to the restaurant. I drowned my loneliness with a colorful and delicious vegetable torte, layers of eggplant, squash, and peppers smothered in red tomato sauce.

Ready to Journey On

There was no reason to linger in *Pontevedra*. Restless, I was ready to journey on. I smiled at the permission I gave myself to travel by train and save myself a day's walk to *Padron*. But I had less than an hour to catch the last train, so I had no time to spare. Rushing back to *Hotel Ruas* I packed and checked out, then walked the short thirty minutes to the train station and climbed on board.

Ahhhh. I was on my way with the power of the train moving me forward. On my way to *Padron*!

Thankfully, the travails of my pilgrimage had been replaced by the gifts of Pontevedra: Mother Mary, the Holy Spirit, the Olive Tree, the Dove, and the Seagull.

I rested in my seat, joyful and buoyant, brimming with light—a confident and sure-footed pilgrim. My purpose was fulfilled and my way clear.

But soon the rumbling unease of the train, the uncertainty of what lay ahead, and the simple desire for this journey to be over had me yo-yo-ing between time and space, dimensions and consciousness, emotions and life.

Patience became my lesson again.
Always patience.

It took only a few minutes for the unfamiliar travel by rail to set in. It was a foreign mode of transportation for me, a Californian used to traveling alone in my own car at my own speed in my own direction, free to move freely on the freeways. Ticketing and timetables put me on high alert. My unease on trains trickled into the cracks of my discomfort being a foreigner on a foreign continent—yet alone.

In faith, I knew all was provided for, yet I still lacked security and confidence. Moving back and forth between dimensions, summiting the peaks of higher consciousness, and diving into the depths of third-dimensional duality rocked me. Consistently remaining in the realms of higher consciousness took practice. Like a wobbling toddler learning to walk or a landlubber adjusting to his sea legs, my footing in multiple dimensions was yet precarious.

Ghost Town

By the time I disembarked at the *Padron* station, a quilt of clouds hung low in the sky. The sun—and my joy—had stayed behind in *Pontevedra*. The train station was dank, dismal, locked up, and abandoned, with no town in sight.

Two other people stepped off with me, but their surefooted stepping showed me they were certain of their direction. They disappeared before I was able to ask questions or even follow their example. The dusty station gave off an air of 1800s American Wild West—not at all what I had imagined while planning this trip (yet again). Then the train's horn blasted, announcing its departure and was gone in a flash. I was left standing in the dirt. Alone.

I noticed the station's fading pink stucco building was covered in graffiti. It shared space with the even more dismal *Hotel Rosalia* on the other side of the tracks, both in the middle of nowhere. No street entrance, no taxis waiting for straggling passengers, nothing. A ghost town. I crossed the tracks at my own peril.

Before I checked out of the *Hotel Ruas* that morning, I'd asked the *senorita* at the front desk to call ahead to *Hotel Rosalia* for a reservation, but the phone rang and rang again, unanswered. *Have I been diverted to a place that would drain my soul of all the Light I had just imbibed in Pontevedra?* I struggled to withhold judgment.

The Snake's Message

Crossing the train tracks, I hoisted my pack and pressed on, scanning the shadowed ground. And there at my feet was a snake. Immediately I sensed it wasn't threatening. Small, maybe six inches or so, and tannish brown, it was unlike any species I'd ever seen.

**No, not a scary snake,
but it was a snake all the same.**

I kept my eyes on it. Still, it didn't appear alarmed by me as it slithered slowly with nowhere in particular to go—like me. I noticed the snake was invisible to the two others who walked over it. *There must be a message for me in this. But what?* I knew he was a messenger, but I'd grown weary of this game that required me to figure it out on my own. I plunked down on the curb where the snake had just vacated and wished, "Someone, just tell me!" And as clearly as if an Ascended Master was sitting by my side, I listened to my inner wisdom.

> *The snake is an affirmation of transformation. You have been called to certain places on the* Camino *to cause transformation. You are not necessarily here to be transformed, even though you are gifted with many states of transcendence for your diligence. The snake is always symbolic of the Law of One. One purpose of your journey is to reveal the Oneness of God's True Light and Love. Your journey is one of service and the opportunity of transformation for others. Some you meet will accept the gift you carry, some will not, and that is their free choice. How it is received is not your concern. You are asked only to walk the path of Light.*

The depictions of Mother Mary stepping on the serpent, or the serpent tempting Eve to cause separation, misinterpret the snake's energy. The snake represents the shedding of old beliefs to reveal the dormant energies of Light and Love. The snake is ascension. He holds his power through his slow course, basking in sunlight to receive God's energy.

He wanted you to know that even here in this abandoned place transformation happens. He was reminding you of your purpose. Let go of your doubt.

Listening to my inner guides ignited my resolve. Suddenly, my gait was fast and purposeful. I pressed on.

Better to Walk

At the *Hotel Rosalia*, there wasn't a soul to greet me except a loner outside smoking. He immediately informed me I needed to return at 8:00 p.m. I thought it was better to walk than to sit on the dusty curb until then, so I crossed back over the tracks and set out in the direction described in my guidebook to *Iglesia de Santiago y Padron*. This is the church where it's believed the remains of Saint James were transported after he was martyred in Jerusalem. His remains still rest in this church.

I knew *Padron* was the starting point of Saint James's ministry. But I was not inspired to visit the *Iglesia* or nearby *Monte Santiaguino*, landmarked as the place where Saint James first preached the gospel. From my guidebook, I concluded that both places had become tourist outposts influenced by religious dogma. By the time of James's ministry, the spirit of Christ's teachings had become veiled through misinterpretation, translation, and the early decrees of Christianity.

I have no doubt that Saint James' intention to preach the Word of Christ was pure, but the message had become subjective.

No, the way of Saint James was not my *Camino*, and *Padron's* historical significance did not express the energy that resonated with my concept and my love of Christ. For me, being in *Padron* so close to the beginning and end of James's human life was stifling. So were the rules symbolized by his mummified *human* energy of 45 AD. I would have preferred the presence of his *eternal* energy.

It took all my energy to stay present so I would not be pulled back into a time of past lives of my own. I could think only of moving through this place as fast as possible. Once again, I was sucked into the vacuum of suffering and negation, and I couldn't find my way out. If the sun was in the sky, I guessed it would be setting by now, but I felt void of Light inside and out. The way *was* hard and painful.

**If only I could raise my consciousness,
I could rise above its illusion.**

But for the time being, I was stuck.

Locked Out! Again!

The chaotic energy of the city of *Santiago* was only twenty kilometers away, and I could feel it. For the next thirty minutes, the allure of a brief rest inside the warmth of *Iglesia de Santiago y Padron* kept me moving toward it. But when I finally arrived, I found the church locked. Locked out! Again!

With no relief or rest, I bundled up against the wind and rain for the three-kilometer walk to another hotel, *Hotel Scala. I'll count my blessings elsewhere.* The wind whistled in my ears, my hair flew wildly in the gray sky. The festive music and family laughter of *Pontevedra* only a few hours ago no longer buoyed me. I felt like I was back on the *Camino*—the gray, wet, cold *Camino*.

The sun that had been shining that morning had definitely set.

Chapter 30

Aurora greeted me at the front desk of *Hotel Scala*. Sweet Aurora named after the stars. She beamed when I recognized her celestial name. The lobby was empty, the *café* deserted. No games were being played in the game room. A TV could be heard entertaining itself.

Aurora, who was schooled in English, efficiently checked me in to Room 226, clean and ready. Even though the hotel was empty, it seemed Aurora ran the front desk as if it were fully occupied. I quickly unpacked, sent Jim a text, and then retreated to the downstairs *café* for a meal, postponing planning the next stage of my journey until later. For now, I was thrilled with my clean bed. At least the bland spare space gave no room for imaginary demons to interrupt my needed sleep.

Sipping my bottled water, I calculated that I'd been on the *Camino* thirteen days and had traveled 213.7 kilometers.

As the evening wore on, boredom set in. *This place is just a stopover, a bus stop. How can I make the most of my time? The food is subpar, the room adequate. It is a place along the way to tomorrow, nothing more. Or is it? A space holding space.* This was not my place, the final non-stop before I made my way to *Finisterre.*

I passed the time journaling until my pen ran dry. *Another pen out of ink.* I had been measuring my days by the remaining ink. I had only one pen left.

My Pathway Home

For days, I had spoken no more than a few sentences except for the few precious moments when I found a landline and cried out to Jim. But even with Jim, our conversations were fraught with unease. Trivia shielded us from our real thoughts, stifling our words. *How's the weather?* Our unspoken worries disconnected us.

I was so far away from our home together, and he was so far from me on the *Camino* in this environment of uncertainty.

We danced around it—both trying to be okay. *I miss you, Jim! How fast can I get home to you?* In that moment, my longing thoughts were interrupted by a text message from our son. Jimmy had sensed it was time for me to come home and took it upon himself to make sure I did. My return itinerary had been left open, another unknown piled onto the unknowns I dwelled in. However, my return flight required me to backtrack 329.8 kilometers to my starting point in *Porto.* Instead, Jimmy had rerouted my itinerary to depart on Friday from *Coruna,* only an hour's bus ride from *Finisterre*. A swift two-hour flight to Madrid followed, then Madrid overseas to Chicago and a cross-country flight home to San Diego. Twenty-six hours. Set. My pathway home!

It felt good to have a return itinerary. Grounded. Certain. Paradoxically, I felt lifted by concrete details. I would complete my pilgrimage in *Finisterre* and then head home. No backtracking; I'd take a direct route to the arms of my beloved family. An air of Peace breathed over me. *So close.* Finally, I could see beyond the veils that clouded me in aloneness.

But, perhaps, I was getting ahead of myself. I was still in *Padron*—and a long way from home.

With Aurora's help to decipher the timetable, I found a bus to *Santiago* departing promptly at 7:45 tomorrow morning. There, I would change busses and travel the last three hours to *Finisterre*. Once off the bus, I could easily walk three and half kilometers to the cape and *O' Semaforo* Lighthouse. *So close.*

My stomach twirled, a butterfly flying home.

Understanding My Why

I had been so near to understanding my why—*Finisterre, Cabo Fisterra*—the last known end of the world. That's back when the world was flat and fear kept man shackled to his birthplace. This was the last known place on earth where man could step before sea: The end of exploration, opportunity, and adventure—but not the end of mankind's dream.

Cabo Fisterra was confined and contained with no unlimited abundance or infinite majesty in this reality. Barren rock jutted into tempest waters, frigid and ferocious. Here, nature battled nature for meager resources—and for life itself.

And yet, for me and some restless souls before me, *Finisterre* was the beginning, an invitation to dream and explore beyond boundaries.

For me, *Finisterre* was a leaping point of Faith.

Faith to grab hold of that thread that tied me in knots and, at other times, spread out like an endless silver strand. It beckoned me to follow the *Camino* of the Milky Way unbound by trodden paths. It invited me to step into eternity, challenging me to trust that there's no end of the world, knowing we live simultaneously in all universes.

We're able to move freely in a twinkle of an eye to other galaxies and star systems and universes—*and to the sacred space within.*

Back to the Infinite One

The Milky Way had beckoned me—and many other earth-weary souls before me—to follow the path Home. Home. Back to the infinite One. Home. The place Eternal where there is no end.

Yes, this place called *Cabo Fisterra* had historically been labeled the end of the world, a finite reality that held humanity contained and boxed by limited imagination. It also held people in place as tightly as gravity clenched them to Earth.

Finisterre was once the place where dreams of an infinite universe ended and civilization began. Civilized, our world grows small. We're told to stop searching. Quit dreaming. Settle down. Make a living. Be content with what we have.

Here, I felt close to my answers and to shattering the shackles of my mortal being.

For me, *Finisterre* symbolized the solidifying of our mortal being and the end of remembering our eternal God Being.

Moving On

I awoke at the hotel to a chilly and damp Monday morning, the thermometer hovering around four degrees Celsius. By the time I stood at the side of the road on high alert to flag down a bus, the sun had not yet crested. There was no distinct bus stop, just a wide turnout. The road was busy with trucks and cars carrying workers to their Monday morning jobs. Diesel fumes invaded my senses. I stood stiff like an on-duty soldier, bracing myself from the wind rush. *Peregrinos*, walking two by two, shuffled by. They were cloaked in ponchos, their backpacks protruding from beneath, looking like a line of hunchback turtles. With

Santiago, their prized goal, less than seven hours' walk away, the pilgrims were plentiful.

When the bus finally landed in front of me, I fumbled for *dinero* and, with cold and stiff fingers, peeled off the correct fare. I checked and double checked this was indeed the bus to *Santiago*. After exhausting the driver's patience, I scooted in next to the half-asleep regulars en route to earn their weekly wages.

My thoughts drifted, changing with the scenery. In a flicker, my dad appeared—twice. I knew it was him. He first entered in my dream last night, but I didn't remember until the bus was rocking back and forth down the narrow road. In my memory, it seemed impossible to forget him, loudly clad in a coral-colored golf shirt. Dad was at Disneyland, full of fantasy and fun, wearing rose-colored glasses and grinning wide, trying to get me to do the same.

Dad lobbied again for my attention as the bus passed a farm equipment dealership. Ironically, the store yard was lined with the same tractors he'd sold in Montana. And then last night's dream returned in all its Technicolor—stark against the gray. *Be happy! I love you and will never leave you!*

With his undying optimism and joy of life that surpassed the grave, he had searched and found me in the shadows.

My tears broke free in a torrent. More tears. Endless tears that paved my journey. I could not recognize if they were sorrow or joy, but the immense release felt good all the same. So I let them flow. And just to make certain I knew he was at my side, the bus flew by yet another farm equipment store yard. Farm equipment: the best and most solid sign of Dad I could imagine!

Santiago Grit

Through the filmy window, everything that came into view was gray and gritty. The rain could never wash away the decades of grime. Road time was marked by stops and starts until finally we arrived at the *Santiago* station. Rows upon rows of busses came and went, in and out of a garage-like hangar. Diesel fumes mixed with wet cement and transient body odor. Once again, I felt out of my element.

I offered a silent pilgrim's prayer between changing busses at the terminal, which was as close to the *Catedral Santiago* as I would come. There was no need for me to go farther for I felt *Santiago* had long ago exchanged its heart and hope for the constant stream of pilgrims' coins. Then I purchased new tickets with a different bus company and joined other pilgrims who had completed their pilgrimage to *Santiago*.

Their end was my beginning.

Mythical Creatures

The way to *Finisterre* required passage through twelve kilometers of an area called the Moorlands.

This stretch of land contains megalithic tombs and 4,000-year-old prehistoric stone carvings called *Pedra Longa*. Predecessors walked these paths centuries before the Christian era dawned. The forerunners to Christianity are the reason I'm so drawn to the *Camino de Santiago*, not for its religious markings but its alignment to the Milky Way. The mystical and isolated Moorlands are steeped in legend and lore. Here, time stands still. And legend lives on.

One mythical and legendary being is Vakner, described as a terrifying creature who lives in the deepest and densest parts of the forest. He has an evil nature, appearing both animal-like and man-like.

**Should you come in contact with Vakner,
your blood will run cold.**

The Catholic Church used Vakner to create a sense of foreboding and increase its success at converting people to Catholicism. Vakner, the Church claimed, was a ghastly, evil creature who would attempt to destroy anyone entering the woodlands to practice pagan rites.

Yet even more terrifying than Vakner is the myth surrounding *Estadea* and the Company of Souls. *Estadea* is the place where departed souls wander the woods in search of unwary travelers. When they come upon these innocent souls, they take on their bodies for their own. If you're traveling in the Moorlands in the dark of night, you may see lights flickering here and there over the mournful, marshy countryside. It's the sign of these invisible beings who will try to lure you into opening your hand to receive their ghostly light. Should you accept it, you are consumed! You will have joined the Company of Souls condemned to wander.

That means these souls—and you—will wander the Moorlands until another unsuspecting stranger enters this wasteland and poses an opportunity for you to assume his or her body as your own. Until then, you will spend eternity drifting where the ghostly lights flicker. So it can happen that you may simply disappear from life. Grim.

Powerful Moorlands Energy

Safe on the bus, I still wasn't prepared for the powerful energy of the Moorlands and its ruin. I could only imagine how much worse I would have felt if I'd walked through this soulless wasteland.

My best efforts to shield me from the denigrated energy were not enough. I felt overcome. Bundled in gloves, hat, and my down jacket, still I was freezing. Too cold and drowsy to ask for help, I simply couldn't move myself to ask the bus driver to turn on the heat. It dawned on me he was the sort who might chill the bus and its passengers on purpose. So I sat frozen and immovable.

Then the gnawing doubt of being on the wrong bus began eating away at me. I knew it was impossible, and yet this force feasted on my fear of being lost and heaved me into panic. Then, worst of all, before I slipped into a coma-like trance, I lost my favorite hat. Finally, as the bus neared the sea, the suppression I felt lifted.

In the context of duality and polarity, evil force is undeniable. And I rarely use the word "evil" for I know in God's Truth, evil does not exist. However, in the third dimension of duality, a universal belief in evil has made it extremely real.

Not until we transcend duality into Oneness will evil lose its grip and be seen for what it is—an illusion.

Espousing that the human experience is only an illusion with its war and hate, lack and poverty, disease and death can be misleading. However, when one lives in the grasp of mass consciousness, universal belief is very real. Only when we experience illusion as a mirage and we can truly see its hypnotic attraction does it finally become powerless—and just that—an illusion. *This is transcendence.*

In duality, the force of darkness appears as mighty as the power of Light. I could not escape the force of this maligned energy. And much to my peril, in times of danger I tend to forget to call on Archangel Michael and his legions of Light for protection. *If only I had thought to ask!*

Spell Lifting

I was finally close to *Finisterre,* and the hills greeted me with flowering Goldenrod. The slick road reminded me of the earlier rain. Awakening from my haze as the spell was lifting, I could actually smile. The last hours' fear and anxiety of being on the wrong bus dissolved. *It is all part of the energy of the Moorlands.*

These dark and dense energies had made my passage difficult, exerting every effort to make known their aversion for Light beings like me. In my God Presence, I could see that these beings, like all of us, were simply seeking love. But in the lower consciousness where they reside, it was unwise for me to readily extend my helping hand. *The third dimension is a polar world. It is the reality I am presently experiencing, so play by its rules!*

From my window's view, everything was a composition of monochromatic shades of gray. The sea was a depthless, deep charcoal, the sky a steely thunder. The clouds hung heavy and low, a quilted ceiling. In contrast, the white shoreline reached to the gilded hillsides of blooming Goldenrod.

While traveling through the Moorlands under the spell of delusion, I wondered if I would ever come out of it.

How would I ever take another step?
I'd been so drowsy. It seemed so real.
I'm so grateful to Archangel Michael!

The Pilgrims' Uniform

On my final leg to *Finisterre,* the bus stopped at a makeshift terminal curving out of a village street. The doors swished open to eager pilgrims pushing their way for a seat back to *Santiago.* There was a certain look to a pilgrim—wind-burned skin, tousled hair, weathered clothes. They looked scruffy and derelict, yet in a healthy sort of way. Beards were the norm.

Pilgrims wore and carried myriad outdoor equipment bought just for this pilgrimage that would likely end up in attics, never to see the great outdoors again. No luggage, only backpacks. And boots—all kinds, sizes, and styles of boots. We pilgrims were a tribe, and we wore our ceremonial dress in sacred honor of our journey. I'd met only one American on my path, Dr. Nic. Few Americans chose to travel so far to walk for so long. *We were the novelty.*

As I pushed forward to make my way off the bus, I was deluged by hotel hawkers bidding for pilgrims to fill their empty beds. No order, only chaos. I moved to retrieve my backpack from the bus's underbelly— the first time I'd been separated from my pack since foolishly giving it to Franco. It didn't feel good to be parted, and I eagerly wanted reconnection to all I presently owned. Given the uneasiness of traveling by bus and rail, always nervous about my connections, misreading arrival times, departure times, and transit times—the last thing I wanted was to lose my possessions. *My favorite hat. Where is it?*

Granted, there were comforts and advantages to walking. The yellow arrows were never far away and didn't require tickets or timetables. Walking the *Camino,* I had no schedule to adhere to and all I ever needed was in my pack *always* on my back.

But in the madness, I'd left behind my hat. This was the second time I'd lost something; the first time, I'd lost my *credencial* when I was tricked by Franco. *This is different. I've lost a friend who's been with me from the very beginning, a companion.* I consoled myself, knowing I'd soon be home where other hats would take its place. Home! Where a choice of hats were stacked in my closet! Lots of hats!

But that's not the same as losing the hat I'd worn on the *Camino.* I was the young child who'd lost her blanket, grieving for it as if I'd lost a best friend.

Chapter 31

A few meters of walking and just minutes from the bus station, I set out to search for the tourism office, a good place to get my bearings. But like the churches on this trip, one had yet to be open. I continued to believe if they had been open, the people there would have been helpful.

In *Finisterre,* I found the tourism office located in a ramshackle building a few doors from the bus stop. On the door hung a limp handwritten note that had fallen victim to the weather. *Abierto a las quatro* (open at four). It was a long time until *quarto,* so I pressed on.

I'd found hotels were the best place to ask for help—next to churches and *turismos.* In fact, hotels seemed better because they were always open. So I entered the one-star *Hotel Finisterre.* The owner was kindly, much kinder than his one-star designation would signify. I asked in my broken Spanish which *rua* would lead me up the hill to the *O' Semaforo,* and just in case I misunderstood his directions, I asked again.

Because he was so kind, I lingered a bit longer.

"Mas?" (more questions?)

"Yes . . . *Sí.*"

"*Donde está autobús a Coruna?*" He informed me where and when I should meet the bus two days from then. This vital tip helped settle my homeward journey so I could leave the future behind and stay present.

"*Gracias!*"

"*De nada. Buenas tardes.*"

Christ of the Golden Beard

Outdoors again, I felt invigorated after the frigid bus ride and suffocating diesel fumes. After fifteen days, outdoors was more home to me than indoors. With fingers on my mala beads, my mantra of gratitude kept rhythm with my steps as I climbed the last three kilometers to the *O' Semaforo.* I sang a tune. My merry soul lifted, a happy journeyer at last.

A quarter way up the steep climb was *Igrexa de Santa Maria,* the Church of Saint Maria. Feeling emotionally dirty from traveling through *Santiago* and the dark energy of the Moorlands, I paused. *A quiet prayer inside this roadside chapel would balance my energy and dust off my travails.*

I learned of evidence that Jesus had walked this land. He would often travel with his friend, Joseph of Aramathea, to *Britannia,* with *Finisterre* being a likely stopover for trade and provisions. While Joseph traded tin from the mines, Jesus would sit with his Druidic teachers. In my reverie, I could feel His presence.

Inside the church, I saw an ancient effigy of Jesus on the cross called *Cristo da Barba Dourado*, the Christ of the Golden Beard. I knew it has been historically associated with miraculous healing powers. Divergent beliefs blurred in the presence of this statue when both the prayerful Christians and spiritual Druids witnessed the inanimate statue grow a beard and perspire.

Cristo da Barba Dourado is believed to have been sculpted by Nicodemus, the friend of Jesus who, along with Joseph of Aramathea, helped prepare the body of Jesus for burial.

I found the story of how this statue came to this small chapel in my guidebook— interesting folk-lore—similar to the miracle of Jesus calming the waters in Galilee. It read:

A ship sailing to England while passing Finisterre encountered a storm so severe that all would surely perish. In the cargo hold was the sculpture by Nicodemus. During the crew's last attempts to survive they threw the figure of Jesus into the turbulent waters along with their final prayers. The seas miraculously calmed and the ship and its crew harbored safely to shore to cheers of celebration. It was a miracle. Days later, the statue floated ashore and found its place in the Church of Saint Maria. Annual celebrations continue to mark this miraculous event.

Christian Shrines

One way the early Christian Church converted pagans was to overlay a Christian symbol—statue, cross, or chapel—over the original Druidic sacred site, remaking them into Christian shrines. I discovered firsthand nearly every sacred portal I encountered was overlaid with a Christian replica. *If the exclusive shroud of Christianity is folded back to allow the original Light of nature's holy places to shine through, would we once again unite in the allness and Oneness of God? It may take some time, but I believe Chief Joseph who said this:*

**"All paths are the right path
and all lead to One."**

In the time of Saint James, *Finisterre* was one of the foremost Celtic sites of spiritual practice and ceremonial ritual. Therefore, it was entirely reasonable to assume that Saint James specifically chose *Galicia* to share the gospel for its richness of mystic and majesty. Or perhaps Saint James chose *Galicia* simply to follow in the Master's footsteps. Either way, it provided a good place for conversion.

Unlocked!

I turned the heavy brass handle, and the massive door easily swayed open into this dwelling place of Faith. Disbelief followed. Unlocked! After a few moments, I adjusted to the shadowy interior and made my way to the altar and the statue. I seemed invisible to a tour group who crowded forward, jostling me for a better glimpse of *Cristo da Barba Dourado*.

Being in this space, I had no doubt the miracles were real and this was a Spiritual portal visited by Jesus, Druidic Spiritual Masters, Nicodemus, Joseph of Aramathea, Saint James, Saint William, and countless unnamed devotees. Its synergy created a portal to God and Spiritual awakenings for anyone ready to walk through dimensional doorways to higher consciousness. *A profound place for me.*

After the Father concluded his dialogue, the crowd of tourists retreated to the vestibule, leaving me alone with the statue of Jesus. Underneath the cross appeared to be saintly mummified remains encased in glass. Another sepulcher. *So absurd for the clergy to encourage praying to a spiritless body reduced to dust. Someday, the invisible Spirit within each of us will be recognized and death will be seen as the illusion it is. Then there will be no homage paid to soulless material remains.*

The Father was tidying up behind the altar while visiting with a local parishioner. I shyly made my way toward him and stood with outstretched hands, extending my pilgrim's passport. Without even a sideways glance, he stamped my *credencial de peregrino* with no thought to what he was doing, never wavering to acknowledge me. I wanted so badly to tell him thank you! I wanted to bow before him for giving me my first church stamp on my long, long journey and bless him and thank him and gush. But he did not give me that opening. *I want him to see me, but he does not. I am just another foreign chore intruding on his time.*

With my precious *credencial de peregrino* in hand, I walked back to the alcove toward the cross of Jesus and the mummified body beneath—and I sat. I couldn't withhold my feelings any longer. Tears fell; sobs broke free.

**What am I feeling—heart breaking
or heart opening? It is all the same.**

Ready to Listen

Outside the church, the rain had ceased. I stopped to remove my jacket and scarf. And I searched again for my hat—just in case. I began the climb up the hill, scouting out the places I would explore the next day. The hill was steep and the going slow. Shortly, I halted for refreshment and reflection. *What just happened? It is big! I know that much.*

And as clearly as if he'd just sat down on the rock beside me to share my apple, I felt

the presence of Lord Sananda. It was just a feeling, an impression, that he came to impart something important. *With no companionship, communication, or familiarity of home, the* Camino *is the perfect break from restricted thought forms and rigid judgments that hold me captive to my ego. I am ready to listen.*

Every footstep that had led to this moment, the solitude and the aloneness, the doubt and uncertainty—all of it—had prepared me to die to my personal identity.

The priest's rebuff finally awoke me to "enough!" Lord Sananda had my full attention. I was ready to let go of everything keeping me separate from God and my divine heritage—from who I truly am. I was prepared to become one with the Christ Consciousness. On a hillside in Spain with Sananda as my witness, I reaffirmed my life to God and All That Is. I had just died to myself and come out on the other side.

Looking back, I don't know how else I could have explained it. I wasn't alone after all.

The Physics of Enlightenment

Fully conscious of the spiritual initiation to Light and Love I had just passed through, I knew my physical body would require recalibration to adjust to these higher frequencies of Light. This would take time and integration. To rush such a physical shift in consciousness could cause physical harm, much like electrocution. This was the physical aspect of enlightenment I'd learned from Joshua David Stone.

Stone's research points to the possibility of enlightenment when the physical body replaces denser matter with higher vibrational frequencies of Light and attains a 51% Light quotient. The higher states of consciousness require a greater measure of air and fire than the carbon-based energies of earth and water. One aspect of the physical enlightenment process is to reverse the denser earth and water elements in the body into the more etheric elements of fire and air. *In-Light* brings the Light of the firmament into one's physical body. This is a bodily process, one that requires both physical and spiritual transformation.

Enlightenment is not finality. Rather, it's a starting place for the Christ Consciousness; the oneness of God's Divine Nature and human nature expressing Itself in our daily lives.

O' Semaforo Lighthouse

Finally, *Finisterre*. I walked to where there was no land left to travel. *Finisterre*—the end. I had truly walked to the end.

At the entryway to *O' Semaforo* Lighthouse, I grabbed the door handle and was catapulted forward by the wind, nearly falling into the *café* and not at all graceful. Wind, my new companion and one I'd learn to respect—was making herself known. And Rain was no match to Wind's force. *Another reckoning with nature has begun.*

I was eager to secure my room for my three-day stay. I had been guaranteed only one night, and again uncertainty unsettled me. *What would I do for the remaining days?*

"Thy Will, not mine," flitted through my mind. But *I* wanted it so. *I* wanted my room. *I* wanted security. I wanted it to play out as *I* had planned.

Yes, I had gone with the flow, twisting and turning, adjusting and flexing. Yet being so close to the finish, I yearned for consistency—even a *little* consistency. My anxiety was taking its toll and making me weary. Was I falling ill? This question ran through my mind while checking in. And then I received the news: Yes, I could stay the last two nights at the Lighthouse. *Worry is such a waste!*

Chapter 32

Desorio, the innkeeper, led me up a short circular stairway to a round hallway that opened to three guest rooms. My room was in the center. Opposite its entrance was a sitting room. The ceiling was painted royal blue. Everything was round like a lighthouse should be. Through walled-in glass, guests kept watch on the endless sea.

My room was sparsely furnished and tiny, built to withstand the bombardment of wind and rain and weather. The walls were thick cement, the lights caged in metal, the windows reinforced with iron bars. Rock solid. Nothing rattled this above-ground bunker, and I immediately felt safe inside.

Although I'd been up since four in the morning, my excitement to explore chased away any weariness. After unpacking and settling in, I was ready to discover whatever awaited me in the few daylight hours left. The wind was keeping the rain clouds out at sea, but when I stepped outside, its gusts took my breath away. Soon I realized the Lighthouse was a busy tourist destination and this well-known end of the world had become a bottleneck. Bus after bus rounded the bend sharing the road with souvenir vendors and parading passersby. I'd swung to the other side of the pendulum—from solitude to soirée.

I skirted the crowds down to a hillside toward the bluff that jutted out into the ocean. Four hundred feet below, cliffs sheared the water's edge where the Atlantic swell unceasingly battered the headland. I was drawn there, but it required passing the Pilgrim's Memorial before I could reach its precipice.

The smell of charred remnants alerted me to the monument before I stumbled upon it. After a pilgrim's journey, it's a ritual to burn clothing or other items symbolizing old behaviors and beliefs held before the pilgrimage that no longer served one's higher purpose. The Pilgrim's Memorial is a sculpted bronze boot fixed in bedrock bordered by blackened rocks encircling an open fire pit. It represents a ceremony of transformation by fire. To me, it looked like a trash heap.

Its symbolism resonated with me, and yet, I couldn't accept the burning of one's boots.

After all, my boots got me here. Next to my backpack, they were precious to me. *No, I am still attached and couldn't let go of my beloved boots. Not yet.*

Over and over I heard the words circling in my head, "The Pilgrim's Memorial is a decoy. It's a diversion. Keep going to the bluff." Few people venture beyond the Pilgrim's Memorial. Rocky and steep, it wasn't a trek for the skittish. Still, I kept going.

Not far from the brass boot was the International Peace Pole. "May Peace Prevail on Earth" is inscribed in different languages on each of the four sides of this internationally recognized symbol of Peace. There are thousands of Peace Poles in nearly every country. This one is unobtrusive, just holding space. Nothing much.

Again, I had an eerie feeling this was somehow a decoy steering tourists away from the stargate. Thousands of pilgrims walked the *Camino*, each with a purpose unique and individual to him or her. Wistful memories of my pilgrim friends swirled in my head: Dr. Nic in search of a love in harmony with his faith; Donatella, walking the way of the medieval Saints in search of the Divine Mother's love, protected by Vittorio; the sea-loving Germans, Klaus and Renata completing another adventure; the native Celtics charting the Milky Way. And my own pilgrimage—to find my way *within* to Home.

The International Peace Pole serves beautifully to awaken many hearts to Peace for the first time. The stargate held another awakening to those who were beckoned to the bluff.

Capricorn and Pan—Heaven and Earth

As I passed the fire pit and approached the bluff, I came toe to toe with five mountain goats. I slowly edged away, giving these wild ones their space. But rather than having concern for my close proximity, they seemed to motion me closer. *A sign! Indeed I was at the stargate.*

From our experience on the Chief Joseph Trail, we discovered similarities when entering sacred portals and stargates—first, at each location was a Gatekeeper attended by a Guardian or Guardians. The Gatekeeper usually came in the form of a rock outcropping or tree and a Guardian who would often appear as an animal, bird, or insect—in this instance, the goats. Pan, the god of nature is symbolized by the goat-like satyr. The constellation Capricorn is traditionally depicted as a sea-goat with a fish tail. Capricorn and Pan—Heaven and Earth—were guiding me to a Spiritual pinnacle point. The Pilgrim's Memorial served as the Gatekeeper to this stargate, guiding approaching pilgrims to leave their denser energies behind before entering the stargate's heightened energy. It sometimes gently deterred the unprepared.

One of my quests on the *Camino* was to reunite all soul aspects into my physical embodiment. Goats look galactic to me; their rectilinear irises, so uniquely different from our rounded variety, provide a clue to an other-worldly origin.

The goats' invitation was clear, but was I ready to embrace my galactic presence?

Glimpses of supernatural realities flashed before me. The wind—or was it the goats?—kept me off balance. Was I ready, could I or did I have the courage to walk through the doorway of omni-dimensional consciousness? Nothing made sense, and yet I understood.

Even with the winds billowing and the rain belching, the bluff remained peaceful and calm. I learned that when turbulent air suddenly stills, it's a sign of peace and the proximity to a sacred vortex.

Beyond the Mind

I had walked fifteen days and nearly four hundred kilometers, each step taking me closer to the Light of Home. I had said good-bye to my ego personality and parted ways with my ancestral lineage. I had nothing left to surrender. Every step required me to recognize and acknowledge those dark aspects of me, the ones I couldn't admit even to myself. If I could finally let go of the lies of unworthiness and those feelings of not being good enough and unlovable, I could accept my God Presence as who I truly am. Then I could receive the dimensional frequencies of God and Light that are my birthright.

Every experience in all my lives, in all dimensions, led me to this pinnacle moment in my forever search for God and Home. My wrenching dark nights of the soul, and now my solitary and soulful journey on the *Camino,* were preparing me for what was to come. This spontaneous knowing was coming to me so rapidly, I didn't have time to think. I moved beyond the mind. My knowing was channeling through Source—crystal clear Truth.

Later, in hindsight, I knew I could use my mental faculties, step back, and examine all of what was transpiring in a state of wonder. In that moment, though, I was overtaken by a Spiritual power greater than I had ever experienced.

I was in the arms of God and I was safe.

My curious mind was fed from a stream of unimportant minutiae, possibly to keep it occupied so Spiritual Grace could descend. *There is nothing I need to know.* Pan, Capricorn, and an invisible team of Light Beings assisted me through the stargate. They mapped the way through the twelve dimensions of this Universe and guided me to higher consciousness—from Earth to Oneness—encoding a Divine blueprint into my physical being. My very own spiritual yellow arrows.

I was shown the way Home. And once this pathway was charted, I would never be lost again.

Chapter 33

After a time, I regained my Earth's footing. I was atop *Cabo da Fisterra,* surrounded by water and wind. I couldn't tell if it the wind was pummeling the water or the water thrashing the wind. With my body nearly seventy percent water and rapidly shifting into the ascendancy of air, these powerful elements swirled and swayed me. The energy remained intense.

As the sun was setting and my day done, I was in a transcendent state, alive, blissfully calm and grounded as I carefully made my way off the bluff back to my room in the Lighthouse.

The wind whistled through the vents of my room, reminding me I was captive on the cape—captive in a good way—air and wind reminding me to breathe and go within. There was no going *anywhere.* I was isolated and immersed in an unfamiliar, rarified energy of the galactic realms. I was on top of it, in it, around it. There was no other place to be. Only the unrelenting rain and wind—water and air—kept me grounded to Earth.

It was challenging to adjust to what had happened on the bluff. My emotional body was especially vulnerable, and I teetered on thoughts of senselessness. Yet the instant I surrendered into stillness, I opened into enlightenment. *I am not crazy after all!*

How much Light could my body hold? It could very well be my shattering! Something was happening. I could feel it, but it wasn't physical. I was conscious of moving through a tunnel of Light, propelled by the wind. I lay on my bed and trusted that whatever was taking place was orchestrated by the Holy Spirit and supported by the Ascended Masters.

**Archangel Michael was protecting me—
of that I was certain.**

This tunnel was my way Home—everything I'd yearned for from the moment eons ago when I separated from Oneness into duality. I was at the culmination point of all my Spiritual desires integrating divinity. I held on to every shred of sensibility I could muster. *This is what I have prayed for!*

Surrendering To It All

I lay prone surrendering to it all. Finally, I relinquished my search for a God personified, a God separate and apart and outside of me. I released, finally, the religious-inspired notion that God's totality could be contained in a person or depicted as a personality. I saw that God could only be an all-encompassing Consciousness of everything: the Creator, the Oneness. And in that Oneness, we are all It.

And I saw who I am, a spark of this Divine Consciousness, one and the same. At last, I gave up the search outside of myself for what *is* me and found God within. Spirit surged through me as unlimited Grace. Home was not a destination on the *Camino* nor an allocation nor a *Fonte de Vida*. It is Grace within my own body. This is why I walked—to light the way with Grace.

I am a soul journeyer walking in Grace.
Home, always Home on whatever path
I choose. I am One.

There is no end. There is no beginning. The map Home has no gridlines, latitudes, or directions. Home has no location. It's not a birthplace, a house for only family, a town for only residents, or a country for only citizens. Home, in the universal sense, has no walls, doors, or borders.

I am Home. I am now Home in my physical body. I found Home in my heart through the door of aloneness. I cannot go where I already am. I found God, whom I had confined to heaven, within me.

Wherever I am, God is. Wherever God is, I am.

All that I can conceive is Home. Home is —me, and I am Home. The final paradox—leaving home to go home. The shattered untruth. My path was not the prettiest, the easiest, or the shortest, but it delivered me to who I am—at Home, with God. My pilgrimage on the *Camino* opened me to the Universe, allowing me to let go of my limited self. I discovered my galactic being, my universal being, my I am Presence, and my God Presence. And in this realization, I became One. No longer the fragmented, forgetful human; now the whole and complete Christ Self. Shima.

**Oh bless my pen that makes sense of it all,
weaving a story around emotions that run deep.**

I came to know this: It is not others who can break our hearts—not husbands, wives, or partners nor outside events and circumstances. They cannot. Only *we* know how to pierce ourselves in the deepest way possible to shatter love. And only *we* can pick up the pieces. Only *we* have the authority to go that deep within ourselves to break our own heart. And that can't be done for others. The heart is personal. Only *we* have the private privilege to pierce it.

Flowing Rain

That night, I ate a dinner of apple pie. *I've survived a surge of ascension.* Then I sank into the darkness of a moonless night, waiting for sleep to move me deeper into the void, the place where faith resides. The wailing wind and the lighthouse beacon rhythmically passed by my window, reminding me where I was. I awaited sunrise when I could return to the bluff.

Early morning dawned Light. Yesterday's sunshine didn't make it through the night, but I did. The struggle blocking me lifetime after lifetime from owning my Christ Self had lifted. *My resistance shattered, I had transcended.*

Before this revelation, I could *see* the highest vision but was unable to walk over the threshold to *experience* It—the most painful suffering of all to *see* but not *be*. This time as I stood at the threshold, I entered. It took years of preparation and weeks walking through unrelenting rain in a foreign land with no compass or companions to confront my buried fears. And finally those fears let loose. My flowing tears and Mother Gaia's rain kept in tempo as illusion and miscreation were torn from their tethers. In communion with Mother Earth, I weathered both my internal and external storms. I faced and fought the obstacles in my body, revealing a new Light body free of old emotional traumas and the debris of ignorance.

I have found my way Home.

Finisterre, Cabo Fisterre, and *O' Semoforo* were the culmination of my *Camino*—the culmination of my life's Spiritual journey to date. In the overwhelm of my experience, I sought to understand. My pilgrimage and its challenges were necessary to heal the wounds held in my heart. With an open heart I could receive Grace and Wisdom. On the bluff with the mystical goats, I was given a prevue. This glimpse freed me from my ego interfering, allowing my total surrender into the divine consciousness and acceptance into Light. Home.

Venture into the Rain

I awoke rested. The foul weather, however, thwarted a sunrise ceremony on the bluff, so I redirected my plans to hike up *Monte Facho* in search of the sacred stones *Piedras Santas* and the hermitage of Saint William *Ermita de San Guillerme.* I prepared to venture into the heavy rain bundling up methodically and sequentially so I wouldn't overheat before stepping out.

In my snug little cocoon my hood kept falling over my eyes. *Stay dry or see—I couldn't have both.* Every choice a compromise. Oh, how I wished for the weather to break. And with that thought (or perhaps it was just my imagination), the rain pounded in reply. I forged on in good faith following a sliver of light, hoping that I'd stumble upon the ten-ton granite boulders that supposedly could be rocked with a finger. *It would be a lifetime opportunity to walk in the energy of these sacred stones.*

I started up the steep path leading to the summit. Rain, heavy rain, but so far no mudslides or washouts, so all was well. My feet held firm. Forgive my ceaseless mention of the wind and rain, seemingly boring and redundant, but their power was all pervasive, so all consuming, they cast their pall on my entire world.

It was not far before I rounded a bend and discovered two enormous boulders. On top of the boulders sat a third rectangular rock, also enormous. It seemed impossible that this architectural marvel could be created by natural causes, or even how man could undertake such a feat. *Not by man, not by nature—then by whom?*

I was immersed in the energy of its sacredness and determined to push through the harsh conditions. I scrambled around the rocks as best as I could without slipping, taking in this mystery with all my senses. I later learned this site was a holy place of prayer used by ancient Druid priests. To me, the three stones in perfect balance symbolized the Trinity.

**The vibrant energy there was so tangible
I knew I was experiencing the power of
nature undiminished by time.**

Rain Dance

I searched for shelter to bring out pen and paper and memorialize my find, but it was impossible and I would chance losing all of my notes. Instead, I opted for the recorder on my iPhone, but even that wasn't working until I realized signals sent through touch couldn't be deciphered through my gloves.

By now, rain was sheeting down, the wind pushing it sideways. This storm was unlike anything I'd yet experienced. I knew I could be in danger and yet the electricity in the air, or perhaps the infusion of Light within me (or simply because Mom never allowed us to play in the rain) made me giddy.

I was free! And so I danced!

The rain knew no boundaries. It found its way into the workings of my iPhone. It seeped into every unsealed crevice, my under-layers, my boots, and my socks. My only concern was not being cold and wet in the moment, but would I be able to get dry later?

As I felt the first signs of dampness against my skin, my better judgment told me to turn around before it was too late. The cost of wet boots was too high a price to pay for this moment of childlike delight.

Foolhardy! The night before, I had connected to the Milky Way and transcended the Earth's relentless weather. There was no need for me to venture out until the rain lifted, the clouds parted, and the sun shone again. My connection here was with the stars and the Cosmos. And when I finally succumbed to my foolishness for being out in indefensible weather, I experienced a miraculous realization of why I was there. I was connecting with *galactic* portals, not *earth* portals. My mission was to map the way home through the Milky Way and the stars. The wind blew harder, the rain shifted sideways and turned to hail. It was ferocious yet invigorating. Still, it was time to call it quits. The weather triumphed, forcing me to turn around.

When I had arrived back at the road I'd traversed earlier, it had been washed out. I stopped to consider my options. The hillside to the left was steep and overgrown with heavy scrub. Impassable. To cross the washed-out road would destroy my boots. Not an option. To the right was a fence, tall but scalable without my backpack. As I stood in the pouring rain pondering my course, a sign appeared loud and clear.

Tributaries of water flowing from the hillside had created symbols in the sand. I knew immediately they were Pleiadian Light symbols from my previous sightings on my Chief Joseph Trail at Swallow's Hill. These galactic markings were as legible as if I were looking at words spelled out in the English alphabet. Their message reminded me again that reality included the celestial realms. Accessing celestial dimensions through planetary or physical means simply wouldn't work. In other words, *there was no reason to be out in the storm.*

Pleiadians at Play

Of course! Oh, for the Grace of God, the messages were clear and direct. Finally, I had *eyes* to see! Light language—plain as day. I grabbed my phone to snap a picture of the Pleiadian glyphs, but my cell phone screen appeared as an old-time photo negative. *Pleiadians at play?* I switched from the camera to the voice recorder, and the Pleiadians' mischief continued. My words came through garbled in a language I couldn't identify.

First, the reversed negative image on my camera and next the strange language on the recorder. Ha!

Common sense told me these strange occurrences were caused by the rain, and I chastised myself for being so foolish. But I knew there was more behind this coincidence, for I had experienced extraterrestrial playfulness firsthand on my Chief Joseph pilgrimage.

The Pleiadians and other galactic beings are highly skilled with technology, seemingly able to alter electronics to make contact with us Earthlings. These electronic glitches affirmed that I had many invisible companions walking beside me, and everything was divinely guided. They showed me with my own eyes I was not alone, that I was guided and protected. With that, I experienced a joy of brotherhood.

I saw what before I could only trust and feel.
I was not alone. I never had been.

With a quick acknowledgment to Mother Earth and her ultimate power—*Yes, Atlantic Ocean, you are bigger than me*—I spun around looking for another route to the Lighthouse. Journey OM.

Chapter 34

The rain lightened, almost misting, but I was concerned that my folly might have ruined my phone. There was no denying my boots were wet. How long it will take them to dry? That was the question. Back in my room, I placed my boots near the radiator and appealed to Desorio to dry my clothes. He was somber and forlorn, reluctantly accepting my wet bundle. Being in a place of such enlightenment, I didn't understand his sad nature, and as hard as I tried, I couldn't break through his morose shell.

Still early in the day, the thought of staying inside the Lighthouse fortress stifled me. Perhaps when I dried off enough to forget my most recent excursion, I would head to the village where I could carry out regular, normal, day-to-day activities, *la oficina de correos*, *la farmacia*, running errands and such. In the meantime, I huddled in front of the tiny radiator with my *café con leche* and waited out Mother Nature. In time, the rain lightened and again I tried walking to *Finisterre*. But the wind had picked up where the rain left off and blew me sideways, so I returned to the Lighthouse. There, Desorio called for a taxi.

Candido picked me up promptly. When I slid into the back seat of his smoke-filled four-door, my sense of unease overpowered the foul tobacco smell. *Only a short ride, better than walking in the wind and rain.* But my intuition said otherwise.

Candido, as it turned out, was not an honest man. His transient fares gave him ample opportunity to evade integrity. Knowing he would never see who he cheated after the short rides, he took advantage of each person. That day, I became his prey when he charged me fifteen euros for a five-euro trip. It was a small indiscretion—sure—but his dishonesty jerked me hard. When I asked him to wait while I stepped out of the taxi to check the bus schedule, he took on three more passengers in my place. Had I not left my shawl on the seat and his new fare kindly ran to return it to me, I would have been left on the side of the road.

At that point, I stood my ground and demanded he fulfill his obligation to return me to the Lighthouse. The new passengers, unaware they had solicited a taxi already engaged, were distressed by our heated exchange, judging me an angry American and reluctantly offered me a seat in *their* taxi to avoid further conflict. I sulked silently in the backseat wondering what dimension I had just thudded into after being so engrossed in love and Light a few hours earlier. How quickly could I lose my bearings?

I was tired of being misunderstood, tired of trying to speak a language I didn't know. Conversations between foreigners were stilted—just enough to meet my needs, *"Quiero, tengo, por favor..."* *I want, I have, please..."* and if I couldn't sign or speak English, I moved on. My energy to communicate was spent, so I gave up. I was over it. If I couldn't commune with the ascended realm, I wanted to be home where I belonged, with Jim, where needing to know something was not a matter of survival.

Heightened Frequencies

My trip to town was a sobering reminder that my time in the celestial realms while residing on earth would be fleeting. I was adjusting to the heightened frequencies surging through my body. Candido's vibration was too discordant for me to easily shift my consciousness. I was relieved to return to my little Lighthouse quarters where I nestled in my sleeping bag, the radiator on high.

Finally, my body warmed up. The thought crossed my mind that my excessive use of heat would cost Desorio his profit, but after too many days of layering and bundling I chose not to deny myself this small luxury.

I passed my time journaling. Already the names and places and challenges that seemed so recent and acutely real were drifting away. My journal would be my only record of my steps out of darkness and into Light.

Finite experience would dissolve into the non-reality it was, and all that would remain would be Truth and the Reality of God.

The rest would be forgotten. I was memorializing this finite experience in two-sided tape, fountain pens, ink, paper, and paste. My ink cartridge was half-full. *Which would run dry first—me or the pen?*

Miracle Moments

It was a little after five and the twilight sky had shifted to a smoky gray. The hours between Spain and California spanned my day's end and Jim's day's beginning. This had become our time to talk when I found myself in a room for the night with a landline.

We were enjoying a leisurely chat, no thought of minutes and dollars and poor connections entered our minds. As I savored the soothing sound of his voice, a knock on the door interrupted our call. I ended the call, our goodbyes abrupt, and greeted Zanetha, the young woman who tended the *café*.

On our first meeting, Zanetha and I discovered that our respective language fell short, so we communicated with our eyes, our smiles, and our gesturing hands. With a flurry of arms and stilted words, she managed to tell me that an *el hombre* in the *café* would like to meet me. *El hombre,* a man? But who? She pointed to *Monte Facho* through the barred windows.

Monte Facho, yes! The special place on the mountain. How did she know I was interested in the mountain when I could barely order *"café con leche, por favor?"* Much to my happy surprise, Zanetha intuitively knew I was here for Spirit, not tourism. *Yes, the miracle field was wide open.* It is impossible to conceive in our limited human awareness, but it was clear that everything was being choreographed by God's Presence.

Each of us plays a unique role in the Divine Plan unfolding, and when those pieces come together, this is when God becomes real.

This was Zanetha's part, connecting me to *el hombre.* What followed next gave me no doubt that everything, *everything,* is divinely guided. My years of searching and seeking, my trials and initiations, the dying to my social identity, the freeing from my ancestral lineage, the piercing of my heart—closing, breaking, opening—and now walking the *Camino* through Portugal and Spain to the sacred mysteries at *Cabo da Fisterra.* All this led to this one reunion. *El hombre* José and me.

Meeting José

Before departing, I had encouraged myself to be open to the unexpected and willing to explore places not marked on the *Camino's* map. *Be open to meeting someone.* These liberties fortified my certainty that I was not a pilgrim in the traditional sense; my way was different, and not to be influenced by history or the way of other pilgrims. This continually challenged me and I found myself in constant comparison, first with Vittorio and Donatella, and then with others.

Like me, the man I was about to meet, knowingly or unknowing, was also spiritually guided to our meeting. Our meeting was the synchronicity of Law and Light coming together in holiness on earth. How he was told or who and what to look for I will never know, nor does it matter. José found me and I found him. That simple. And we both held keys to the divine plan.

Hastily, I grabbed my raingear and headed downstairs to the *café*. Zanetha was back tending bar for a boisterous crowd stacked three-deep. Our eyes connected and revealed all we needed to share—no words required. She had done her part connecting José and me in a mystical and supernatural way, and I showed my gratitude.

When I entered, I was drawn to a handsome, middle-aged Spaniard standing at the bar drinking an espresso. Slight in stature and impeccably groomed in a casual, approachable way, he emanated a quiet, assured demeanor. His silver hair was freshly cut, every strand in place. His small mustache was trimmed short and blended well with his clear, olive skin. I deemed him a healthy sort, physically fit under his blue jeans, sky-blue windbreaker, and sturdy brown leather shoes—all this in spite of the fact that he smoked. But I had grown more accustomed to the fact that many Europeans enjoyed tobacco. He didn't use cologne to mask it, either. Tobacco *was* his cologne.

His name was José. I don't believe I ever caught his surname. It didn't seem important then. Now, as I write this, I wish knew it.

Depth of Spirit

A gentle Galician with a regal air and the visage of Peace—this was José. Yet nothing outward about him revealed the depth of his Spirit. He walked the earth as José. But in his God Presence, he was certainly something more, something other. Of this I was certain.

Born and raised in *Finisterre*, José grew up surrounded by these holy treasures and he guarded this sacred land with mystical reverence. He came to the Cape every day to walk in prayer. "It is my place of tranquility," he explained. I don't know how we communicated; his English was spare and so was my Spanish. Yet we found a deep coherent understanding.

Early on, I would welcome each new encounter with openness, unaware of any subsequent danger I invited. Unwittingly, I had stepped into harm's way. I learned not to foolishly trust that everything was a spiritual sign. So my reserve wouldn't allow me to fully trust José, but intuitively I felt a connection and safeness with him. I had managed this far without experiencing actual harm; however, this time I would not be so quick to jump at Spirit's call.

Yet, we both knew we were being guided by God in that moment.

"How do you know me?" I asked.

"I just know."

"Yes," I responded, with the same knowing.

And with that, I returned to my room to slip on my rain gear and hiking boots, making ready for my second excursion up the steep and slippery slopes of *Monte Facho*.

José led me down the walkway to his car. We paused at a yellow arrow painted on a roadside signpost. *"Este es primero,"* he said, pointing to it. "This is the first yellow marker on the *Camino Santiago*. It is marked 0.0 kilometers. *Este es la comenzar y terminar."*

"The beginning and the end," I answered in translation.

"I will show you places that are holy and sacred. They are not for everyone to see. You will not find them yourself, so I will take you by car to *Piedras Santas*."

I'd already discovered I was no match for the elements. This thought made me laugh a little, thinking of so many rainy days. And then, to find the hidden pathway on my own, that would certainly be futile. José could be the one to show me the way. And yet—I halted before entering his car. *El hombre,* this man I didn't know, on an unfamiliar mountain road, in challenging weather. An uneasy twinge rushed though me. *I feel safer on foot than restrained in a car—confined.*

Then I shook off that thought, mumbled a quick prayer to Archangel Michael, stepped in, buckled up, and let go of my fear.

Unspoken Communication

José's car was impeccably clean. A sign! A good one, I decided. The smell of cigarettes was countered by pine tree air freshener. By European standards, his new car gave a hint of social status. Yet his air of humility balanced any perceived nobility. It did not escape me that he selected New Age music rather than Spanish radio. The primal beat and chanting invigorated me, and blissfully the words were in English. I smiled. He smiled. I began to respect this holy man and, in our unspoken communication, I let him know I could truly see him, *see* him.

At first, José only spoke when I spoke. He seemed comfortable in silence. No chatter. I settled into my seat, with only the low sounds of the radio and the hum of the engine propelling us up the road. When he finally did speak, his words came out slowly, allowing me to insert my English word next to his Spanish. In this way, we both managed to learn a bit of each other's tongue. Back and forth we bantered in this bilingual way—the first time I'd experienced real communication in a foreign language.

Before long, I learned he had a twenty-eight-year old *hijo,* which I mistook for grandson until I realized it was his *son,* nearly the same age as Jimmy, our son. Perhaps I'd offended him by assuming he was older than his age, but he gave no such clue, only smiling lightly when I told him about my *hijo* Jimmy back home. I learned he was divorced. When he shared this, a hint of sadness clouded over him. Whether it was from religious guilt or the genuine feeling of loss, I couldn't tell. As a man of Spirit, though, I guessed the latter had tendered his tone. These days, he cared for his mother and spent time in the tranquility of the Cape. The gentle easiness of his life was enviable.

After our brief initial exchange, we drove in silence. We came to the place where the road had been previously washed out. The puddles that had made my hike on foot impossible had become passable by car. The Pleiadian symbols had long since been washed away, meant only for my eyes in that earlier moment. Then another messenger appeared—a Harrier hawk. A hawk! He flew overhead and landed on an electrical wire that hovered over the road. A second Harrier joined him, and they began to dance on the tight wire.

"Look at them." I pointed to the great birds. But then I second-guessed my intuition and their message. *Was I clear? What are the hawks telling me? Go forward? Beware?* I sat back in my seat, opening to my intuition, and putting the symbols together: electrical wire and hawks, electrical wire and hawks. *They are showing me grounding power. Yes. Grounding.* Their coming in a pair revealed the harmonizing power of masculine and feminine joining heaven and earth.

**I journeyed on in confidence,
certain that the Ascended Masters had a
hand in bringing José and me together.**

There was still a large puddle, a small pond really, covering the low spot on the road. "Do you think we can make it through?" I was surprised by my shrill tone, the alarm bursting out of my mouth fast. But José didn't flinch and smoothly drove through it.

"*Si,* I've done this before." He gave a small laugh. "Every day I come here. I know this road. There is no problem. *Tambien,* okay."

Of course, he was right, and we were on his turf. I sat back and let go a little more. Shortly after, we arrived at the three boulders that had caught my attention before—the henge that could only have been positioned by supernatural means.

"Stop! *Por favor,* we must stop here!"

I must have sounded demanding, but I knew we had to stop. "Can you show me the way to the top?" I turned to him and smiled. He parked fast, pulling along the shoulder of the road. We bolted from the car and clamored up to the boulders, with José speeding way ahead.

"*Venga,* come, come," he called out into the cold wind. He then reached back, offering me a helping hand. He tried coaxing me farther, but I held back in the safety that my sure-footed-ness would allow. José was a pro, accustomed to this place, these stones. He scrambled back down, quickly, and grabbed my hand to help me breach the space between trust and the boulders. My experience with Franco surfaced, cautioning me about accepting too much assistance.

"Come. Don't worry," he said in English. "It's okay." And something told me that it was, that his intentions were of the highest order. And so I accepted his hand. It felt warm and comfortable, like a friend.

The wind whipped up around us. But no rain. It was a clear wind, buoyant and fresh, a wind that rejuvenates. It slapped at my face, waking me up. The exhilaration moved through me like an electrical current. But it wore me down quickly, too.

José soon sensed I'd had enough and motioned me back down through the boulders and to his car. He blasted the heater, the warm air pushing through the vents, soothing to my hands. Before long, we were rumbling up a winding, narrow road. Spiraling upward, he pointed the car toward the peak of *Monte Facho*. The end of the road. We had arrived.

Chapter 35

One the holiest and most revered places of the ancient world—*Ara Solis.* This holy place beckoned believers to eternity and enlightenment beyond the perennial Light of the Sun. Belief held that it was the closest point to the melding of two worlds—finite and infinite.

Since prehistoric times, people had come to *Ara Solis* to worship the Great Force beyond human understanding—a place of sacred worship to a transcendent power. The *Piedras Santas,* located at *Ara Solis,* were the natural altars where these two worlds met. For this reason, countless Roman legionnaires made a final journey to this chosen site to end their earthly lives.

José stood before it as I came up from behind.

"Piedras Santas," José announced. *"Piedras Santas."*

We stood at the precipice, the wind still whipping. The sheer drop from mountaintop to sea bottom was steep, plunging down, down, down. The awesome gap made me sway. One misstep and I could have easily tumbled to my demise.

I looked to José. He only nodded, and then he

pointed to three groupings of immense boulders that appeared strategically placed.

"Stop, *ahora*," José instructed. In his half-gesture half-speaking way, he went on to explain. "Think of an intention. When you reach the *Piedras Santas*, you state your intended desire. Then I will show you what next."

I took a few moments and dove deep into my heart for my innermost desire. I knew there were many ways to say what is all the same. And there was but one desire: To be with God, to be Home, to be Peace, to be Love. I anchored the word Peace in my consciousness for I knew when I arrived at *Piedras Santas,* all ability to remember could very well allude me.

I held still in a state of Oneness, no thought. Forgetting these were stargates where heaven meets Earth, my destiny and purpose eluded me.

I forgot that I was Shima; I let go of all identity with the world. In the dance of being in my God Presence, I simply AM.

Grace and gratitude overwhelmed me. *"Gracias José, gracias, gracias, gracias!"* I called into the wind, repeating *"gracias, gracias." If I only could share in words what my heart and soul are bursting to reveal.*

Alone in my thoughts, I moved in and out of dimensions. I didn't know if it had been seconds or minutes until I heard José calling out, *"Ahora,* now let us walk." A jolt moved through me, I looked to him, his hand out, motioning me forward. For a short while, I had left my body.

Sacred Portals

José led the way, walking fast ahead of me. I followed, my eyes on his back so I couldn't gauge his reaction to the impact this sacred place was having on me. At one point, my mind took over and asked, "Should I map the landmarks and directions and establish my bearings if I am ever to find this place again?" And then I let the thought go. *There is no future in the present. I cannot predict if I will ever be called here again.* So I let it go.

Only in this moment had the Universe chosen to reveal her secrets to me.

If it weren't for the Holy Spirit, these sacred portals would be hidden. Clearly, no one could find the way to these places unless they were guided.

With eyes to see and filled with Grace, these mammoth stones stood ready to unveil their mystical powers to me.

After arriving at *Piedras Santas,* José circled around the cliff-side and moved high above the water's edge below. Inching my way along, trepidatious and timid, I fell behind.

"Aqui," he called out, his voice fighting the sound of the wind. And then he pointed to one boulder.

"Aqui! Here," he said it again. And there it stood,

the rough granite surface that bore the worn mark shaped in a cross six inches by six inches. It was polished and pink in contrast to the course gray granite.

"*Este es mas cinco mil anos.* Five thousand years. *Peregrinos* have come for thousands of years to ask and receive holy gifts from the divine. After their prayers are offered, the pilgrims sign the cross on the stone."

The ancient ceremony had worn this granite giant smooth. José marked the cross with his finger and guided me to do the same. My fingers dropped into the groove, the smooth granite cool and vibrant to the touch.

I remember a similar tradition at *Catedral Santiago.* Through the ages at *Portico da Glori,* the Entrance of Glory, millions of *peregrinos* placed their hands on the solid marble entryway to mark gratitude for their safe arrival. Their fingers had worn through the solid rock leaving indelible holes. *How similar.* I realized my ceremony here at *Piedras Santas,* and the one I passed over at *Santiago,* were the same. It was the same mark on stone, the same intention of gratitude.

**One ceremony in nature, the other
in a church, one pilgrim's way or another's.
All is One.**

My Wish – *Desear*

"Ahora, es tiempo a desear, to wish." José guided my hand to rest at a certain place on the boulder. "Now," he instructed, "move the rock, two times. Ask for what you wish for, and it will come to be." I followed his instructions, repeating my mantra of God and Love and Peace.

Then the boulder began to sway. Back and forth, it rocked.

I guessed it to be easily ten tons, the size of a car, yet there I was, with one fingertip rocking it back and forth, this ancient giant! I moved my hand a few inches to the right. And the boulder held firm; it would not budge.

"Ah!" I looked to José, both of us nodding with excitement over this marvel. I experimented moving back and forth, here and there. But no doubt there was only one spot, one exact spot where Spirit would reveal its enchantment. In this exactness, this impeccability, I found God. My heart expanded in love.

**Yes, I am transcendent. I am complete.
I am whole. Home.**

From atop this mountain I experienced past, present, and future—California and Spain. All time and space had become one, converging and collapsing into each other.

To the Two-Sided Mountaintop

After *Piedras Santas,* memories of the day began to fog, my recollection sketchy. I knew we were no longer on the hidden pathway and back in view of the familiar yellow arrows. I strode along behind on the dirt road.

I had come to trust José and dutifully followed his lead as we traveled from spot to spot in and out of the car to the top of *Monte De San Guillerme.* The pinnacle of this mountain was two-sided. Far below, it was bordered by the sea and, that day, matted in clouds and framed by a slate sky. Beyond it, I could see the picturesque red tile roofs of *Finisterre.* Water lapped both shores, the inner sea nestling up to the sandy beach and the outer Atlantic frosted with whitecaps. The village separated the tranquil from the tempest.

On the Atlantic side, a tiny fishing boat tossed back and forth in the rough waters. Even so far away, I could feel the waves' stormy turbulence.

"Pequena barca," José said, interrupting my thoughts. "It is normal for these fishermen," he explained. *"Toda dia, toda dia."* As if he knew what I'd been thinking.

"Ahora vamanos a Ermita de San Guillermo." Now we will go to the hermitage of Saint William.

"Si, yes, yes, *si."*

We set out toward the hermitage, walking briskly through the forest. I marveled at the tall pines, similar to California's Torrey Pines. It gave me a sense of familiarity and warmth as they immediately transported me home. The feeling of moving through time and space and dimensions was becoming so natural, I hardly gave it a second thought.

Ermita de San Guillermo, which is mentioned in the tourist guidebooks, can be easily accessed by foot or car. Because of its alignment to *Ara Solis* with its sacred natural landmarks, it was also the place missionaries chose to preach in their efforts to convert pagans to Christianity. The hermitage of Saint William dated back to the 5th century. Christian lore noted this location was specifically chosen by Saint William for the multitude of people who came here to worship Spirit—a transcendent power beyond human understanding. For this reason, it was a potent and perfect vantage to discredit pagan beliefs.

I have no doubt it was with honorable intention that Saint James, Saint William, and others chose this place to convert the pagans; yet I could not help but feel that the missionaries' zeal—in their attempts at conversion fueled by their fear that the moral fabric of ignorant souls be torn by paganism—only created judgment and a deepening separation. This was a place at the opposite end of the spectrum from *Ara Solis* and *Piedras Santas.*

Sun's First Rays

We clambered around a giant boulder and came upon what looked like the back wall of a cave. It faced due east—well planned, I thought—to receive the illuminating sun's first rays. It was protected from the westerly winds ripping across the headland.

Off to one side and in front of the cave's entrance was a six-foot rectangular stone resting two feet above the ground. It was carved smooth in the undeniable form of head and torso. Saint William's bed. (By the size of it, William was a small man.) Another smooth oval carved stone served as his washbasin. With all the rain, it was filled to the brim. Wilted spring flowers collected from the hillside had been left as offerings on a makeshift altar along with pinecones, feathers, and rocks—evidence of the many Pilgrims and tourists who had come before us.

José stood alongside me as I pondered the illogical layout of the house. *Why would the bedroom be out in the open air away from the protection of the cave?* He could no longer stifle his amusement. He pointed to three square carvings in the rock overhang, remnants of where the roof had been attached long ago.

"Oh, I see, yes. The roof!" I looked toward the space where it once was. Now in its entirety, I could easily see how it once was a lovely home—the inner cave opening to the outer living area covered by a canopy of thatch and carpeted in pine needles. *"Ahora,* alas," he said, "only families of rabbits live here, *los cuneros."*

"No Beso!"

I moved to the bluff and sat next to José while he smoked. The fresh air and wind carried away the smoke with my thoughts. He paused and snubbed out his cigarette. I looked to the earth at my feet, dank and moist from so much rain. Above me, I saw a small break in the clouds, a patch of blue showing through. And then before I knew it, I felt Joses body closing in as he turned and kissed me.

A kiss.

"No beso!" My body jolted back.

He pulled away, too, respecting my feelings. I stood, pretending to brush the mud from my pants and then excused *him*, sensing that a misunderstanding had arisen from the joy of being in such a sacred space.

**Sometimes, feelings of spiritual ecstasy
and carnal desire become confused.
Overwhelmed in the bliss of Oneness,
he must have misunderstood.**

While I accepted José's misguided feelings (for my own safety), I still chose to take measures to fend him off. Whenever I could feel him moving from his Higher Self into his ego, I created the obvious boundary that respectful men do not cross—coveting another man's wife. I spoke of Jim and God and honor. And behind my shield of noble words, I felt safe.

I felt a mutual respect between José and me, but still at the forefront of my thoughts was caution. *Alone with this man in the countryside and in a foreign country.* I wished I could let go of these feelings of anxiety and settle into the comfort of Jose's presence as I had with Dr. Nic. But his attraction to me was there—unmistakable. With Nic, I felt no sexual tension, just a bonding of two souls reuniting. Sadly, Franco and those of less integrity had shuttered my open heart.

Then the rain hissed down demanding we leave. The energy shifted and so had the elements. The wind whipped us, biting and harsh. And I was no match for the descended energy of the hermitage.

Chief Joseph and José

We returned by way of the washed-out road. The Pleiadian symbols were completely erased. They were meant just for me this morning. Next to the washout were stone ruins, remnants of a house.

"Que es este?" I asked. "What is this?"

"Está casa es la casa primero, the S-O-S," José said. "The family living here would signal warnings to the ships at sea."

On a downhill route with switchbacks and steep ravines, he drove with expertise as we barreled back to the Lighthouse. But we weren't finished. He walked me to a few of the obvious tourist sites, the ones I had discovered on my own, including the bronze boot and the Peace Pole. Next, we wandered around to the back of the Lighthouse marked off to tourists but not to José. This was his boundless backyard. We stood in the elements at the cliff's edge staring to the bottom of the sea. It was ominous, steep. The wind howled as I stood close to the edge, too close for comfort, even with José's arm around my waist. I had already learned that my weight could easily take us both down in an unbalanced moment.

I begged off and asked to return from the deserted cliffside. We hiked back to the sidewalk where the tourists were parading up and down the avenue. And then in one of the most significant moments of my pilgrimage—I came full circle—Chief Joseph.

José halted midway on the sidewalk, causing the steady flow of tourists to ebb around us. Puzzled, I looked toward him to gain understanding, but we couldn't hear each other over the roar of the wind and chatter. Instead, his hand gestures directed me.

In truth, no words were necessary.

He pointed to a gap between the cement sidewalk, the gap where the grass and weeds grew. He motioned for me to line up my toes along the border. I complied. Then he took my chin in his hands and raised it—just so.

He stepped back.

I stood still as a statue, not sure what I was to do or what he was showing me. I stood frozen in place and set my sights straight ahead.

And on the face of the rock wall . . . There was Chief

Joseph staring back at me eye to eye. Chief Joseph. There he was. Plain as day.

So many times on this journey, I'd felt overcome with awe, causing my tears to flow uncontrollably. So again. Amid the throng of tourists, there was only me and Chief Joseph—transcendent.

I was moved in a whoosh of emotion
to a time eternal, a time beyond time,
and the space of no beginning or end.

I stood in a place I had forgotten, the place of Home. Still in the present but observing the past, I had the other-worldly experience of remotely viewing life *before* me: Shima, *before* my *Camino* when the untruth of duality kept me chained to my human self, *before* I learned that being unlovable was a lie, the untruth which forced me to believe me unworthy. And now this, my realization and resurrection into the fullness of my Christ consciousness.

On the *Camino* I walked with Spiritual Masters who guided, protected, and, yes, challenged me.

I asked for guidance to lay down the illusion
of my social identity and ego personality.
I asked to be shown the doorway to Oneness.

I was tested to surrender all I thought was *me* but really never had been me at all. The *Camino* challenged me to see the *all* of me, inspiring me to view my wholeness with divine eyes. Each step unbound, untangled, and dismembered—all the self-created littleness I had created lifetime after lifetime.

Three weeks and hundreds of kilometers led to this moment. With Chief Joseph and José as my witness, I had come Home.

Chapter 36

I pulled myself back to the present and tried explaining to José my relationship with Chief Joseph, their similar names, José and Joseph. I wanted to tell him about the Stargate Pilgrimage through Oregon and Idaho and Montana and the similar rock outcroppings that we had discovered on Chief Joseph's trail. But none of this was necessary.

José knew.

All the same, he patiently listened as my words gushed out between floods of emotion in the jumbled language of English, Spanish, and Spirit.

I walked the pathway of Mother Earth to the immortal Light of the Milky Way. Its stars beckoned me, and I followed their direction. The stones underfoot cried out—the same stones still warm from the footprints of Jesus and James and William and the holy women before me. They invited me to walk the Way of Peace, in harmony and love with divine Truth—the immortal Truth that's inviolate from age, reason, or perspective.

In the end, I discovered every one of my pilgrimages, regardless of continent or country, was the same pathway showing me how to *be* a divine human being. There is only One Way and it is eternal. I was complete. My destiny fulfilled. Journey OM.

José left me with this suggestion: "Perhaps tomorrow we will meet again and I will show you *Muxia.*" He paused. "In the sunshine." He smiled.

"Perhaps," I offered back as we waved our goodbyes.

But we never met again.

Expanded!

When I returned to my room, the space was too small to contain me—my field of energy had so expanded. I opened the door and windows. Restlessness took over. Time was on the short side. Less than three days to home, but I knew I must be careful not to rush ahead of myself. If I tried pushing time, it would only push back. The feeling of not being with my beloved Jim could easily take me into the whorls of sadness, so I sank into where I was—in the "now" of another blustery night on the Cape.

I sought a place of normal, but how could anything ever be normal again? I couldn't even sit. Unsure of what to do, I paced. I fathomed. *What has just happened?* Everything was quickly becoming dreamlike, surreal, and beyond my ability to grasp. I couldn't think about anything else yet it was beyond my comprehension. Meditating wasn't an option; I'd been alone with my thoughts for far too long. I did my best to ground myself by organizing my room, my toiletries, and my backpack. I tried to write in my journal but couldn't. *Where would I begin?*

Finally, I remembered food. Food! I was famished. And food would certainly ground me. So I prepared for dinner as if going on a date with my new self. I took time to dress *up* by donning my cashmere shawl. I carefully applied lip-gloss and escorted myself down the stairs to the restaurant.

Dinner Date

The dining room was small, like all things at *O' Semaforo*, with five tables impeccably dressed in white linen. Since my arrival to *Finisterre*, my meals had consisted of *naranjas, café con leche*, snacks, and apple pie. The last real sit-down meal was Saturday in *Pontevedra*, which seemed like a lifetime ago. This night, I would be served a meal at a table with linen, silver, and china. Perfection.

I was excited about this date with myself. It was too early by Spanish custom for dinner—only six o'clock—but Desorio opened early to accommodate foreigners like me who were more accustomed to bedtime at ten than late-night dining. On this evening, the dining room was empty. Alone with only my thoughts, I let go a deep sigh. The place offered menus, but they were only props. Desorio informed me he would be serving me the plate of the day and I would like it. *Ah! Having no choice to make feels like a relief.*

Smart enough to tell by his tone, I knew this was not the time to request a vegetarian meal. He poured my sparkling water, and I savored it as if it were the finest champagne. Catching my mood, Desorio had taken on the demeanor of a seasoned waiter, serving me with professional formality. There was no place for chit-chat with this waiter: Serve and be served.

The first course was an appetizer of small green peppers stuffed with white rice covered in a red sauce (what we in America recognize as Campbell's Tomato Soup). The second course was Hake, a local fish caught fresh that morning. Desorio was correct. The fresh, flaky, and delicate texture of the fish melted in my mouth. I loved it.

Found Home

For a second night, I was set to sleep atop the celestial pathway to the Milky Way. But this night would be different. The energy of it would not shock my system for I knew where I was going. I had found the way Home.

The next morning, I again felt quarantined in the confines of my quarters, so despite the unwelcome weather, I bundled up and walked in the only direction possible, down the hill. I had reached the end of land, no longer the end of the known world, but still, I had no destination. I walked simply to walk.

I noticed a cement cross more than six feet high along the roadside, invisible to me on my many treks back and forth before. *How did I miss it until now?* But there it was like a sentry along the road. *Does it represent the same custom as in the States, memorializing fatalities?* Yet this cross was much grander than the tiny memorials at home.

The invisible power of the Church loomed large. An electrical tower had been built around the monument; its steel gridiron caged the cross. These two unlikely companions drew me into symbolism and meaning. My pilgrimage had taught me this: *Nothing is as it appears.* Every circumstance holds layers of meaning and hidden messages. And this was the message the tower and cross conveyed to me.

Followers of a religion or belief system can become caged by dogma and lose their freedom that God intends.

Those who rigidly followed doctrine, without allowing and accepting their own inner guidance can easily become limited by others' beliefs.

Simple Realizations

The Church teaches that the way of the cross is suffering; the crucifixion represents sacrifice, either for the sake of salvation and redemption or for getting closer to God. *Is this what Jesus was truly trying to demonstrate? I think not.*

I no longer believed suffering was God's way. Rather, it's a misguided method to keep loyal followers imprisoned in a mentality that prevented the real God virtues of freedom, joy, peace, happiness, and bliss to enter their lives. Just my thought.

As I continued walking, another simple realization entered my thoughts. I noticed after spending time with José that I wasn't inhibited by the language barrier anymore, and I had intuitively stopped greeting passersby with *"Hola, buenas dias."* ("Hello, good day.") Instead, I was simply thinking of acknowledging them. It wasn't a conscious decision, just a letting go of trying to speak a language I couldn't, which opened communication into a realm of higher consciousness. We simply understood each other in the language of Universal-Speak—a smile.

Life just became a great deal simpler.

Market Scents

I was charmed by my newfound understanding as I stepped out of the downpour and into the *supermercado*. The rain had caught me off guard yet again. I shook off like a wet dog before entering.

Then like a child unattended in a candy store, I bee-lined to the produce, drawn by the loamy aroma of unwashed vegetables still sheathed in soil and precious fruit priced so high it sat ripening on the shelf too long. I'd been living on *café con leche, queso,* and *pan*. I tried to limit the bread, but it was the staple of the country, simple, cheap, and irresistible. Made fresh each morning, it was nothing like I'd ever eaten in the States. The earthy scent of alive and natural food filled my being. I took a moment to simply inhale.

Nothing in America could replicate the sensual mix of moldy cheese, hanging meats, overripe fruit, and musty root vegetables. Divine.

I chose one *manzana*—only one—because apples were heavy, and every ounce I carried made a difference. I found my place in line to pay and was offered the simple grace of going ahead of a wizened old woman. Unlike times before, her kind gesture did not add my tears to the puddles. I acknowledged her in Universal-Speak—I simply smiled. She had learned (and was teaching me) there is no hurry in life. Every moment counts, even standing in line.

On the *Camino*, every moment melted into the next, days slurred into weeks, time slowed. With my little understanding of the language and the culture, I had to learn even the simplest things as a child would. Every encounter required me to meet it head-on, eye-to-eye. I accepted every small favor as the greatest gift from God.

Everything was magnified and, in the moment of every experience, I thought I'd remember it for the rest of my life.

Practice Patience

Next, I made my way to the post office and joined the long, seemingly motionless line. It became an opportunity to practice what I had just received from the wizened one: patience. Postcards mailed, I walked a short ways to an internet *cafe*. I was tempted inside by thoughts of e-mail, television, and news, but it took no time to discern it wasn't the place for me.

Still, I ignored my intuition and entered the dark *cafe* where another lesson in enlightenment waited. I used the restroom and then felt obligated to pay for its use, so I ordered a *café con leche*. My stomach churned before my last sip. *I chose to ignore my well-being for the sake of another's expectation, the sake of appearances, and my feeling that I was beholden to the cafe owner for using his bathroom.* A paid-in-kind mindset surfaced from my subconscious. How long I'd held this untruth, I didn't know. I let it go. The lesson: Listen to my intuition and honor my body.

I could finally see how *every* innocuous experience gave me an opportunity to choose God, which meant choosing Self. Simply walking into a *cafe* and knowing to turn around without entanglement was a choice point. I had become a strong direct beam of Light on the *Camino*. I didn't cower by the scowls of the Spanish men or cast my pearls before them. I no longer cared what they thought of me, nor did I seek their approval. I had been gracious in every way, letting go of false notions of obligation and only exchange energy through the beneficial presence of my being.

Beholding to another was not choosing God.

Should I make the uphill climb back to the Lighthouse on foot? Rather than opting for a swift return by taxi, I bolstered myself with good reasons to walk. For weeks, it had been my main mode of transport, and I'd come to look forward to the rhythmic motion of body and soul. With this decision made, I stepped out and at once the wind ranted and the showers commenced. And then another realization—the force of the elements was Mother Gaia's way of clearing diverse energies accompanying the busloads to *Cabo da Fisterra*. The alchemy of wind and rain purified and protected Mother Earth's immaculate energy.

Desorio informed me that the *café* and restaurant were closed today, that I'd have to find a meal elsewhere. This bit of news discouraged me after anticipating warmth and food and shelter. I didn't know why the restaurant was closed; he gave no reason. It was just closed and that was the way of Desorio.

I smiled a hungry and dejected smile. *"Senor, por favor,* I can make do with *la naranja,* a piece of *pan,* a slice of *queso,* and *agua. Por favor,"* I proffered.

He knew I'd just made one trek on foot to town so he agreed to these rations. Later, he motioned me into the restaurant and served me salad and apple cake. He didn't join me in my meal, but I knew he had softened.

It was 4:22 a.m. on Thursday, May 3rd—my last hours in the Lighthouse. The draw toward going home kept sleep away. At 6:15 a.m., my alarm would sound and at 7:00 a.m., I would get ready for the final walk down the winding mountain road to *Finisterre*. I held on to the expectation of a dry, reverent walk to seal my journey, but it was slashed by a torrent of wind and rain. *Would I ever learn to let go of expectations, no matter how small?* I surrendered to the wind gnashing to gain entrance to my room and went to brush my teeth—that fresh clean feeling of Colgate wind or rain couldn't steal. Fresh breath felt good to me, bringing me even closer to God.

The Small Things

What I looked forward to at home were the small things. The thickness and softness of toilet paper, clothes washed in a machine and dryer instead of a bidet and towel rack. Starbucks. Windless, rainless silence. And the absence of faucets dripping. Inhaling fresh air absent of cigarette smoke. Speaking without thinking. *Being* without being vigilant. Raw food, alive food. Down pillows and comforters. Trusting again in the protection of my beloved Jim as I surrendered into his arms.

Simple things that made my life rich.

And the things I would cherish and honor from the *Camino?*

Those would come when time had softened the punches and sanded the edges. That's when I would remember the kindness of old women, the friendship of Dr. Nic, the appreciation of each country cobblestone painstakingly placed by hand, the similarities to San Diego kindled by bridges and blooming eucalyptus. Knowing—really knowing—rain and wind up close and personal. Learning the healing remedy for blisters. And mastering the skill of the backpacker's way: expert and organized and compact.

Peace in the Rain

In those final dark hours before dawn, the weather lashed out one last time—but it was only the last for *me*. This was the way of the *Cabo da Fisterra* and would remain constant long after my departure. The rain pounded, the wind howled, the windows rattled. Never—ever—ending. That was the way—at the end of the world they call *Finisterre*.

I was at peace in the rain knowing I had endured a journey orchestrated by the constant devotion of my Higher Self to open my heart. I saw home drawing close and, in that moment of completion, deep fatigue set in.

I railed at God, "I retire. I am done. Traveling to these places has wearied my bones. Take me from this journey and ask me to travel no more."

And just as I finished my entreaty, I caught myself.

"Thy Will is my will; my way is Thy Way—always. And so, if Thy Will is just that, for me to journey to foreign lands or wherever you guide me, then please, align mine with Thine and give me strength to journey on. Allow me Peace All Ways, Home All Ways wherever the next *Camino* or the next trail of Chief Joseph leads. Near or far, Thy Will Be Done."

Gratitude

At 5:12 a.m.—one hour and three minutes until my alarm would ring—I had one more thing to do.

> *Dear José,*
> *I trust our difference in language will not bar you from receiving this note of appreciation and my gratitude for the kindness you have shown me. You are a very noble and honorable and holy man, and I am privileged to have met you. I am not a "peregrino" in the traditional sense. I do not follow the way of Saint James. I follow the way of the stars, the Compostela, the Milky Way, and the path of God to home. You showed me this way on Monte Facho. For this kindness, I will hold you forever in my soul.*
>
> *Before I departed on this journey, I was told by my guides I would meet someone who would show me the hidden pathway. You are that holy man who protects this sacred pathway and the Wisdom it holds. I thank you. Gracias.*

In America, I have connected with Chief Joseph, the Chief of Peace, who lived in 1877. When you showed me the Indian in the rock face, I knew my connection to Cabo da Fisterra was destiny. Profound destiny. And so, I have walked hundreds of kilometers to arrive at this one time and place with you. José. Joseph. Thank you for being my guide.

May God always be within you, before you, and behind you. May the stars light your way and the wind clear your path. I wish you Peace All Ways.

Your friend, Shima

I made my way down the dark circular staircase for the last time to say good-bye to Desorio and ask him to messenger my letter to José. It was still hours away from sunrise and everything was dark inside and out. I found Desorio in the corner of his office, illuminated by his laptop. The light was enough for me to see his eyes dart back and forth from his computer to me. He was thinking—weighing the unreasonableness of my having to walk in the dark and pouring rain—rather than (the nuisance) of giving me a ride. He knew there were no taxis to call at this hour.

As I handed him my letter meant for José, the protective shell surrounding his heart broke open. In our last moments, he softened with kindness, even a smile. And we headed to his car together.

Chapter 37

It was a short wait before the bus arrived—just time enough to let the anxiety of travel take hold. A young woman in her early twenties shared the bus stop with me and two older women.

"Por favor, está el autobus a Coruna?" ("Please, is this the bus to Coruna?") The younger woman seemed to have no patience to answer such a foolish question, but her silent thoughts spoke loudly enough. "Why would we be here at this early hour, away from the warmth of our bed in this dreadful weather if it wasn't the bus stop?"

She dismissed me with a cough and a turn of her shoulder. Then one of the older women stepped in and assured me, *"Ah sí, el autobus a Coruna."* ("Yes, it's the bus to Coruna.")

In my journey, I realized, I had gone from steps to legs. The next bus would take me to *Coruna*—the first of the many legs in the *last* leg of my journey home. Time and distance slowed by the *Camino* had rapidly accelerated fueling my exuberance. But my future-thinking enthusiasm was short-lived, and I found myself once again subdued when I stepped on the bus.

The smell of all things *bus* smacked me—a stench years in the making, the kind that permeates every pore—a stale air concoction of diesel, cigarettes, body odor masked by overused cheap perfume, and Pine-Sol. I found a seat, gripped its metal bars, and looked forward to when I could breathe deeply again. For the time being, my lungs refused to inhale the smoke, diesel, and years of grime and grit. I didn't know what was worse: the smoke or the toxic concoction.

A Younger Version to Respect

The young woman I spoke to at the bus stop sat down in the seat in front of me. She coughed and coughed and coughed—that hangover cough—again, the kind of cough known only by one who has been there. It was the cough of staying up too late, emptying the bottle of wine, and smoking one too many cigarettes. Her friends were likely still lying in their beds while she braved the brutal morning bus ride each morning. Her nights out weren't filled with joy and laughter and celebration; they were nights of drowning. I could feel her pain as if it were my own. *Her life's story is indelibly written for those with eyes to see.*

And yet, I admired her. She was responsible. She got up with only a few hours' sleep and was on her way to a job; its duty keeping her from spiraling down further. *I know these things about her; I see a former self.*

I silently acknowledged this woman with compassion. I respected her greatly. She was not well and yet she was accountable to her job. I saw the sadness in her eyes that had become *her*. For some unknown reason (perhaps to give solace to a former aspect of me), I again asked the silly question, *"Está el autobus a Coruna?"*

This time she answered, acquiescing to our unspoken sisterhood.

Hypnotic Reverie

I stared out the window as we passed through village after village. The hypnotic rumble moved me into reverie, and I began to see through the eyes of my husband as a young man living in Portugal. I could picture him walking the narrow streets, past the ancient buildings on cold, dank days. The air smelled of smoke and poverty. I could see him trading his boyish smile for figs and oranges offered by a *Portuguese* mother—an old woman's simple act of kindness substituting for the absence of his own mother's love. *If Jim's love for this foreign country was so great, how much worse was it at home for him?*

On the Bus

It had been three hours since Desorio drove me down the winding Lighthouse road—my last good-bye to *O'Semaforo* and *Finisterre*. I saw the sun starting to rise. I only knew this from looking far into the distance where a thin line of blue sky hit the horizon. Overhead, it was still gray and cloudy.

Gray to blue—how symbolic of
where I had been to where I was going.
The blue sky was calling me home.

An old man boarded at the next roadside stop and
chose the seat in front of me. With that, my view
ahead was only his small, bald head with a few lone
hairs poking up from his wizened scalp. I turned to
look out the window, but his presence extended beyond sight. The smell of him told me his unseen story:

*It was a big undertaking for him to travel
to Santiago, the big city. Someone or
something more important than his daily
routine called for him to leave the comfort
of his old age. He had taken time, pains-
taking time, before his morning departure
to wipe away the day-before activities
with a lavish spray of his favorite cologne,
the one saved for special occasions. Still,
the cheap cologne mixed with the old-man
smell didn't conceal what couldn't
be washed away.*

I realized how different hygiene was in Spain than
back home, and I treasured my cleanness. The smell
of him *and* the bus made me eager to return. Yet the
stench went beyond annoying. I began to feel nau-
seous. It grabbed my gut and twisted it. The lurching
rumble along the winding road didn't help. I squirmed
amid these overwhelming sour odors, making it near-

ly impossible to catch a decent breath. I covered my face with my shawl, hoping my own seventeen-day Shima-scent mixed with wet cashmere would soothe my discomfort. *At least it smells familiar.*

Enduring this small misery, my thoughts turned to gratitude for the winds of *Cabo da Fisterra* that constantly cleared stale energies. *Better the scent of stale cologne than basura, garbage! Yes! It could always be worse!* With this fleeting thought, my nausea lifted. It took about forty-five minutes, but finally I was smart enough to make the move to another seat.

I didn't miss the symbolism in the lessons delivered on this bus ride. *Everything is a choice. I could choose to smell stale cologne or get up and move.*

The choices we make in minutiae sometimes make the greatest difference in the whole.

I reminded myself to be intent in the small choices, for therein lies the comfort.

Last Hours in Spain

Finally, I was through *Santiago* on my way to *Coruna.* This bus driver had a kinder heart than the previous one and kept the heat on high. I was relatively comfortable as I journeyed toward my last night in Spain.

Arriving in *Coruna*, I hailed a taxi to the Marriott, chosen for its signature American name. In less than twelve hours I'd be boarding the first of three airplanes—to Madrid, to Chicago, and to San Diego—the final legs on my journey home.

My pen had been capped for two days, for I had completed my journal and filed my last entry. Or so I thought. Another *ah ha* moment at the airport bookstore awaited me.

Here's how it happened. Before my transatlantic flight, I aimlessly wandered around the airport's concourse with a few euros left in my pocket. I paused from my meandering in front of a bookstore, which didn't appeal to me for the books and magazines—even American authors—were translated into Spanish. Off to the side, however, I noticed a small shelf with a slim variety of English titles. Here, God revealed Itself again.

In the beginning of this journey while walking with Dr. Nic, we would spend hours talking about our favorite authors. Both Nic and I loved Paulo Coelho, and our conversations would always lead back to quoting a memorable line in one of his books. Coelho's books had awakened both of us on many levels and resonated Spiritual Truth common to both our hearts and souls. Authors can do that—unite. They can teach, guide, and show the way by sharing an experience that speaks directly to us, their readers. Paulo Coelho had that kind of effect on Nic and me.

During my preparations, I read every book I could find on *Camino de Santiago de Compostela*. Coelho's *The Pilgrimage* was one of them. Like me, he was a soul journeyer, and his recounting of his spiritual awakening on the *Camino* was so similar to my spiritual journeys that, at times, I felt I was reading my own words. I don't remember the particulars, but I remembered embracing Paulo's exquisite essence. Plus I loved hearing Nic talk about this beautiful, spiritual author. Weeks later, lifetimes really, here I found Paulo Coelho among the handful of English titles.

Looking back, it was a simple moment, one of many synchronous ones, but this time, I grabbed Coelho's book to my heart as if it were the only copy left in the world. I paid for it with my last twenty euros and floated out of the store.

My journey had just affirmed this truth:
There is always more to be revealed.

My Fellow Travelers in Life

At the departure gate, I was keen to observe the other passengers traveling with me. A boisterous group of unruly, twenty-something Irish and British lads had taken over the aisle and consumed the communal energy, their loud laughing and too-big feet blocking easy passage. Because I missed hearing my English tongue, I eavesdropped on their conversations and was jolted into their reality—fraught with cussing and cursing and youthful brashness. *Be mindful what I wish for.*

I stepped away from that group and moved closer to a large family from Africa—eight in total from babies to elders—a family of all ages. All were dressed in finely woven, brightly colored fabrics, scarves, and shawls. Their feet were bound in foreign-bought, leather shoes, shiny and new, and so unlike their native dress; a requirement for travel, I guessed. *Surely they are more comfortable when their sandaled feet ground them to Mother Earth.*

I could feel their unease being encased in colorless glass, steel, and cement—*and shoes.* I imagined the sterile confines felt foreign to their colorful and natural culture, yet they remained perfectly poised, balanced in calm serenity, speaking softly to each other or not at all as they endured their unfamiliar surroundings. *What peace, in stark contrast to the boisterous lads.*

The elder matron held her prayer beads, so likewise I took my mala from my wrist and joined her in our soul sisterhood. And with each bead on my mala, one by one, the women I had met on my *Camino* appeared—the old woman who fed us oranges, purposeful Shea and and devoted Donatella; robust Renata, dutiful Zezenia and the Spanish grandmother so fearful of me walking alone—And now this grace-filled African matron. My tears gave way! *Ah, yes! Good to have met you and be in your presence!*

I had learned the meaning of Self-Love, and In Self-Love I found Peace, and In Peace I am One.

The words of Paulo Coelho's spiritual tome carried me home. I had walked the way of the Masters. Thus, in the stillness of my being, the message of my

Camino was revealed. This was the journey of my soul.
A Journey Home.
    The End
    JOURNEY OM

Reflections

Walking the Prayer

W as the *Camino* central to my ascension process? Was it necessary to dredge the depths of my physical stamina and go such distance to find God who resides within me? It certainly gave me the way to find out. And what I discovered I already knew: the one truth that had been so hard to accept—*Wherever God is I am, and wherever I am God is. I stand on holy ground wherever I may be.*

Back in San Diego, the emotional and physical pains lessened, replaced by periodic pangs of poignancy. My tears dried. The edgy anxiety, my constant companion that had wedged itself into every moment on the *Camino*, loosened. The reality of what happened receded into memory. Only a beautiful sadness lingered.

Walking the *Camino* ripped the fabric of my emotional body and unraveled the fiber of untruth that entangled me. It demanded I say *no* to the doubting mind and forced me to test my faith—not once— but over and again. Could I accept who I am and live forevermore in my God Presence—that place where there is no doubt, no pain? Could I accept the reality that I am perfect just as I am? In being lost, I learned to trust myself. Through blisters I persevered. Alone with myself, I found a loving companion, a kindred spirit.

We are all pilgrims. Life is our pilgrimage. Daily living is the unfolding of lessons to be learned along the way. Awareness is gained through experience until we are finally able to paint a yellow arrow for another and help point the way.

On the *Camino*, God spoke to me directly and indirectly. The *Camino's* sacred sites—some forgotten and forlorn, others gilded in gold—opened my eyes to see nature beneath and Spirit beyond the man-made shrines. Transcending my senses, I learned to fully *see* and *hear*; I tuned out life's demanding cries and in the silence I heard the rain whisper and wind squeal. God spoke to me: "*I* am with you. Wherever *I* am you are. *I* can never leave you, for *I* am you. You are home."

I returned empowered and enlightened. I was shown a passageway into the Interior Castle of which Saint Teresa de Avila spoke. I found my way home—yes, home to San Diego--and more. Truly Home wherever I may be. The doorway was opened fully. The Light would forever shine and I could not turn my eyes away from God's Love.

There was no going back. No need to retrace my steps.

If I Could Say to You

I think of the fellow pilgrims I met along the *Camino.*
And if I saw them again—this is what I would say:

Donatella

"Donatella, your yearning for the love of Saint Amma
will likely take you to her Sanctuary where you will
wait endless hours, perhaps even days, to receive her
special hug.

"Your love for Amma is a reflection of you. She
rekindles in your heart that which you are. It is not
necessary to go outside of yourself and stand in line
for what is already the beautiful and loving you—the
essence of the Divine Mother. Like me, Donatella,
you will discover this for yourself. The embrace you
so keenly seek from Amma is the same embrace your
husband and daughters seek from you. They too, will
wait hours, days, even lifetimes for *your* special hug. It
is all the same.

"This is the special gift of your *Camino*: The realization of your family's love, the realization of Self-
love, and the realization you already have what Amma
gives. In this we are alike.

"I admire you, Donatella, for your convictions,
your Pilgrim's way, and your strength of character to
follow your heart. That is the mother's way. Amma's
way. Your way. This is you, Donatella, and I am grateful I received your hug."

Dr. Nic

"And, you, Dr. Nicandro Castañeda. And the yoke—
a passage in the Bible that gives you permission to
follow your heart. You look for dogma to tell you
what you already know while your Spirit cries out
for freedom.

"I wonder . . . is the biblical interpretation of the
yoke misleading? Is there a different way to understand the yoke? Are we looking in the right places for
what our souls try to show us? Perhaps if loving partners are of the same belief, they could only follow side
by side in a straight line. Would that limit them to a
single dimension, to only one point of view? Would
that make their world small?

"What if the perfect balance of the yoke is the
opposite—the yin and yang, the masculine and feminine, the Light and dark? If joined in a marriage
of two individuals different and diverse from each
other, could they spiral to the realms of heaven together? I wonder."

And I remember you, Dr. Nic, sharing your fears
as you said to me, "If I rid myself of my devils, I'm
afraid my angels will flee as well."

In response, I tell you this: "Have no fear, Dr. Nic.
Face your devils. And your angels will Light the way."

Shima

And finally, I think of me—Shima. And I say, "I love
you, Shima. Welcome Home."

Home but Between Worlds

Before departing, I had dedicated my *Camino* to accept all and allow all—and resolved to never, ever judge. My mind, however, was not so willing to give up its judgmental role. Like the reverent monk alone in the silence of his sanctuary, who had seemingly mastered Peace, only to find when he stepped out in the world his peace dissolved in the chaos of the marketplace. I, too, was a master of allowance and acceptance as long as it aligned with my way. Stepping back into life as I knew it before the *Camino* would be my test.

**Mastery is determined by how quickly
Peace returns in the chaos of the marketplace.
Mastery is constancy.**

Days morphed into weeks. I was still between worlds and had not fully settled back into a routine at home. My heart had been shattered open. Every feeling and emotion was laid bare. My vulnerability embarrassed me, yet endeared Jim, and in a way it brought us closer as we learned to live in this new transparency.

I cried. Easily. It was the music—always the music—on the radio, on the popular singing competition *American Idol,* even on the background music playing in stores. Music reached inside me and wrenched the sobs from their hiding place. I did not try to stop it. I listened. Alone, I turned the volume on high and let loose. After so many weeks, I got so comfortable in my aloneness that it embarrassed me for anyone (even Jim) to see the depths of my heart.

Jim did his best to adjust to my new being, but I could tell even he was confused. In the back of his mind was always the uncertainty I may not return home. Or I would come back in such a different vibration that I'd be intolerable for him to be with. My absence was an opportunity for Jim's own personal inquiry. Was he willing to release and transmute any limiting beliefs? Could we both accept and allow a renewed vision of our sacred heart reunion? Could we celebrate a transformed life? Together?

Lightly at first, I shared my sensitivity and embarrassment with Jim, but he readily saw through me. He guided me, saying, "Stay silent. Remain soft. Let no one force your sword. Don't reach out. No need to return calls. Like waves, let feelings swell and withdraw. No need for you to go out."

Jim's words were few but deep. He was the wise one. I listened. It was all new to me.

I read and then re-read others' experience on their life-altering walks; Paulo Coelho's *The Pilgrimage*, Shirley MacLaine's *The Camino*, and Cheryl Strayed's *Wild*. I watched the movies *Into the Wild* and *The Way*, and I tried to connect in the only way one *can* truly understand another—by walking a similar path. They were me; I was them. And when I became One with their experience, I would admonish myself for daring to compare my lowly experience with their exalted passages. The more I begged to understand the meaning of my journey, the louder my Higher Self sounded to simply accept what was True: To no longer look outside of myself; to never seek the opinion of others for validation; to trust that what I had done was True.

Danger—Imagined or Real?

When I accepted the call to walk this path in search for Oneness and ascension, every pilgrimage I'd ever made in every lifetime surfaced. One upon another, they converged into a superimposed hologram of all my lifetimes.

Was I ever in danger? Were supposed threats real? Or, simply imagined? Yes, some people and the weather posed potential peril, but I could see and face *those* foes. It was the eerie feelings of energy devoid of God that threatened to cloud my consciousness. This caused me the most fear—fear that I couldn't fully grasp. Yet intuitively, I knew this energy was not there to *support* me but rather *thwart* me. Perhaps my greatest risk was my *unconsciousness*.

I was immensely grateful Archangel Michael was at my side as I traveled these unchartered dimensions until I could confidently discern Dark's deception and temptation.

On the *Camino,* I had the opportunity to see the illusion of sin. Most of my anxiety stemmed from lingering memories from this life and past lifetimes. Even though many memories had nothing to do with my life as Shima today, the experiences recalled were just as real. Experiencing danger, real or imagined, was the catalyst and an essential process for purging the false self and accepting enlightenment. I knew if I could *feel* the fear and stay with it, I could release it once and for all. In the terror of those moments, I accessed deep, deep wounds from other lifetimes. The echoes of ancient atrocities held me hostage and could have easily led to insanity. I held on to my idea of God even though I wasn't sure my idea of God was even real.

Yet, this is what I had asked for—Oneness with God and ascension—and these last dark nights were the passageway. I had lived many lifetimes for this time of revelation, to at last see Truth beyond the veil of illusion. Abuse and persecution, martyrdom and crucifixion, drowning, burning at the stake, and all of the suffering I felt necessary to become pure enough for God to love me was simply not Truth. Not Reality.

**By discovering what God is not,
God is revealed.**

I laugh to think I had naïvely believed I'd be anointed, "enlightened" with a crown and holy scepter, never considering that Mastery would require *feeling* the darkness, experiencing fire of obliteration of the false self, and letting go of every perceived comfort that was not God. Maybe that naiveté is what kept me on my path. To go into the heart of purity required single-minded focus and unyielding faith.

What if there was no God on the other side?
What if there was nothing?

Every pinnacle point I successfully reached required absolute faith—without question. Yet, before I could transcend the cliff of unknowing at the once-claimed "end of the world," I had to cross the slippery scree of my past. I knew that one misstep, one lapse in consciousness, and I would plummet from my ascent. To conquer darkness I walked in ignorance, unconscious of Reality, in separation and my own perception of hell— with this single focus—until I could see the Light.

This was my quest of Almighty God to do what
lifetimes could not do—face my self.
And the *Camino* made me do exactly that.

Step by Step in My Dreams

Details of my journey were fading fast. In the process of integrating my experience, I sensed I was losing recall.

When you become it and are it—
when you are just being—all separation
disappears, and without separation,
there is no individuality or identity. It just is.

After crossing so many time zones and dimensions, it was easy to slip into timelessness. To stay grounded, I recited the time and place every time I passed a clock like this: It's Saturday, May 5th at 2:03 a.m. in San Diego, California.

I am roused from my sleep with snippets from my journey. I resist fully waking. The down comforter molds to my body like a cloud and I am warmed by the radiant heat from Jim. But I know if I do not pen these divine messages, they will be lost. My Guides do not awaken me lightly and when a precious flow of words is ready to spill, I must rise. A writer learns to value this inspiration from within and above. So I get up, pull on my jeans slumped where they dropped the night before, and move from cocoon to keyboard. What was tickling me awake, just out of my grasp?

Slowly, excerpts from my dream surfaced—first, a wash of warmth, then rocking and swaying and moving. Everywhere Light. I feel it fill me up. The warmth floods hot, turning to sweat. I am vibrating. I awaken just enough to ask, *"Is this a dream or is this really happening?"* Then I intuit: "I'm adjusting to a new vibration, recalibrating into a new cellular matrix." I am conscious and I am not. If I try to think too hard, I will lose the little bit of awareness I have. I am in the space between awake and asleep but conscious enough to know I must surrender fully to receive these gifts offered to me.

My *Camino*—Walking to Remember

I walk in my dreams. This dream is no different than the others; I'm still walking. Every pilgrimage I have ever made in every lifetime is blending through, one on top of the other. And now the *Camino*. Step, step, and remember. Step, step and recall, cleansing and clearing lifetimes of missteps.

I Arrive—
   Getting off the plane in *Madrid* and navigating
      the massive, foreign *aeropuerto* buoyed by the
      uncertainty of travel.
   Taxiing to *Hotel Central Parque.*
   Learning the color-coded ways of the *Metro.*
   My initiation into rain. And more rain.
   Finding the *Catedral* and receiving my first
      Pilgrim's *credencial.*
   Stamp. Step.

I am Lost—
  In *Ponte de Conde* and okay with being "lost."
  Step. Retrace. Step again.
  Blessings for my journey at *Megalitco do Fulom.*
  Silence. No cell phone. Cut off from Jim.
  Meeting Dr. Nicandro Castañeda. Food and
    friendship and open hearts.
  Step.
  Rain. Blisters. Tired. So tired yet enduring
    another blistered step.
  Sweet, sweet orange juice dripping down
    our chins.
  Barcelos, Hotel Borgeis, and a rained-on carnival.
  Step, step.
  Step, step, kilometer after kilometer.
  *My body is humming now. I am warming from
    the heat of vibration. I am dreaming and I am
    awake. The hum becomes a sway, step, step,
    rocking now, warmer, sweating, step, step.*

And I Shiver—
  In the enslaved castle *Casas dos Assentos.*
  Rest, no rest. Cold and conflict.
  I Meet—
  Pilgrims walking through my dreams.
  Klaus and Renata, Reverend Thomas and Shea,
    Donatella and Vittorio, Franco and Zezenia,
    Desorio, Zanetha, and José. Yes, José.
  And Dr. Nic.

And I Taste—
> The taste of love.
> *Queso* and *pan* and *sopa de legumes*. Oranges,
>   sweet, sweet *naranjas* fed by a Portuguese
>   mother.

And I Say Goodbye—
> *Ponte de Lima*. Nic. No words to say goodbye.
>   Perhaps we'll meet again.
> Step.

I am Alone—
> Alone—walking alone in the rain. I slog in aloneness.

I Yearn—
> For a kind word, a companion. Anything familiar.
> I step.

I Cannot Speak—
> A foreign tongue. A stilted language that isolates
>   and separates. *Donde, por favor, obrigado, que,*
>   *perdon—*
> Step.
> I resist. I accept. I surrender.
> Step.
> God's Will to carry on.
> Step.

I am Protected—
Saint Germain, Archangel Michael, Lord
Sananda, Pleiadians, companions and
protectors. Step, step.
The rhythmic stepping enters every cell, filling every
molecule, replacing what was with what is.
Light, lighter, step, step.

And I Cry—
Tears. Puddles of tears. Rain. Water. Wet.
Step, step.

And I Fear—
The meanness of life. *Arcade, Hotel Isape—*
cold and forlorn.
Stepping into doubt.
Surrendering. Allowing. Remembering.
Flashes, bits and pieces, random remembrances
slipping in and out of consciousness as I am
transformed. Old memories erased, replaced with
awareness I can barely grasp.
I am pulled to consciousness.

And I am Loved—
Jim—my link. I call. He answers. He takes me in
his etheric arms and keeps me whole.

And so I Persevere—
  Rooted in unwavering Faith.
  I resist the pull of home. I am not done. I will not
    return without fulfilling my destiny. Step.
  Sleep, wake, pack, walk, unpack, sleep, walk,
    pack. Repeat.
  Step. Step.
  Determination replaces doubt.

And then Sunshine—
  Pontevedra, Hotel Ruas, and reprieve. Spanish life
    and sunlight. Plazas and people. Wine and
    laughter.

But the Clouds Return—
  I watch the families' glee. Not mine. Separate.
    Happiness saddened by my aloneness.
  Wanting what they have.
  Step, step, step to the next stop.

I Travel—
  Trains, then busses. On again. Off again.
  *Holding back my despair while hoping the next
    destination will lift the pall of aloneness.*
  Swoosh. The snake.
  Padron. The Ghost Town.
  Hotel Rosalia. Abandoned and alone.

And I Walk—
　To another locked church.
　Cold. Wind. Gray. Forlorn.
　Step, step.
　Hotel Scala and Aurora.

And I Phone—
　To America
　To anyone! Frantic for a lifeline.
　There is no answer. *I am my only lifeline.*
　Just a stop, just one night, keep moving—
　　　tomorrow *Finisterre.*
　Sleep. Awake. Go.

Morning Comes—
　Doing things I would never do—never in America.
　Waiting roadside for a bus.
　Step. Choices. Consequences. Step. Step.

I Arrive—
　Finally—*Finisterre.*
　Glimpsing miracles.
　Wind, rain, stargates. Wind, rain, José. Wind,
　　　rain, Chief Joseph.
　Shattered, surrendered, ascended.
　Filled with Light knowing who I am and the whole-
　　　ness of my being, I am circling, spiraling, my feet
　　　no longer touching Earth. I'm soaring, spiraling,
　　　trying to remember. What awakened me, urged
　　　me to write? What are feelings spelled in words?

Almost Home—
    Twenty-six hours.
    Coruna—*Madrid*—Chicago—San Diego.
    Another bus. More travel.
    Marriott—room service, laundry, TV.

Home—
    Stillness.

Awake—
    I am fully awake now. I have not moved. Eons
    passed in minutes. The dream is over. *Camino*
    Shima Shanti finished. It's just me now, but
    am not alone. In God's Presence and Christed
    Self I am whole and complete. I am Light
    beyond being.

I am Peace.

www.ingramcontent.com/pod-product-compliance
Lightning Source LLC
Chambersburg PA
CBHW020453100426
42813CB00031B/3353/J